TEACHING ENGLISH

J. H. Walsh

TEACHING ENGLISH

TO CHILDREN
OF ELEVEN TO SIXTEEN

An Account of Day-to-Day Practice

HEINEMANN

LONDON

Heinemann Educational Books Ltd
LONDON MELBOURNE TORONTO
SINGAPORE CAPE TOWN
AUCKLAND IBADAN
HONG KONG

First published 1965
Reprinted 1966

Published by
Heinemann Educational Books Ltd
48 Charles Street, London W.1
Printed in Great Britain by
Butler & Tanner Ltd, Frome and London

To

My Own Teacher
PROFESSOR P. GURREY

Contents

WRITING

READING

MISCELLANEOUS MATTERS

Foreword

THIS BOOK is intended for beginner-teachers first; then for more experienced teachers and other educators, who may turn over its pages in the hope of finding something which relates to their purposes; and then for examiners, particularly for those who are planning and conducting the new examinations. In it I have described in detail, and with examples and illustrations, some of the more useful day-to-day practices in the teaching of English (this has been my principal business), and have also written about the work of preparing children for examinations, as well as that of preparing better examinations for the children. The ages of the children I have in mind are from eleven to sixteen; the range of ability is a wide one, though excluding slow-learning children.

By far the larger part of the book is concerned with Writing and Reading. Six chapters are devoted to Writing, the first three of them to the work of the younger children, and the last two to that of the older. Into them I have incorporated about fifty examples of children's work, some from each year: the best of these are numbered from 1 upwards, and will, I hope, give help to teachers who are trying to establish their own standards. The chapters on Reading are arranged in the same manner as those on Writing, and I have attempted to make my suggestions as definite as possible by applying them to well-known books, plays, and poems. The final three chapters deal with miscellaneous matters.

Of this book's several limitations, I feel that I should specify two which I have myself imposed on it. First, in setting out to write a book on the day-to-day aspects of my subject, I have deliberately avoided dealing with the more exciting sorts of lesson—the free writing, the writing of poetry, the impromptu acting and miming, and the critical study of newspapers and popular fiction; not because I do not value such things, but because they are already given sufficient prominence in educational journalism, with the effect that the more ordinary, but still very necessary, kinds of work are a little overlooked. Secondly, I have been unwilling to include in this book accounts of any lessons which I myself do not give, or have not at one time or another given; and this means that the lessons described here are in the first place appropriate to a particular school and to particular children. But these limitations admitted, I hope that intelligent teachers who are prepared to adjust and adapt will find here a book of much general usefulness.

I should perhaps offer an apology for writing yet another book on the teaching of English; there are already several good ones on the market. My excuse is that 'English' nowadays covers a very wide field, in which a great number of teachers are at work; little wonder if the books already available differ markedly in substance and approach, and if each of them offers something new. It is my hope to have written a book which is different again, and one which makes its own small contribution to the literature of the subject.

J. H. W.

September 1964

Acknowledgements

IN DEDICATING this book to my old tutor, Dr P. Gurrey, I have tried
to express my special indebtedness to his wisdom, friendship and
example. My debt is only a little less great to Mr Denys Thompson,
with whom for many years I have been privileged to work on *The Use
of English*. It was Mr Thompson who, in 1955 and 1956, first printed
the four substantial articles on which I here draw, and who more
recently proposed and promoted the publication of this book.

I must also acknowledge the help I have received from three other
friends. First my headmaster, Mr R. R. Pedley, himself a specialist
teacher of English, who has so often endorsed my views and projects,
and given strong support to my department. With his permission I
here reprint some writings which have already appeared in school
publications. Then two of my colleagues, Mr R. D. Cole and Mr F.
Tomlinson, who for long have worked close to me, and along lines
similar to my own. Both of them have given me generous access to
their pupils' work; if I had not been ashamed to do so, I would have
printed more of it, and less of my own pupils', and in doing so would
have made this into a better book.

Lastly I would like to set down my thanks to my wife, who has given
me so much help with this, as with everything else I have written.

For permission to reprint matter drawn from copyright sources, I
am indebted to the following:

Miss Ruth Pitter and The Cresset Press Ltd for 'The Hut' from *Urania*;
Miss Elizabeth Morse and J. M. Dent & Sons Ltd for an extract from
Chang; J. M. Dent & Sons Ltd for an extract from 'Youth' from *Youth
and Other Stories* by Joseph Conrad; Mrs Helen Thomas and Faber
& Faber Ltd for 'Birds' Nests' from *Collected Poems* by Edward
Thomas; Miss Diana Ross and Faber & Faber Ltd for an extract from
'The Winged Horse' from *Wild Cherry*; Faber & Faber Ltd for 'Song
of the Mad Prince' from *Collected Rhymes and Verses* by Walter de la
Mare; Longmans, Green & Co. Ltd for an extract from *Sea Hunters*
by Frank Robb and for the grammar exercises quoted in Chapter 13;
Macmillan & Co. Ltd for 'Afterwards' from *Collected Poems* by Thomas
Hardy; John Murray Ltd for an extract from *The Four Feathers* by

A. E.W. Mason; Thomas Nelson & Sons Ltd for an extract from 'The Red Room' from *The Short Stories of H. G. Wells.*

In addition I should like to acknowledge my indebtedness to Mr R. D. Cole for permission to print the examples of writing numbered 2, 10, and 25, and to Mr F. Tomlinson for permission to print 11, 21, 23, 33, and 35. I regret that I have now no record of the source of 8, 9, and 19.

CHAPTER I

STORIES

Story-writing today—The incentive to write stories—The value of story-writing—Writing to a prescribed plan—Other approaches to story-writing—Reading and broadcasts as stimuli—Fantasy—Veiled autobiography—Self-discovery

'EVERY CHILD loves a story. He loves reading stories and he loves writing them.' That would be a pleasant way of starting a chapter on story-writing. It would be pleasanter still if it were true.

It is not true, of course. It probably never was; but it is certainly much less true today than it was thirty years ago. Consider reading. Most teachers know that nowadays there are children who rapidly outgrow their liking for fiction. 'I've read all the stories I'm ever going to,' declared a thirteen-year-old boy (an intelligent one at that); and thereafter his reading-list consisted only of non-fiction titles. And it is the same with story-writing. Give a class of children, even eleven-year-old children, a half-dozen story titles to choose from, and there will often be one child who sits puzzled, scratches his head, and at last asks, 'Can I write something else, not a story?'

Remarks such as these point to a change which has taken place, of recent years, in children's reading and writing habits. Many parents look upon this change as a good thing: the time formerly wasted on fiction can now be spent in acquiring knowledge of a 'factual' kind—the kind which leads to prowess in the television quiz-contests. Many teachers deplore it. But it is no part of my intention to enquire what has brought the change about; I mention it only in order to make my first point—that beginner-teachers must not expect their pupils necessarily to feel the same enthusiasm for writing stories as they themselves did when children. Besides, this point once made, it must also be said that a great deal of story-writing is still going on in schools. In this chapter I shall first consider what makes children want to compose stories, and what advantages they gain from doing so. After that, I shall go on to suggest some means by which teachers can secure better stories; and then, with the help of examples, I shall show what I think to be the best kinds of story.

The question 'Why do they want to write stories?' is not an easy question to answer; but it is an odd fact that story-writing is one of those activities which, so to speak, 'carry their own incentive with them'. Probably the immediate incentive is pleasure—the primitive pleasure of shaping a story, and in particular the satisfaction which comes from completing it. The drive towards completion, towards wholeness, is very strong. It must be a common source of amusement to teachers (it has certainly often amused me) to find a pupil who, through a desire to finish what he has begun, has been betrayed into a homework story of inordinate length, extending many pages beyond any reasonable requirement, and flatly ignoring the merciful provision that 'you may leave your story unfinished if you want to'. For the final six pages, the handwriting deteriorates into a scrawl, the page margins are unruled, and the simplest words are misspelt or are left out altogether; and one dares not enquire at what late hour on Sunday evening the writer tottered off to bed, his self-imposed task wearily accomplished. Yet he needs no pity, for he has known the story-teller's excitement and his sense of achievement. We find ourselves passing on to other questions: 'What is the good of it all? Apart from this satisfaction, what other benefit has the writer derived from so great an expenditure of energy? What is the *value* of story-writing?'

Now it is perhaps not difficult to say what story-writing *ought* to do for a child: it surely ought to do what the reading of good fiction in effect does do—provide a space in which he can move about freely, experimenting with new emotions and situations, and thus preparing himself for the shocks and stresses (anticipating, too, the delights) of later life. The reading of good fiction does this; and the writing of stories can do it too, especially when it is undertaken under the influence of good fiction previously read: in his writing the child reshapes the situations he has read of, adapting them to suit and satisfy his particular needs. But a child does not necessarily do this every time he takes up his pen; on the contrary, most of the stories which children write are trivial enough, and show small evidence of having satisfied any needs whatever. Is this to be wondered at? After all, much of the fiction which children read is bad fiction, and from bad fiction they can derive only a distorted idea of what the world is like; so that their own stories are nothing more than a striving to come to terms with experiences which are of the crudest and most superficial kinds, or which ordinary people simply do not have. It is a fact that I seldom find myself able to commend a child's story wholeheartedly, and seldom want to keep a copy of one; and I suspect that my experience in this matter is that of other teachers as well.

To put it briefly, one often feels that the writing of a story has done little enough for the child as a person. On the other hand, it may have done something for him as a writer.

For above all else, story-writing gives the child a chance to write *at length*, to write *in quantity*; and at an early stage, copiousness itself is a virtue. The time spent on lengthy fictions (crude they may be, unoriginal, influenced by bad or frivolous reading) is not time wasted if the act of writing brings with it increased confidence and fluency, which are absolute necessities for the child who is later to write willingly and with skill. There is an interesting parallel between the teaching of story-writing and one of the best-known methods of teaching handwriting. I am thinking of the Marion Richardson method, according to which the children are first taught to make 'writing patterns'—a kind of glorified scribble which gives copious practice in easy movement; only after they have acquired fluency and a sense of continuity are they shown the formation of the separate letters. In English composition, similarly, it pays to insist at first upon copiousness rather than upon accuracy: the wise teacher is at first content if a child can carry an extended piece of writing to a conclusion, and defers till later an insistence on more acceptable subject-matter and a greater exactness of expression. Of course, there is the unwise teacher as well: *he* works in the opposite direction. To his unconfident beginners he declares sternly, 'What I want is one page of perfect English—not six pages of rubbish.' Often enough, what he gets is one page of rubbish.

I shall not dwell further on the benefits to be derived from copious story-writing. Obviously, the more a child writes, the more opportunity he has for meeting, tackling, and by his own efforts overcoming various tiny obstacles of expression—most good writers being, in spite of all we teachers may prefer to believe, to a large extent self-taught. If the value of the work is but granted, the next question arises of itself —what steps must we take to secure good stories, or at least long and fluent ones?

Now for some teachers this is no problem at all. The child's story is built up according to a prescribed plan: (*a*) a dramatic opening—an incident or a snatch of conversation; (*b*) an explanatory passage, making it clear how the opening situation came to be as it is; (*c*) a return to the opening situation, developing it further; (*d*) some explanation as to who the chief characters are (this gives the teacher a chance for instruction in the writing of character-sketches); (*e*) a new and startling incident to conclude Chapter 1. And so on, chapter after chapter. It all looks very sound, and no doubt produces some worth-while stories. But the method is open to criticism. For one thing, it allows the story to develop out of the prescribed plan, and thus in effect puts the cart before the horse: ideally the plan should develop out of the preconceived story. For another thing, it takes the whole business of story-writing too seriously—more seriously than it deserves, I feel—and presupposes a long story of several chapters. Not every such story is carried through to its conclusion with the zest with which it is started; and anyone who remembers starting long stories in his childhood may also remember that few of them were brought to a conclusion.

Then what, alternatively, is the teacher to do to help the young story-writer?

He can do three things. He can give attention to the most difficult part of the work, which is getting the story begun. He can read the finished story, comment on it, and commend what he sees good in it. And he can allow the children to read their stories to one another, and to exchange criticisms. In a later chapter, I shall write about the marking of compositions and the exchange of criticisms; here I shall confine myself to 'getting the story going'.

It is worth while experimenting endlessly, trying this or that, observing the results, and keeping in mind the methods which have been successful. There is, of course, the approach through titles pure and simple. One can make much play with titles suggesting secrecy, or promising revelations of the unknown: 'The Secrets of a River', 'What's in the Cellar?', 'The Hole in the Wall', 'The House with the Crimson Doors', 'The Monster that Survived', 'The Stone Idol in the Forest'— all that sort of thing. Often it needs only a few words to stir memories of lively or even sensational reading, the matter of which is absorbed into a new story, or adapted with such skill and taste as the child can command. With these evocative titles one may classify evocative opening sentences: ' "It is a fearful creature indeed," declared Sir Andrew as he surveyed the huge ape in the steel cage; "I wonder how long we shall manage to hold it." ' (Obviously they are not going to hold it for very long.) Or this one: 'Until the summer of last year it was thought that there were no more lost cities to discover. Then, in July . . .' Such openings have the power to suggest the lines along which the story may develop, without prescribing them exactly. Or, again, there is this, a story-opening which, at different times, has been variously treated by different pupils: ' "It is a very queer machine indeed," announced Professor Maxwell proudly; "you would be surprised at the things it can do." ' Professor Maxwell's machine has at different times been a time machine, a space machine, a machine for taking one into the fourth dimension, a dish-washing machine, and a machine for ducking fourth-formers! Or, to give a final example, this one: 'We had always wondered what Mr Craxton kept in that locked shed of his, and one day we resolved to find out.' Mr Craxton's shed has been known to house contents as varied as moths, mushrooms, a time-machine, an atomic submarine, a nuclear warhead, a ray-gun, explosives, 'hydropetroloxide', silver bars, horse-dope, a flying saucer and a machine for converting Mr Craxton into a superman.

So the teacher experiments, constantly adding to his list of titles and opening sentences. I do not intend to give lists here (I have done that elsewhere); but I ought to add that one cannot expect any single title necessarily to appeal to all the children in the class. Story topics are best prescribed in batches of six or seven.

Together with these titles and opening sentences I would classify the short passages of prose or verse which the pupil is required, not necessarily to introduce into his story, but to use as starting-points for his invention. The instruction to the pupil is, 'Write the story which comes to your mind on reading the following.' A suitable prose passage might be this one:

Only the small chimney, smoking in the thicket, revealed the presence of the dug-out, almost roofed over by the roots of the beeches, and hidden by deep snow. Darkness was approaching, and the snow was falling thicker than ever, as she pushed aside the trails of ivy and crept in.

Or this more fragmentary one:

An old coal mine—disused silent workings—dark tunnels and dripping water. Listen to that echo! Anything, *anything*, could happen in such a place!

As for passages of verse, a quick search through an anthology will easily reveal suitable material; and I have had success with scraps such as this:

> We crossed a height of breezy down,
> And came upon a hidden town;
> For fifty years no human feet
> Had walked the pavements of its street;
> But feet of . . .

Those feet, at various times, have been the feet of goblins, rats, ants, phantoms, ravenous wolves and Martian monsters. And here is another:

> I saw a crazèd face, did I,
> Stare from the lattice of a mill:
> While the lank sails clacked idly by,
> High on the windy hill.

And another:

> The western tide crept up along the sand,
> And o'er and o'er the sand,
> And round and round the sand
> As far as eye could see:
> The rolling mist came down and hid the land——
> And never home came she.

And another:

> He laughed: 'If one may settle the score for five,
> I am ready; but let the reckoning stand till day:
> I have loved the sunlight as dearly as any alive.'
> 'You shall die at dawn,' said they.

The success of the story depends partly on the pupil's examining the passage closely, and picking up as many of its implications as possible.

I must not omit to mention that published novels and stories—*The Invisible Man*, *Fighting the Flames*, *The Secret Garden*, *Secret Waters*, *The Gorilla Hunters*—are useful in providing titles for the children's own stories, especially if they have not read the originals. It is also possible for children to make deliberate use of the characters and the material in books they have read; I am thinking of the obvious 'The Further Adventures of . . .', where the gap is filled by the name of whatever hero the writer happens to favour at the time. An advantage of this approach to story-writing is that it allows not very imaginative children to lean heavily on the originals: I have seen some 'Further Adventures of the Swallows and Amazons' which were written by two girls of very moderate ability. And again, there is the possibility of the teacher reading a short story to the class, and inviting them to make it a point of departure for their own narratives. After reading the chosen story, the teacher writes up two or three story-titles which (as it were) stem from the original one. I have not tried this with any class of my own, but I have made use of sound broadcasts which have been devised with this sort of intention, and I would not like to leave the subject of story-topics without saying a few words about the use of radio in the classroom.

I have in mind such radio series as the one called *Listening and Writing*, where the work of an adult author is used to stimulate the child into writing stories of his own. During one programme, two short stories were broadcast, both about horses. The first, by Liam O'Flaherty, told of a little boy's vision of a large black horse in the skies; the second, called *The Winged Horse*, was by Diana Ross, and it began in this way:

A winged horse once alighted in a field and began to eat grass.

It had not been grazing long when a man came along the road and seeing it there stopped in amazement and then climbed over the fence which divided the meadow from the road and went towards it, resolving to ride upon it.

When the horse saw him coming it raised its head and said to him:

'What do you want?'

'I want to ride upon your back,' said the man.

'Why?' said the horse.

'Because if I do I shall reach my destination the sooner.'

'And what good will that do?' said the horse.

'Why,' said the man, 'it will save time.'

'For what purpose?' said the horse.

'Why, everyone wants to save time,' said the man. 'Even you ought to know that that is reason enough.'

'Well, for such a reason as that you may not ride on my back,' said the horse.

And it tossed its noble head and snorted through its nostrils.

After a pedlar, a soldier, a philosopher, and a lame old woman had in turn pleaded vainly (though each for a good reason) for permission to take a ride, a child approached the horse, and put out its hand to touch it.

'What do you want?' asked the horse, when it felt the child's hand.

'I want a ride,' said the child.

'Why?' asked the horse.

'For no reason at all,' said the child. 'Except for the ride.'

'Well,' said the horse, 'get up on my back and I will give you a ride.'

So the child got up on its back and the horse leaped into the air, and galloped about the sky, and when it came down again and the child slid off its back:

'That was a good ride,' said the child, and stroked the horse, and patted it, and then with a shining face climbed over the fence and went running down the hill to tell its mother all about it.

And the horse looked after it, and shook its head, took a mouthful of grass, unfolded its wings, and leaping up returned once more to its pastures in the air.

After the broadcast was finished, the listening class were given two or three titles for stories of their own, among them 'A Ride Just for Pleasure'. Here is what one twelve-year-old boy wrote:

(1) *A Ride Just for Pleasure*

He was cropping the short lush green grass when I saw him, a big white muscular horse, an ordinary horse you may say. But this animal was different, for he had, folded on his milky white back, two wings! I stood staring at him for a moment, expecting him to run away as soon as he saw me, but instead he paid no heed to my presence, and I was allowed to come closer. I reached out with my hand and patted his thick, muscular neck. Then I decided that I would like to ride him.

I edged myself closer and then gingerly clambered upon his back, and then, laying down low, I urged this magnificent creature into the air.

His wings stretched themselves out, and he galloped into the air. I marvelled at the ease in which he performed this action; and I had to hold my breath in amazement as the green meadows and fields fell away from me, and I rose steadily into the rich blue skies.

The fluffy white clouds floated by us as we climbed higher, and the atmosphere grew fresher and fresher until my cheeks were quite red, and my hair, and the horse's mane and tail, were blown backward by the wind. Through breaks in the silvery cloud I had a most magnificent panoramic view of the world below. The horse turned and galloped higher and then dropped again, and I had a wonderful feeling of satisfaction as we plunged earthwards, the wind, now behind us, blowing my hair forward.

He wheeled once more and then the horse came to land, and I felt rather sad that my marvellous ride was over. The horse landed on all four hooves, snorting through his nostrils. I reluctantly slid from his creamy soft back, and as I departed I stroked and patted him.

(Second Year)

I think it will be agreed that this story has good qualities. The boy has picked up the suggestions of the ride on horseback as already contained in the story by Diana Ross, and has developed them in a very personal way: he conveys a feeling of the *presence* of the horse ('thick muscular neck'), and of the horse's quality when *seen* ('milky white back') and when *felt* ('slid from his creamy soft back'); and he imparts to the account of the ride a sense of enjoyment, expressed in the description of the red cheeks and the blowing mane and tail. One or two conventionalities of expression and one or two errors seem in the circumstances hardly to matter. The writer's gusto communicates itself even in the flow of the words, as in—

> I marvelled at the ease in which he performed this action; and I had to hold my breath in amazement as the green meadows and fields fell away from me, and I rose steadily into the rich blue skies;

or in—

> The fluffy white clouds floated by us as we climbed higher, and the atmosphere grew fresher and fresher until my cheeks were red, and my hair, and the horse's mane and tail, were blown backward by the wind.

These are two sentences which, for their balance and rhythm, an adult writer might be pleased to write. Of course, it may be urged of this story that it develops only a small part of the broadcast story which preceded it, but the fact I would emphasize here is that without the broadcast the child's story would never have been written at all.

I have already suggested that, while the making up of stories plays a part in the education of children as writers, their stories are usually not good ones when judged as representations of life. From a technical viewpoint, too, they are likely to be inferior, for the child who writes a detective story, a spy story, a war, Merchant Navy, cowboy, caves-with-treasure, or space-suit story, is competing with professional authors who may have spent a lifetime in doing this sort of thing really well. All the same, there are two kinds of story in which the child, in spite of his inexperience and his modest equipment, can hope to shine; one of these is the fantasy—the slightly-more-grown-up fairy story of which 'A Ride Just for Pleasure' is an example; and the other is the 'veiled autobiography'. I will speak of the fantasy first.

In writing a fantasy, the eleven-year-old child is on his own ground. It is not only that he has recently emerged from a childhood where fantasies are treated as real; it is also that, having but one rule to follow, he is not bound by the various restrictions which make adult writing so difficult to imitate. This one rule is that he must take the fantasy seriously. If he is able to do this—if he is able to ignore the impossibilities and the absurdities and to treat the fantastic incidents as something 'real and present'—he has a chance of being an artist in his own small way. This ability is possessed, I think, by the writer of the story about the horse; and it is also possessed by the writer of this, written to fit the title 'The Cat that Talked':

(2) *The Cat that Talked*

It was a nice warm day. The sun shone down and there was not a breath of wind. My homework was completed, my other jobs finished, and now I was having an enjoyable time playing 'catch' against the wall of our garden. Slowly I sensed a feeling that something was watching me. I looked around; the rhythmic 'tap tap' of the ball against our wall was cut off abruptly. I saw my audience sitting quietly behind me, its green eyes piercing down into my heart. Suddenly the cat raised itself off the ground. It yawned, and stretched its limbs lazily as though stupefied by the glare of the sun.

I stared back at it and it stalked forward, covering the ground easily with its long, black-velvet legs. When it was in front of me, it sat down again. Then to my surprise it did the most remarkable thing I have ever known a cat to do. It talked in a soft childish voice.

'Stroke me!' it commanded, without flickering its delicate eyelids.

'You—you spoke!' I replied, bewildered.

'Of course I spoke! I'm no dumb-puss! Stroke me, you puny human!' it shouted, as though in a fury with not being obeyed. Unsteadily my quavering hand reached out and slid down the creature's back.

'Ah, that's better,' the cat murmured, completely soothed. Then it spoke again.

'I permit you to take me in as your cat,' it stated.

'I'm sorry, I can't. I've got two cats already,' I replied.

'Can't! Can't! You won't take me in instead of that moth-eaten white low-born cat there?' it screeched, as it saw our gentle harmless white cat, Tatty, appear. 'Well, the absurdness of it!' it continued. 'I condescend to permit you to take me in and you won't? There are a lot of people who would pay—yes, pay—to have me. So I will leave you, you ungrateful human!'

With that indignant statement the bad-tempered cat disappeared.

(First Year)

It is worth while observing the matter-of-fact approach to the situation (H. G. Wells does the same sort of thing—gives an everyday setting by way of introduction to his most extraordinary occurrences): the day is warm, homework is finished, the writer is playing a game of 'catch' against the wall. The cat, when it arrives, is given presence and personality; the conversation and other incidents, while admitted to be astonishing, are made 'real' by the circumstantial details. When I first read this story, I found it interesting to compare it with the work of the other children treating the same subject; for while the others struggled to explain away the phenomenon (one boy even introduced a ventri-loquist), this child brushed aside the whole necessity for explanations: he went straight for his fantasy, and set out to make a living thing of 'the cat that talked'. I should perhaps add that he was one of the most intelligent boys in his class.

Now I have already admitted that we can do little to *teach* writing of this kind; but we can occasionally provide the right topics, and when at last the work 'happens', we can allow it to be read to the other members of the class, and can single it out for praise. What we ourselves value the children will soon learn to value too. Nor is the gift for such writing confined to eleven-year-olds; a similar but more adult sort of fantasy may emerge in older children, as it does in the following example from a second-year boy. The title chosen was the title of an H. G. Wells short story—'The Door in the Wall':

(3) *The Door in the Wall*

A small door—a red door—a plain door—the door in the wall. When I first saw the door, this was how it looked to my eyes. It was an extremely plain door. One of the plainest doors I had ever seen. The most unusual thing about this door was where I found it. I found it at the bottom of my grand-aunt's garden. It was a very big garden, at least six acres of woodland, field, and cultivated land. Around the garden was an enormous wall, at least ten feet high. The door was in the wall at a point where the wall's height had surprisingly dropped to a height of seven feet. There was a small alcove going into the wall with the door fitting neatly into it. Only once had I seen over that wall, and when I did, I could only see continuous marshland on the other side. To my knowledge, nobody had ever opened the door to get to the marshland, until one day when I was in the garden.

I had seen this door three times before this day, but had never been able to open it. Then suddenly, as I approached casually, it swung open. I have never found out why it did open and I do not think anyone will. Slowly I crept through the opening and got a tremendous shock. There was no marshland in sight.

In front of me there was a pleasantly cultivated garden, with dahlias blooming and cherry trees blossoming. I now knew why there was no marshland. I had come through the doorway into my grand-aunt's garden. Yes, I had entered where I had come from.

But there was something different about the garden. The stately Georgian mansion could be seen in the distance. The cultivated fields and numerous paths were there. Then I knew what was missing—sound. There was not a single sound except the crunch of my boots on the gravel. I walked towards this 'second world'. Suddenly I saw some gardeners; I ran to them quickly and then stopped. For these gardeners were immobile. They could not move.

I rushed here and there over the estate, but everything was stationary. The birds, the clouds, the grass did not move. Even the sun was in a fixed position.

I entered the house. I found my grand-aunt at her desk, still as a statue, in the middle of a letter to one of her daughters. I ran quickly out of the house down the garden: everything was still, immobile, incapable of movement, stuck in the position that it was in when I opened the door. Quickly I hurried to the wall, to the red door, to freedom.

But there was no door in the wall.   (*Second Year*)

The course of this story is clear enough. The boy goes through the red door, and steps from his own world into—his own world again, with this difference, that it is frozen into immobility. When he tries to return into the living world, he cannot find the red door, and he is imprisoned, apparently for ever. The whole has the quality of an evil dream—it is a dream of death or of separation, perhaps, or a claustrophobic fantasy. But I do not think we need try to explain it (it is doubtful whether even the writer could have done so); it is a self-sufficient little adventure into the land of nightmare.

I said earlier that there are two sorts of story in which the school-child can hope to excel. The fantasy is one, and the other is the 'veiled autobiography'—the story in which the child treats, in an indirect way and perhaps not always intentionally, some aspect of his own inner life. I am not thinking primarily of those long unsubtle outpourings, the direct expression of wishes and aspirations; though these also are of interest, and the writing of them is sometimes thought to have therapeutic value. I can recall examples of these too. I once heard a teacher tell about one of her pupils, a disturbed child, who kept spreading amongst the other girls of her class a number of untrue stories about her friendship with a master in a near-by grammar school; the girl was set to work on a long novel, in the writing of which, it seems, she worked her way back to emotional normality. And I recall a pupil of my own, young Stebbing, a pleasant intelligent boy (a stutterer too), who wrote novels of three-exercise-book length in which an exceptionally handsome and powerful hero, not entirely unlike Stebbing himself, lured away a succession of pretty girls to a succession of desert islands. But the stories of both these children leaned heavily on adult fiction; and the kind of story I have in mind is something much shorter and more personal. Here is such a story: the title proposed was 'The Hole in the Wall', but the writer changed it to suit his purposes.

(4) *The Hiding-Place*

When Jimmy was young and he knew lunch was nearly ready, he used to go to that bush to hide from his father as a game. His father would come and fetch him, scrambling just as Jimmy did through the hole in the fence which backed on to the field at the back of their garden. He used to pull Jimmy out of the bush and jokingly call him a rascal. Jimmy used to giggle and smile, and they would go home through the hole in the fence for lunch.

During lunch sometimes Jimmy used to notice his father being very quiet, and even at his young age guessed that he was thinking about his mother who had died when he was born. When Jimmy became a little older his father began to speak harshly to him, but seemed to be trying to restrain himself from doing so. When Jimmy hid in the bush his father was angry when he pulled Jimmy out, although, by the time they had reached the fence, Jimmy's father had returned to his kind self, though Jimmy noticed it was only because he was restraining himself. Jimmy also noticed that he went in that quiet trance more often, and although he was not particularly perturbed, Jimmy often wondered why his mother's death had such an effect on him.

By the time Jimmy was seven his father was going to the pub every night, leaving Jimmy in the care of their next-door neighbour. In spite of being drunk his father was still restrained, and he went into a trance very much more often.

One night his father came to collect him from the next-door neighbour's as usual, and put him to bed, but to Jimmy's surprise he went out again. Jimmy waited all night for his father to return, for never before had he gone out a second time. But his father never returned.

The next-door neighbour was a very kind person and she looked after Jimmy. Her son and he became great friends and he led a happy life with them. He did, however, fall into trances, very much as his father had, thinking of the hiding-place which had given him so much fun.

Jimmy led a happy life. He went to university, married a nice girl, but throughout his life he often thought of that hiding-place which had given him his first memories of happiness.

(Third Year)

It may be asked wherein lie the merit and interest of this story. Certainly not in the writer's manner of telling it; rather in the events themselves and in the situation which they adumbrate. In changing the 'hole in the wall' to a hole in the fence, the writer reveals that the incident of the hiding-place has a personal significance for him; he is writing of something which really happened. I shall not attempt an interpretation of the story in detail—the interpretation of children's stories is a hazardous business, and lacking full information the interpreter may easily draw false conclusions. For instance, in this case it would be wrong to conclude that the writer's mother was dead or that his father was a drunkard. Nothing of the sort. But we may think that the writer is here expressing, in a shadowy way, one of the plights of early adolescence—the plight of the sensitive child who discovers that a formerly affectionate father has banished tenderness from his relations with his son. It is a common enough occurrence: the father who was gentle, playful and kind suddenly decides that the time has come for his son to put away childish things and be toughened into the life of a man. The father's changed attitude (here expressed by the drunkenness and the fits of abstraction) is the more bewildering because it has no apparent cause, and the boy is troubled with fears, anxieties and a feeling of lost love. This particular story, which returns twice to the incident of the hiding-place, seems to me a little elegy for the tendernesses of early childhood.

Such writing does not often come my way. As I remarked in the early part of this chapter, what story-writing ought to do for a child it frequently fails to do. Yet through so much that is derivative and commonplace, a personal accent does sometimes manage to make itself heard; once in a way, we do indeed find a child experimenting with new emotions and situations, and in doing so, as I said before, preparing himself for the shocks and anticipating the delights of later life. There are moments of real self-discovery; as in the following extract, the concluding lines of a long whaling adventure:

> ... Three days passed before 'Thar she blows' echoed again from the crow's nest. Hosia took up his position with Simonen at the harpoon. The *Catalina* rapidly overtook the whale. Hosia let out a scream of terror, for his eyes beheld a hundred-foot-long monster, with green scales and large razor-sharp teeth. Eino witnessed a tail, about as thick as Cleopatra's needle, sweep away the catwalk and the two harpooners, whom they never saw again.
>
> The monster, like a submarine, turned and swam towards the whaler. It raised itself by the *Catalina's* bows, the huge eyes seemingly gleaming with approval at the recent events. Eino snatched up an old hand-harpoon and flung it at the monster's head. It let out a piercing shriek as the harpoon struck its eye, and it sunk swiftly into the black depths of the Antarctic, leaving behind a trail of blood and a shaken crew.
>
> 'Well done, boy,' said the captain and crew alike.
>
> The boy only stared into space. Bloodshed and killing he didn't like.
>
> 'I wish I hadn't done it,' he uttered.
>
> (*First Year*)

What is particular and personal to this conclusion is, of course, Eino's revulsion from the act of killing the whale, (' "I wish I hadn't done it," he uttered.') The young writer is making a discovery about, and confirming an attitude in, himself; and the importance he attaches to the

discovery is shown by the way in which he makes it the climax and end
of his story. Questioned as to the origin of his work, the writer said that
he had read many whaling stories, but had decided that his own should
be a Finnish story, and so had 'got the Finnish names out of Whit-
taker's'. The ending, he confirmed, was his own invention.

One more example, this time the conclusion of a 'desert-island' story.
I had no need to question the writer of this one, for he wrote it in
class under my own eye. The narrator tells how, while exploring his
island, he came across a beautiful cove amongst the rocks.

> As I dragged myself along (I was weak from loss of food) my thoughts
> wandered so much with the beauty of the cove, that I almost forgot that I
> was hungry. Finally, however, I found some scraps of coconut to quell the
> aching of my stomach. I slept, that night, on a rock ledge, and from this
> vantage-point I could view the whole cove. Below were magnificent palms
> with their great fronds acting as some shelter from the scorching sun. All
> round were rock cliffs, like tall guardians watching silently over the scene.
>
> Suddenly I spied something which I had not seen the day before. It was a
> mast of a ship, showing outside in the sea. The rescuers had finally arrived.
> Now that I had stumbled upon this beautiful place, I had been unafraid to die.
> But now I was to leave the cove, to go back into society again, and to leave
> this paradise of Nature's unharmed.
>
> (*First Year*)

In a story not otherwise noteworthy there occurs that one remarkable
statement, 'Now that I had stumbled upon this beautiful place, I had
been unafraid to die.' It represents a discovery the writer has made about
himself and about people in general—the strange way in which, in the
presence of beauty, a man may temporarily lose, or at least know a
lessening of, his fear of death. It is through discoveries like these that
children make small steps towards maturity; and it sometimes happens
that such discoveries are made and confirmed as a sort of by-product
of story-writing.

It may be thought of this chapter on story-writing that there is not,
after all, a great deal of practical advice offered to the teacher who needs
it; but in fact, if a teacher takes story-telling seriously, if he gives his
pupils scope for practising it, if he can distinguish a good story from a
bad one, and if he commends and gives publicity to a good story when
he sees it, he is doing as much as can be expected of him. Some teachers
do none of these things, believing that story-telling belongs to early
infancy, and that it should be beneath the dignity of the older child to
practise it or of the teacher to countenance it. I think these teachers

make a mistake. For after all, story-telling in childhood is a form of play; and if play is one of the means by which a child helps to turn himself into a grown-up, so, surely, is story-telling—whether by 'grown-up' we mean an adult writer or an adult person.

CHAPTER 2

ACCOUNTS AND REPORTS

*Writing accounts and reports—Value and incentive—The use of
classroom demonstrations—Rewriting and revising—The making
of compilations—Informal reporting and the school magazine*

IN THIS chapter I intend to discuss the accounts and reports which
children sometimes write as classroom or homework exercises, or for
a form or a school magazine. Such accounts as these—accounts of
things seen or done in the classroom, in the home, or in the world
outside—obviously differ from the fictions discussed in Chapter 1; and
they also differ, though less obviously, from the descriptions of experiences which are to be discussed in Chapter 3. In that chapter I shall deal
with highly personal experiences, where the writer reveals not only
a set of circumstances but also his feelings, his perceptions, and the
manner of his involvement. Here I am concerned with mere factual
accounts, where orderliness and lucidity are a first requirement, or
where in any case the writer himself does not much intrude.

As with story-telling, there arise the questions of value and incentive.
What is the value of this sort of work? What advantages does a child
gain from doing it? Put these questions to an ordinary adult, and if he
has any ideas on the matter at all, he will probably not hesitate over his
answer. Writing reports and accounts compels a child to 'order his
thoughts', to 'practise clear thinking', and to 'use straightforward
English'. It is seen as the most practical of all the kinds of written work
—as the kind most likely to fit a child for his future career. And we are
not likely to quarrel with these ideas, even if we feel that they spring
from too narrow a view of what writing can do for a child. But to tell
children that the proposed work is valuable is not necessarily to make
them want to do it. From a child's point of view, mere reporting is
frequently a tedious and too-exacting exercise; unlike story-telling it
does not 'carry its own incentive with it'; and a teacher may have to
provide incentives in order to make the work seem interesting and

rewarding. It is one of the purposes of this chapter to show what these incentives can be.

One of the simplest and most pleasing exercises for the beginner is the writing up of a classroom demonstration. One or another of the pupils, or perhaps the teacher himself, demonstrates a simple process— it might be a conjuring trick, or a science experiment, or the working of a model, or the effective arrangement of flowers in a bowl, or perhaps the insertion of pin-curlers and rollers in the hair—and the children are then asked to write up the demonstration in detail. Subsequently, some of them are permitted to read their work aloud, and invite the criticisms of the others. Provided that the demonstration is simple enough, this kind of work often has a special appeal for backward or unimaginative children, who are incapable of much invention, but not incapable of recording what has recently passed before their eyes.

With children of greater ability, there are sometimes advantages in reversing the procedure I have just described—in having the account read first and the demonstration given afterwards. The pupil devises and perfects his demonstration during his leisure time, and then writes an account of it as a homework exercise. He brings the exercise to the classroom, and he also brings the necessary apparatus for his demonstration—handkerchiefs, matchsticks, match-boxes, candles, bottles, and paper for cutting or tearing—as well as penknives, or scissors, or any other implements required. First he is allowed to read his account of the proposed demonstration; as it might be this:

The Bottle Fountain

Bore a hole through the middle of a cork, and insert a drinking-straw. Fit the cork tightly into a bottle half-filled with water, and make sure that the straw is under the surface of the water. Blow as hard as you can through the straw. Take your face away immediately because the water may shoot out of the straw at once.

Because of your blowing, bubbles of air rise through the water into the upper part of the bottle. This space already has air in it, so the pressure there is now greater than the pressure of the air outside. When you stop blowing, the compressed air pushes the water up the straw, making the fountain.

(*Third Year*)

Or this:

A Mystifying Trick

This simple trick can be quite easily performed with the following materials: two sheets of newspaper, some glue and three strips of tissue-paper, one red, one blue, and one white. Hold the strips together and tear them into small pieces. Then let them drop on to a sheet of newspaper. Pick the newspaper up and crumple it into a small ball, with the strips of paper inside. Then make a small tear in the newspaper and pull out a complete Union Jack.

The secret of this trick is that instead of there being a single sheet of newspaper, a double sheet of newspaper is stuck together with a complete Union Jack concealed inside. When the ball of newspaper is torn the complete Union Jack is pulled out. The ball of newspaper is quickly tossed away as soon as the flag is taken out from the newspaper to avoid anybody seeing the secret.

(Third Year)

Or this:

Sixpence from Water

This trick uses a sixpence, jam jar, a candle, a saucer. The object is to lift a sixpence immersed in water on a saucer without getting your fingers wet. It is easily done.

Stand the candle in some soft plasticine in the water. Then light the candle, and put the jam jar over the top of it. When the oxygen is being burnt it causes a release of air pressure and so the water is pushed into the jam jar by the greater air pressure. When all the water is gone up into the jar, you can pick up the sixpence without wetting your fingers.

(Third Year)

After he has read his account to the class, the writer invites his classmates to comment on it; and when they have offered their comments, and further discussion has followed, he is allowed to do his 'live demonstration'.

It will be seen from the examples given above what kinds of inadequacy one has to expect: all three reveal disorderliness, omissions, and inexactness of language. In the case of a really badly written piece, a first reading may leave the class utterly confused. If the writer reads his work twice—slowly the second time—and the process he is describing can still not be followed by the majority of the class, some drastic revision will evidently be necessary; and in nearly all cases there will be small faults of expression to attend to. The 'live demonstration', of course, provides a check upon the written account, as well as encouraging the writer to take care over the latter. After the demonstration, all that remains to do is for the writer, or the class as a whole, to rewrite the work.

I say the class as a whole, because it is often a good idea for the teacher to write up on the board a piece of badly expressed work, and, after discussion of its inadequacies, require the whole class to produce 'better versions'. I shall speak at greater length about this in Chapter 4, and shall say no more about it at present, except to remark that this sort of 'communal revising' can be less tedious than each child revising his own work. But whichever way the revision is done, the children will undertake it more eagerly if they know that the results are not to be wasted, but are to be collected into a compilation—a 'Book of Doing and Making', say, or a 'Book of Party Entertainments'. Of compilations, too, I shall have something to say very shortly.

However, before leaving the subject of demonstrations, I should like to make one or two miscellaneous recommendations regarding them. It is important that the children should not be too ambitious: their demonstrations should involve only a few simple processes—such processes as, when written up, do not need the support of diagrams. Card tricks are usually too complicated for children to describe well. Then, all demonstrations should be performable on a table-top, should not require much apparatus, and should not take too long to do; and the use of gas, or of mains electricity, or of any kind of injurious substance should of course be forbidden. (With boys' demonstrations I have found it impracticable to ban the use of water; and the teacher will sometimes be called upon to lend a box of matches or to provide a cloth for mopping up.) And one final point: the children should be discouraged from submitting accounts of 'how to make' or of 'how to do' which they have copied from published books. The work of professional writers is usually detectable.

Here are some revised versions of the three demonstrations described above:

The Bottle Fountain

Your object is to make the water in a bottle shoot out as a fountain.

Bore a hole through the middle of a cork, and pass a drinking-straw right through it. Fit the cork tightly into a bottle half-filled with water, making sure that the bottom end of the straw is under the water. Then blow as hard as you can through the top end of the straw. Take your face away immediately, and the water will shoot out into the air.

When you blow, air is forced into the water through the lower end of the straw, and it bubbles up into the upper part of the bottle. This space already has air in it, so the pressure there is increased. When you stop blowing, the compressed air forces the water downwards and up through the straw, making a fountain.

A Mystifying Trick

You show your audience a sheet of newspaper and three strips of tissue-paper, one red, one white, and one blue. You tear the strips of tissue-paper into small pieces, put them on the sheet of newspaper, and roll the newspaper into a ball, so that the pieces of tissue-paper are inside it. Then you tear a hole in the ball of newspaper, and draw out a Union Jack.

This is how the trick is done. You need two sheets of newspaper, some glue, a cloth Union Jack, and the three pieces of tissue-paper already described. The 'sheet of newspaper' which you show your audience is, in fact, two sheets of newspaper laid face to face, and glued together round the edges. The flat Union Jack is concealed between them. When you tear a hole through the outer newspaper, the Union Jack can easily be pulled out. Remember to toss away the ball of newspaper immediately afterwards, so as to avoid anyone seeing that the pieces of tissue-paper are still inside it.

Sixpence from Water

A sixpence is placed in a saucer of water. Your object is to lift the sixpence from the saucer with your fingers without wetting them.

You need a sixpence, a jam jar, a candle, a saucer, a piece of plasticine, and a little water. Put the piece of plasticine in the middle of the saucer, and place the sixpence in the saucer not far from the edge. Pour in enough water to cover the sixpence. Insert the lower end of an upright candle in the plasticine, and light the top end. Then invert the jam jar and stand it in the saucer of water so that it covers the candle but so that the sixpence is outside it.

As the oxygen in the jar is consumed, the pressure in the jar decreases, and water is slowly drawn in beneath the rim of the jar. Soon all the water has entered the jar, the saucer is dry, and you can pick out the sixpence without wetting your fingers.

I spoke earlier of the so-called compilation—the collection of pieces of writing of one kind, gathered under a general title. After the various articles or stories have been revised for publication, they are written up neatly, illustrated by drawings and diagrams, and bound into a book with board covers, which is then kept as a record, or lent out to the pupils in turn, or placed on display during an Open Day or a Parents' Evening. The making of such compilations is particularly recommended by those teachers who see it as providing a special sort of incentive—as they put it, 'Children will write eagerly for publication, but not for the waste-paper basket.' I do not myself believe that the truth is as simple as that; children *will* write for the waste-paper basket, and eagerly too, if in doing so they can please and satisfy their teachers,

c

or their parents, or an urge within themselves, or all three at once. However, there is no denying that the proposal to make a compilation is usually taken up with eagerness, and that the children are ready enough to revise and perfect their work for it; nor is there usually a lack of volunteers for the work of transcribing, illustrating, and binding. And of all the kinds of writing which can be assembled into a compilation, there is none more suitable than the accounts which are the subject of this chapter. I once got together a 'Book of Short Stories', but I was not very pleased with the results—there was difficulty in finding stories of a sufficiently high standard; while a 'Book of Our Best Work'—a book to which the members of a not-very-bright form were asked to contribute their best pieces of writing—did not seem worth binding or putting on show. By contrast, a 'Book of Doing and Making' was very successful; its practical nature appealed to the children, and the pieces of writing which went into it were not too personal to be unsuitable for public reading. Few were based upon classroom demonstrations, but with one or two exceptions I was satisfied that they showed first-hand knowledge. The compilation was made by third-year boys; it extended over 115 pages; and there were thirty-eight contributions, including articles on Photographing a Dinky Speedway, Collecting Train Numbers, Collecting Cigarette Cards, Cycling and Fishing, To Nottinghamshire by Bicycle, Scouting, Youth Hostelling, Camping, Hiking, How to Catch Rabbits, Bird Studying, Sailing, Gardening, Cleaning a Bicycle, Repairing Broken Chairs, Conjuring, Badminton, Boxing, Swimming, Ice Hockey, A Before-Breakfast Swim, Baseball, How to Make a Beef-Steak Pie, Camp Cooking, A Saturday Meal, Making a Currant Pudding, Cooking, Making a Pond, Making a Mouse Cage, Making a Bird Table, Repairing a Dog's Sleeping-Box, Building a Rockery, Tobogganing, Making a Stand for an Ink Bottle, and Making a Toy Lorry.

As to how, when, and where the making of the compilation should be done, each teacher will have his own ideas. I do not think that all the work can be done in class-time—it leaves too many children idle for long periods of time. But the work of selecting can certainly be done there: each pupil reads out his article (or several articles if he has made more than one attempt) and submits it to the judgement of the pupils' selection committee. (The teacher's private efforts are directed towards seeing that every child is represented in the book at least once.) The actual writing up of the fair copies is perhaps better done during out-of-lesson times. Some teachers insist that each child's work appears in his own handwriting; others are willing to allow the employment of 'scribes' noted for their neatness and accuracy. I have found it best to have the fair copies written on sheets of ruled paper, which can subsequently, when passed as correct, be pasted on to large pages of red, blue, or green 'art paper'. The large pages, when dry, are stitched into a book.

I now come to the kind of account or report which appears in most school magazines—the description of a match, a concert, an outing or other school occasion which is ordinarily among the magazine's basic contributions. Here are chances of publication which any child might be expected to want to seize; yet the lack of zest with which these reports are usually written, even by children of fifteen or sixteen, shows how little the work is to their liking. And yet here should be the school's opportunity to use its magazine not only to give publicity to its best pupils' writing but also to stimulate *all* its pupils into a competitive effort to 'get something into print'. It can be done, too; but not so much by inviting formal reports of the school's great occasions, as by allowing a good deal of informal reporting—accounts of those same occasions as seen through childish eyes. I am not opposed to formal reports; but I do very much favour their being supplemented by some such a magazine feature as a *Schoolboys' Diary* or a *Schoolgirls' Diary*, for which children from all parts of the school can write entries. The best way of showing the kind of reporting I mean is to give an actual example. Here, the writer describes an occasion when photographers visited his school, and took head-and-shoulders photographs of the children, three children at a time:

(5) Being Photographed

Wednesday, November 2nd—Today we had our photographs taken. The school secretary came round to the form rooms telling the forms to go down, one by one, into the quadrangle. Of course everyone took their time, just to miss the next period. There were many combs going through beautiful locks. I was one of the last to arrive. Not knowing much about cameras, I was shocked when I saw it, for it was a tripod affair with a tiny box-like contraption on top.

When at last it was my turn, I went with two other boys, sat down, and waited for the click of the camera. It didn't come. The photographer was mumbling something at me, and then I realized that he wanted me to take my spectacles off. I obliged, not thinking it necessary, for what difference there was with them off or on, I could not see.

Then the photographer said 'Smile, please', and before I could even show my teeth, the click came with me still raising one side of my mouth. So we returned to our form room to await the results.

(Third Year)

This account is admittedly childish, and has some touches of that school-boy facetiousness which is so commonly present in children's published writing, but it does give a truthful version of the facts, and does so in a way which would interest other children. I add without comment two other *Diary* entries, the work of older children—for the school's *Diary* should be open for all who care to offer entries, and in a school with a vigorous life there will never be any lack of material for the editor to consider. No. 6 is an account of a school performance of *Julius Caesar*, written by a boy who shared the part of Calpurnia with another boy, playing it every other evening. No. 7—a little marred, perhaps, by its jocularity—needs no explanation.

(6) *Acting in a Play*

Tuesday, March 29th—This was the first night of our performance of *Julius Caesar* before a full audience (and a shuffling, restless audience of school children at that). Yesterday, at the dress rehearsal, we had all our faults pointed out; but we missed the less kindly criticisms of the boys of the school, who this year were not allowed to be present.

It is something of a disadvantage to be sharing a part, for one finds that one is not really free on 'off' evenings. One's 'other half' continually needs attention: she occasionally loses our wig or our head dress, or somehow manages to smudge her lipstick. Indeed, it is altogether difficult being a girl. Another 'female' member of the cast, who had already shown herself very unladylike on the stage, was later seen most inelegantly clambering about the gym, her dress tucked carelessly into her P.T. shorts.

Part of our duties this evening was to make 'crowd noises'. Every time I appeared on the stage to perform this function I was fiercely accused, by certain of the stage hands, of being there unnecessarily. (Actually we were only too few.) Their language was not particularly Shakespearian, either.

The play finished earlier than was expected, and after we had taken a curtain, we departed to become British citizens once more.

(Fifth Year)

(7) *A Lecture at School*

Friday, November 15th.—We assembled in the Hall today, eagerly awaiting a lecture to be given by Mr W. Jones, in which he proposed to 'Bring Old Cities to Life' with the aid of lantern-slides. The Hall was darkened, and in the spotlight from the humming epidiascope, the lecturer began his talk. It was at first generally imagined that whenever he wanted a picture changed, he signalled to the lantern-operators by making a peculiar noise with his teeth; but we later discovered that he used a toy pistol which made clicking sounds. (He probably acquired it as the result of more recent excavations in the Staff Room.)

In a rather lengthy but extremely interesting lecture, we were shown a number of cities renowned in classical and Biblical times for their magnificence. Some were more beautiful for being presented on the screen upside down, or sideways. It was then that Mr Jones showed his dexterity in manipulating his pistol.

Before leaving the subject of the school magazine, I should like to speak about one other magazine 'feature' which can be used to stimulate the writing of simple accounts and reports. It is not dissimilar to the *Diary* I have just described, only it is more informal still; it gives the children a chance to recount incidents so unofficial or trivial that it is only their importance to the writers themselves which makes one take them seriously. This 'feature' can be called *Round and About in the School*, or *In and Around the School*, and once the children have an idea of what is wanted, there need be no lack of contributions to it. In a single issue of the magazine, *In and Around the School* might comprise some twenty articles. I give below, without comment, one or two brief examples.

(8) *The School Rabbits*

The Biology Club, which is now flourishing, has not much support from the second formers. There are two reasons for this: (*i*) They cannot do gardening (though the senior part would be glad of some slave labour); (*ii*) When they enter the laboratory to enquire about meetings, the order 'Out, or we'll throw you out!' is shouted at them.

The rabbits now have what looks like a successful litter of six. To the boys who clean and look after the rabbits, of whom I am one, the most unpopular task is fetching sawdust from the wood-yard. Today, Friday, November 4th, we got two willing boys who went like sheep. The most popular task is cleaning, because then the rabbits, except the mother and her litter, are handled, petted, and offered pieces of sandwiches. The food supply is rapidly diminishing as the ground is dug up and raked, and the kitchen is being invaded more and more for food. One boy used to go to the kitchen, coming back with a leaf of cabbage and a couple of potatoes. What happens now is that two boys go, and come back with something like four potatoes, four carrots, three leaves of cabbage, and five slices of bread.

(Second Year)

(9) *The Caterpillar*

One day when we had salad for dinner at school, I discovered a small green caterpillar sleeping on my lettuce leaf. I removed it carefully and placed it on the edge of my plate, where it started to crawl around the edge, going faster every minute. The whole table gathered round to admire it as it circled my dinner. Then someone declared that it was a racing caterpillar, and to give it a fair chance we ought to place it on the table.

We did this and watched expectantly. No doubt it saw that we were all expecting a record to be broken, so it just curled up and went to sleep. At this, we seized our forks and gently prodded the caterpillar to encourage it. At the first prong it sprang to life and set off down the table, pursued by eight forks. We decided to race it over the 'measured inch', but as it wouldn't crawl straight, this idea was abandoned. Our little game was finished when someone accidentally cut the caterpillar in half; so we placed the remains on the floor and finished our dinner.

(Third Year)

(10) *During the Lunch Hour*

Once you look at the gamma-ray screen you can no longer think properly; you may only obey the orders of the mad scientist who hopes to conquer the world with his terrible brain-washing machine which no human can resist. That is what I do during the lunch-hour sometimes. I am usually a 'subject' or guinea-pig, and my brain is completely 'washed' by Richard von Hillier, the world's maddest scientist.

I look at the invisible screen while von Hillier pulls an invisible lever. The effect begins to grow in intensity; I can hardly stand it. I pull and tug at my collar for air. I get into a state of animated fever. The lever comes to a stop. I slowly approach von Hillier with my claws raised above my head like an ape. I walk like an ape. I *am* an ape!

'Stop!' von Hillier orders. I obey. He then goes on to give me a series of orders which I obey, for I am helpless to do anything else.

Usually von Hillier will control four of us at least, and we attack robot squadrons. Von Hillier has a concrete wall or dome around him which no living soul can penetrate except aliens of another planet, who are not likely to pay us a visit. Round the dome there is a ray to keep people well clear of him. This, of course, keeps him well protected—but just in case, he carries two machine-guns.

(First Year)

(11) *A Free Ride*

One day, just after the Christmas holidays, a tipper truck came up the rough track to the place where the sewage men had previously been working.

A little while later, the truck was seen to leave, but it did not get very far. The snow lay deep on the track and the lorry stuck fast. When the men asked for help, some boys near by ran up and started to push it from behind. The truck went a little way and then stopped again, stuck worse than before. This time, one of the men asked the boys pushing to climb up in the tipper, in the hope that the added weight would make the vehicle move. This they did, but there was not sufficient weight, more boys being needed.

Everybody in the tipper shouted to all the boys around. They came running from all directions, and within a short time the truck was full. When they were safely aboard, the lorry driver started the engine again. This time the truck did move, and soon they were wobbling merrily along the track to the drive. Just past the junction the driver stopped the truck and all the boys tumbled out, about forty in all.

Then the lorry started, and they saw it out of sight before walking back to the school.

(*Third Year*)

(12) *Chocolate in the Library*

This morning there was one of those odd jesty things that occur from time to time in school. We were working in the English section of the library when the door opened and a crowd of Upper Fifth boys came in, followed by the school secretary and another lady. We began to move off, but no one seemed to mind our being there, so we stopped and listened to what was going on. Apparently the lady was from a chocolate manufacturer's and was testing out chocolate. She gave each of the boys two little packets of chocolate to try, and then they had to go into a corner with her and whisper which they preferred. I thought this was quite an interesting kind of game, and I should like to have known which kind of chocolate won, but the bell went before they had finished and we had to go away.

The last piece is the work of an older boy.

In the school magazine which I know best, *Schoolboys' Diary* or its equivalent ran for sixteen issues, and might well have gone on for longer. *In and Around the School* has run for twenty issues and shows no signs of exhausting itself. The educational value of these features is to be judged not only by the published pieces, but by the many hundreds of rejected pieces which have given their writers the chance to practise, and also to enjoy, a little informal reporting.

To write mere accounts of 'things seen and done' may appear to be not very exciting work, but if the teacher provides incentives of the sort I have described here, it will be undertaken willingly enough. In the more formal accounts, the qualities for the teacher to look for are orderliness, lucidity, and economy of language; in the less formal, vitality, an eye for detail, and fidelity to the facts. It does not much matter that the subjects of the accounts are childish: we can make no greater mistake when training a young writer—or, indeed, when merely training a young person—than to try to 'bring him on', to make him seem older and wiser than he is. If we take seriously the interests and preoccupations of a child at each successive stage of his growth, we do in fact promote that growth—make it easy, natural, and unforced, and bring it in its own time to a comfortable maturity. That is not just a piece of 'training-college wisdom': any teacher who teaches for long enough in one school can prove the truth of it for himself.

CHAPTER 3

'EXPERIENCES'

Writing about 'experiences'—An example of this sort of writing —The field of 'experiences' surveyed—The wording of composition topics—The preparatory lesson—Small value of 'prescribed schemes'—'Working through the experience'—Exchange of anecdotes—The teacher's contributions—Acquiring the vocabulary—Further examples with comments—Fidelity the key to good writing—The danger of exaggerations and witticisms—Incentive and value—Final examples

ALL WRITING is in a sense the writing of experiences, but in this chapter I am giving to the word 'experiences' a peculiar and restricted meaning. As I said in Chapter 2, what I intend to deal with here is those highly personal descriptions of experience in which the writer reveals not only a set of circumstances but also his feelings, his perceptions, and the manner of his involvement. As compared with ordinary reports and accounts they revolve more around the writer's self, they have greater intensity, and they contain more of what might be called the substance of living. More than that, they are the work which the teacher takes most pleasure in reading, and which he preserves in his files long after other work has been given back and forgotten. And they are almost the only kind of work which can be considered in any sense creative—though 'creative' as applied to children's writing is an unsavoury word, long since vulgarized by slick misapplication and by commercial abuse.

Let me at once give an example of the kind of writing I mean. The writer of the following passage describes his experience of 'being form captain'—*viz* of having, amongst other things, to stand before the class in the teacher's absence, to keep order, and to write on the board the names of the naughty ones.

(13) *Being Form Captain*

I do not really know why so many boys voted for me to become form captain, because I am sure I have never expressed my desire to be one. I was rather startled when the votes were read out, although I had heard my name whispered more than once.

After the second lesson I managed to attract the attention of my form master. I told him that I did not want to become form captain, and asked if I could resign. After a few words he told me to try the task until half term. Although I was not looking forward to the job, I agreed.

I felt very reluctant, when my task began, to stand out in the front. A number of jeers from my neighbours forced me there; more unwelcome jeers and laughing made my uncomfortable position unbearable. Indeed, during the first few days I found myself, when facing thirty boys, unable to place my hands in natural positions. To overcome this I began playing with the chalk and rolling it on the master's desk.

I forget when I first exposed a boy's bad behaviour, but I remember that for a short time after the incident my eyes did not wander in his direction. In the beginning, after I had reported boys for their conduct, which I confess I did only occasionally, I felt like asking them for forgiveness. However, after a couple of weeks I began to overcome my first fears and embarrassment, although I knew I was not a suitable form captain. I feel I was justified always when I reported names on the blackboard, although I should have exposed more boys than the ones I did. The flow of names was regulated by what master and lesson we were to have next. Incidentally, I was rather unfortunate in being the first boy to suffer from an application of the thirty-seventh rule of a certain master. This rule stated that if the form was noisy, and the culprits were not shown, the form captain himself should suffer. (I thought this rule most unfair at the time, but I now agree that it is sensible.) I made quite certain that this position should never arise again.

When half-term arrived, I applied for my resignation, which was accepted. I still think, though, that my form would have been controlled much better if they had not been so foolish at first. After my experience I can now say that I will not be embarrassed when asked to control a number of boys again.

(*Third Year*)

The reader will observe that it is not the incidents related here which make this account of interest—it is the writer's own comments on those incidents, and the way in which he reveals his own personality through them. He records his embarrassments frankly—his inability to place his hands naturally, and his attempts to overcome his discomfort by rolling the chalk on the master's desk. He reveals delicacy of feeling when he tells how he avoided the eyes of the boys whose names he had written up; faced with the necessity of betraying those who until then had been his associates and equals, he felt like asking their forgiveness. The whole is an unselfconscious record of the unhappy experience of one who became involved in a conflict of loyalties, and was too sensitive to resolve the conflict by brutal action.

'Being Form Captain' is a 'school' topic—and there are many other topics relating to school life which are capable of evoking writing of as personal a kind. But the field of childhood experiences upon which a teacher can draw for his topics extends beyond the school. It embraces all those events in the children's lives which, because they are accompanied by emotion or strong feeling, are lived with the sort of intensity that facilitates their recapture in words. In this field is to be found the raw material for almost all the best compositions: in the ardours and pleasures of family life—the rivalries and affections which exist between siblings (the birth of a brother, the trials of a baby-minder, the faults and virtues of elder sisters); in the behaviour of members of the family at meal times, or when watching television; in family separations, meetings, homecomings (a brother home on leave, a mother in hospital, a father 'working away'); in private and public festivals (being a bridesmaid, taking part in a carnival, observing a national celebration); in changes in the family's way of living (the father starting a new job, the mother going out to work for the first time, the family acquiring a car or a television set); in family outings or in evenings spent at home; in shopping or in other group activities (redecorating the house, preparing for Christmas); in visits from or to agreeable relatives (baby cousins) or disagreeable ones; in relationships with neighbours (adults and children, pleasant and unpleasant neighbours); in the planning of 'surprises' for parents or other relatives, or in 'surprises' planned by such persons; in hobbies and pursuits, and in the provision for them within the home or the garden; in the making of new friends or in relationships with old ones (days spent together, quarrels, reconciliations); in injustices done to the writer by other children or by adults; in camping or sleeping out (a hut in the woods, a house in the trees, a tent in the garden) and in hide-outs and secret resorts of various kinds; in the ups and downs of school life (wet days, difficult journeys to school, misunderstandings and punishments, special responsibilities, 'first days' at school, bullyings and being bullied, school concerts and occasions, performing in public, receiving prizes and making speeches, new games invented,

practical jokes, impressions of the school building in unusual circumstances, beginnings and ends of term); in disagreeable experiences
(visits to the dentist, or the hospital, or even the barber); in days of
illness or of convalescence; in changes of weather and of the seasons
(the coming of a heat-wave or of sudden snow); in domestic situations
imposed by unlooked-for circumstances (the care of the home for a
day, the responsibility for calling a doctor or an ambulance, being left
alone in the house for a night); in the keeping or the losing of pets or of
domestic animals; in unlucky losses, lucky findings, sudden variations
of fortune, in holidays, journeys, changes of scene; in everything, in
short, which brings with it a sense of novelty, delight, anticipation,
excitement, apprehension, fear, surprise, aversion, gaiety, tenderness,
anger, jealousy, remorse or pity. The teacher who gives the child an
opportunity of recalling 'how he then felt' gives him a chance of being,
if only for some half-dozen lines, at his most eloquent and sincere.

I have set out above what I consider to be the 'raw material' of the
most successful compositions. A great deal depends, though, upon the
actual wording of the topics as put before the children; as I said in the
first chapter, it is worth while to experiment with the presentation of
titles—it is certainly worth while to take trouble over them. A teacher
can merely ask the children to write on 'Birthdays'; alternatively he
can say, 'Write about the way birthdays are observed in your family,
relating amongst other things how the birthday gifts are chosen, how,
when and where they are bought, how presented, and how received
. by different persons.' Generally speaking he will find that the second
sort of title (a set of hints or instructions) evokes a better response from
the children. The careful wording of topics such as these is a first
essential; the second essential is the classroom preparation of the ground
work of the composition.

A not uncommon way of conducting the preparatory lesson is to
devise, with the help of discussion and a number of blackboard headings, a scheme or plan which is intended as a framework for the
pupils' compositions when they come to write them; but a little reflection will show that a 'prescribed scheme' of this kind can hardly be
of more than limited value. Certainly some types of writing—business
letters, for example, or short formal speeches, or the kind of account
discussed in the early pages of Chapter 2—are the better for being written
to a plan; but once we come into the realm of personal and individual
experiences it is clear that one child's scheme is not necessarily another
child's; a prescribed scheme may easily have an undesirably cramping

effect; and indeed, if the teacher attends to the real business of the preparatory lesson, each child's own scheme will emerge of its own accord. The real business of the lesson is not to work through a scheme, but to work over the experience itself, and to consider as many of its aspects as possible. What this involves is essentially an exchange of relevant anecdotes. Let us suppose that the prescribed topic is a description of the pupil's last visit to the dentist, or to the doctor, or to the out-patient department of a hospital—or better still, let us suppose that these three subjects, having something in common, are all being prepared in the one lesson. The procedure is for the teacher and the class to discuss, say, how they usually feel when they arrive at the dentist's door; some different receptionists and their ways of receiving patients; dentists' waiting-rooms, their decoration, furnishing and characteristic smells, and the periodicals displayed on their tables; the deportment of the other patients, including the younger children; the difficulty of concentrating on one's reading when one is expecting to be 'called'; the conversation and professional technique of dentists, and so on. In this discussion, the part played by the teacher is of great importance; indeed, what he contributes to the lesson will more than anything else determine the interest and value of what the children are to write. It is important that he should contribute relevant (or even partly relevant) anecdotes from his *own* life—tell of the queer dentists *he* has known; of how children behave in his doctor's surgery; of a childhood visit to a hospital for the removal of a finger-nail. Let the teacher tell a few of his own experiences: he can be assured of the unwavering attention of his audience, and he is doing three valuable things. First, he is giving his pupils examples of the sort of thing he thinks worth relating; secondly, he is reviving in their minds similar but forgotten experiences which are to provide the matter for their own writing; and thirdly—and this I suspect lies at the heart of the matter—he is breaking down the children's reserve by being the first to relate something personal, something from his own life, something 'of himself'. To children who are hesitant to confide their own feelings he is giving the necessary lead; his ease and sincerity are communicated, and by the time he has finished his anecdote he finds perhaps a dozen hands raised, a dozen children waiting for a chance not to comment on *his* experiences but to relate their own. The teacher listens to one or two of the children's anecdotes; the rest he will read when he comes to read their work.

Admittedly, this sort of thing is easier for young teachers to do than for older ones—the older teachers grew up in times when it was customary to keep a 'proper distance' between the children and themselves; but old or young, there is not the least need for a teacher to relate adult experiences, or indeed anything private to himself or to the members of his family. Anecdotes referring to his childhood will be his chief resource; after all, the experiences of childhood are the chief ground which he and his pupils have in common. Nor need he fear that in telling a little about himself he will suffer a loss of dignity or forfeit the respect of his class; indeed, the opposite is much more likely to be the case.

Another, and often quite considerable, value of this particular procedure (the exchange of anecdotes) is that in the process the children are able to acquire from the teacher and from one another the vocabulary, technical and otherwise, which is appropriate to the topic they are going to treat. The children who wrote of 'the lady' and 'the suction-object' (these are actual examples) might, had their compositions been prepared in class, have found themselves writing about 'the receptionist' and 'the saliva-extractor'; the boy who told how the dentist 'put some cocaine on my gum' might have talked about 'giving me an injection'. I would stress the fact that it is not only the technical words (those given above, and others such as 'cavity', 'forceps', and 'amalgam') which can be acquired during classroom exchanges; there are also the ordinary words—'periodical', 'palpitate', 'expectancy', 'anxiety', 'reassuring', 'cordial', 'adjust', 'intently', 'appointment'. Moreover, each word is learnt in the natural and proper way: it is not first hunted up in the dictionary and then employed in a specially-written sentence; *it is discovered in one meaningful context, and used purposefully in another.* In such a way, surely, nearly all the useful and permanent additions to our vocabulary are made.

I would now like to give some examples of children's work produced under the stimulus of classroom discussions. I will begin with some of the most 'personal' sorts of experience—those connected with bodily or mental discomfort. The first two are the simple expression of common childhood fears.

(14) *Going Home from School*

Dark! I hate the dark! Winter is coming on and the days are growing shorter. Instead of it being light till late in the evening it is often dark when I leave school.

I am afraid that one afternoon I might have to stay at school finishing work, and when I leave, it will be very dark. I have a feeling that the sky is slowly moving down towards me like an immense blanket, and is going to engulf the earth. I am very thankful to be in my home in the light and not out in the dark gloomy wastes of the night.

(*First Year*)

(15) *First Day at School*

On the first day at my Infant school I was frightened at the vast size of it, the awe, the number of rooms. All the corridors leading everywhere, all the rooms bigger than the rooms at home. All the cupboards with mysterious paper and books inside. All the people there. The strange noises. On the first day, when we were all given a milk, I tried to open mine by myself, but it was slippery and I cut my hand on the foil. When I drank it I did not like it much, and it can't have agreed with me because I was ill for the next few days.

I was always going into the wrong class until I finally got my bearings.

I did not have any friends until about a few weeks after, and I was sometimes lonely until Mum came to take me home.

(*Second Year*)

The writer of the second passage makes no attempt to give a connected account—he is content to record such impressions as he can remember. What he perceived and what he felt are not entirely separate in his mind: he was frightened by 'the vast size of it, *the awe*, the number of rooms'. He recalls things which an adult writer would perhaps not think of: 'all the rooms bigger than the rooms at home.' And it is interesting to observe that he attributes his illness to the effects of the milk, and not to fear and revulsion caused by the strangeness of school.

Here is a more ambitious piece of work, written by an older boy on a topic already mentioned in this chapter:

(16) *My Visit to Hospital as an Out-Patient*

As I alighted from the trolley-bus I wondered by which gate of the hospital I should enter—the main or the back gate—for I did not know the hospital at all well from my last visit, having been rushed there in the middle of the night, and having come home by taxi after my operation and recovery. All I knew was that the hospital grounds were very large.

I decided on the back entrance, for I seemed to remember that the Pathological Laboratory, which I was to attend, was nearer there. After checking on the numerous direction boards I was able to find the place. It was situated quite near my old ward, but it was unlike the other buildings in being built of wood instead of brick. In fact it was not unlike a large hut. I knocked and entered.

Men and women dressed in white overalls sat busily testing test-tubes of blood. Bunsen burners were alight on the benches. As I entered, my card was taken, and I was told to remove my raincoat and jacket and sit down.

Many bottles of chemicals were arranged on the shelves as I looked around. I saw a large refrigerator in one corner with the notice—'The nation urgently needs blood donors. Why not you?' Much glass apparatus lay about the benches, and the smell of ether was particularly apparent.

Finally the doctor (I called him this only I do not think it was his correct title) who had tested the B.S.R. of my blood before, when I had been in hospital, came up to me. He had my card. 'Ah, ex-Robin ward, eh?' I replied with a nod, and he told me to roll up my sleeve.

Now before I had been in hospital I would have dreaded having the needle, but now after being made like a pin cushion in hospital I did not mind it. The doctor tied a thin piece of rubber tubing tightly around my arm near the shoulder. I had the skin cleaned with some ether, and then I clenched my hand as I had done before, and looked away: I think it is always better to do this. I felt the fine needle enter my skin. In the next room, which appeared to be an office, there was a sudden outburst of typewriting; I felt myself shiver, not through my blood test but through the bitter cold. I was told to open my hand. Quickly the needle, together with a sample of blood in the syringe, was withdrawn. For a few seconds there seemed to be a gap in my arm. The spot was cleansed and a small plaster stuck over it. I dressed, and meanwhile the doctor filled a small bottle with the dark red blood from the syringe.

That was all, and as I left the hut a man passed in. I walked over to my former ward and looked through the window. Tony, the little boy with the burnt hand, was the only one I knew.

(*Third Year*)

What one notices first about this account is that the writer does not give us a mere recital of his feelings and sensations; much of the experience is conveyed to us obliquely, in terms of what went on around him. His description of the hut, its inmates and its contents is not mere space-filling, either: it provides the workaday background, the background of normality, against which he sets the (for him) exceptional moment. Even when he reaches that moment, he dwells little on his sensations: his discomfort is indicated indirectly rather than directly ('I . . . looked away: I think it is always better to do this'); and only one sentence is given to the actual operation ('I felt the fine needle enter my skin'). Then follows a tiny master-stroke: the moment of intenser awareness is made to embrace not only the immediate sensation but also the world beyond it (the sudden outburst of typewriting in the next room). Repelled by what had occurred, and yet unwilling to admit his repulsion, the writer goes on to attribute his shivering to the 'bitter cold'. He then returns us to the world of normality (' . . . and as I left the hut a man passed in'); for after all, what had happened to him was only a matter of hospital routine.

I would add, of the pupil who wrote the account printed above, that he was not a 'born writer'—not one who showed exceptional ability in English composition; he specialized later on, if I remember rightly, in mathematics or science, and never again wrote anything which showed the same fidelity to ordinary experience.

Fidelity to experience is indeed a first requirement in this sort of writing; though it is not the sort of fidelity which is achieved by a mere pedestrian recording of small detail after small detail. Something—an unerring rightness, born of the intensity with which the experience is relived—impels the child to choose just those facts, incidents and observations which 'tell'; and the things which he most clearly remembers are also the things which are likely to make the occasion live again for his readers.

Topics of the kind I have referred to so far—topics which evoke very personal pieces of writing, with the writer very much at the centre of them—are good first choices for this sort of composition; they are almost certain to stir up plenty of classroom discussion, and a lively exchange of anecdote and reminiscence. Topics which encourage the pupil to look not only at himself but also at his family—to reveal himself in the surroundings of his family—are usually almost as successful, even if the writing is a little less strongly 'felt'. In the following account of 'Bath Night', the writer looks at several members of his family in turn.

(17) Bath Night

As our family is large, the bathing of us all takes a very long time. The youngest two go up to the bathroom first, and are very eager to go, for they are both boys and have many toy boats and ducks to play with in the bathroom. There is also the attraction of being able to splash each other with wet flannels. My mother washes them all over, and after some more splashing they are persuaded to come out and be dried. The greatest attraction for them, apart from the water, is the putting on of talcum powder. A great deal of it is spilt on the floor, but they smell nice so mother doesn't worry.

When these two terrors are tucked in bed, my youngest sister comes up to bath. She takes about half an hour longer than the rest of us, as she has only just learnt to wash herself. Also she has long hair, which is rather a bother because it keeps falling forward and hanging into the water. My next sister, who is still waiting to bath, is glad that Pearl is so slow, because she can then listen to the radio for a little longer. Eventually Pearl finishes, and after being smacked because she has bitten her nails and there are none to cut, she too is put into bed.

The other two girls have soon finished with the bathroom, for they like to read in bed for some time before going to sleep. Officially, it should be my turn to bath next, but to my elder brother's disgust he is sent up to bed before me. He usually climbs the stairs muttering 'Lucky thing, having homework! I bet it's just an excuse to listen to the play on the wireless!' Sometimes he is right, but even so, after a lot of hard work, I think that I deserve to listen to the radio or read before bathing.

Stephen, the brother I have just spoken of, likes lying in the water and going to sleep. It's really a bit risky, but he enjoys it: his favourite trick is to lie quite still in the water, so that when I come up I think he is dead. He never is, of course, but he certainly looks as though he is.

After I have bathed, my mother and father come upstairs, and they usually have a lot to say about our not putting our wet towels away and our leaving dirty vests and socks on the floor. By the time *they* have bathed, however, I am fast asleep. (*Third Year*)

From the apparently random observations, the various characters emerge—the mother the most clearly perhaps (her indulgence of the little boys, the smacking of the sister, and the grumbling about the dirty socks and vests); but also the elder brother, jealous of the favours accorded to his grammar-school sibling, and trying to draw some attention to himself by 'dying' in the bath; while there are side-glances at the younger and elder sisters, which reveal something of the writer's shrewdness of perception.

Here is another 'family' composition, showing the same attention to detail, but a more strongly affectionate feeling, and—except for a possible flicker of jealousy at the beginning—a greater maturity.

(18) *The Smallest Member of the Family*

From the bedroom above the kitchen there was heard a shout, followed by the crash as something fell on the floor.

'Please go and see what she's doing, Michael,' said my mother, 'and if necessary, stay with her for a while.'

As a matter of fact my sister (Maura, three years old) wasn't all that ill. She had only a sore throat, but my mother, being rather fussy, decided that she must stay in bed.

I clambered up the stairs and went into her bedroom. The invalid greeted me with a shriek of laughter.

On the brown carpet of the bedroom were scattered numerous toys—a doll with only half a head, a thin grey monkey, a pink rattling plastic duck, and a teddy bear (this when pushed in the tummy made a peculiar noise and opened its mouth). There were also two rubber squeaking toys; one of these, a yellow duck I had sewn up, looked rather peculiar with its right ear of mixed cotton and rubber.

I picked up all her toys for the fourth time, putting them this time on a cream table fixed on to the wall (the other three times I had put them on her bed, from which she had knocked them down again).

I sat down by her and asked what she wanted to do.

'I want you to read me a story, Michael.'

'What story?'

'*Cinderella.*'

Then she started laughing. I looked around for the book but could not find it.

'Where is it?' I asked her.

From under a pile of bed-clothes Maura produced a rather thin, ragged book headed *Cinderella.*

'Thank you,' I said. 'If you do that again, I'll tickle you.'

Then I started reading the story to her.

' "This is the land where long ago a beautiful maiden lived. Her name was Cinderella. Cinderella lived in a splendid house, but——" '

I continued reading the story. Maura listened very attentively until I had finished. Then she said, 'Now I'll read it to you, Michael.'

She started in a low quick breathless voice.

' "This is the land where long ago" ' (she said 'long ago' with an uplifted voice) ' "a boo-ootiful maiden lived. Her name was——" '

Maura continued the story. I liked especially the tone of her voice when she came to a certain part:

' "Poor—poor—Cinderella. She ran out into the garden—and there all alone—she cried—*bit—ter—lee!*" ' (She said the syllables with considerable emphasis.)

After Maura had finished reading the story, or rather saying it from memory, I asked her what she wanted me to do next.

'Read *Cinderella* again!'

So I read it through again. Then she read it through. I think I read the book through three times and Maura four.

Soon it was getting dark, and after making her shadows on the wall of dogs, swans, rabbits, and so on, I turned off the light, closed the door and went downstairs.

Half an hour later she was still awake, talking to herself.

(Second Year)

Shrewdness of observation—fidelity to experience—the sort of truthfulness which is born out of interest and personal involvement; as I have already tried to insist, these things matter most, and are the first things for us to look for; and once we have learned to recognize and value them, we are less likely to be led into admiring mere 'clever' writing—the kind in which the child falsifies his experience in an attempt to represent himself as a scholar, a philosopher, or a wit. Here are two more records of scenes from family life, both written under the title 'Conversation in the Kitchen'; the first has the naïve simplicity of one who is content to write a faithful record of an occasion, while the other aims at humour, and seeks to show its writer as a 'funny man'. Both writers were in their third year.

(19) *Conversation in the Kitchen*

When I go into the kitchen I hear, 'Shut that door.' I nose round the kitchen for a few minutes and then I say, 'Mum, can I make some cake?'

'Yes, dear. What kind of cake?'

'Oh, I don't know. Something nice.'

'How about making a sponge?' my mother suggests.

'No, I've made that so often. I want to make something I know I like but I've never made before.'

I heave up the cookery book, an old book dated about nineteen-thirty called *Modern Cookery*. I look through it, hoping to find a recipe that has fairly modern ingredients. 'Can I make some coconut oysters?'

'Well, you can have a look, but I don't *think* there's any desiccated coconut.'

I continue to look through the cookery book for recipes which do not have one ingredient which we have not got. My mother then says, 'Why not do your homework today?'

'No, you know I always do my homework on Sunday.'

'Have you got a composition this week-end?'

'Yes, worse luck. And Latin.'

'Decided what you're going to make yet?' asks my mother, changing the subject.

'Oh, I suppose I've got to make a sponge.'

'Now you know you've not *got* to make anything.'

'I want to make a sponge.'

'Oh, all right. You'd better have my apron. And don't make any mess, but if you do, clear it up after you.'

I set myself resolutely to make and complete the sponge.

(*Third Year*)

Conversation in the Kitchen

Mother: Everyone come and help me wash up.

Father: I'm just putting some coal on the dining-room fire.

Big Brother: I'm just putting some coal on the sitting-room fire.

Mother: The sitting-room fire isn't alight yet.

Big Brother: Oh. . . . Shall I put some on the boiler?

Mother: No, you will not; you'll come and help wash up. What are you doing, Ian?

Little Brother: Please, may I watch this television programme? It's very educational; it's all about America.

Mother: What's it called?

Little Brother: The Stage-Coach Robbery at Dead-End Gulch.

Mother: No, you can *not* watch it. Come here and help.

Little Brother: I'm doing my homework.

Mother: You finished that before tea. Come along, do, and the other two as well. . . . Right, now I'll wash up, you two can dry, and Ian can put away.

Little Brother: Where do the saucepan lids go?

Big Brother: Hey, wait a minute; try banging them with a spoon. They make a lovely sound.

Mother: They go in the bottom of the cupboard, on the left.

Big Brother: This cheese grater sounds quite good, as well.

Mother: That goes in the bottom drawer.

Big Brother: If we use a saucepan as a drum, like this . . . and a set of different-sized glasses, like this . . . we could make quite a good skiffle-group.

Mother: The glasses go in the cupboard.

Big Brother: Listen to this tune, mother. Isn't it good?

Mother: Frankly, no. I've got a headache coming on. Now, please, either help or go away; preferably, go away.

Little Brother: Much as we would enjoy helping, I think we'll go . . .

Father: That reminds me—I must go and post a letter immediately.

Mother: It's very curious, but I always seem to get the washing-up done much quicker when I'm not being helped . . . I wonder why.

(Third Year)

The first passage is, if anything, under-emphatic, for the attitudes and feelings of the two persons are implied rather than plainly stated. Yet the mother's affection and concern for her only child are there— expressed in her gentleness, her encouragement, and her suggestions, though modified by mild reproof ('You know you've not *got* to make anything') and by admonitions. The second account, by contrast, reveals—or rather, would reveal if we took it seriously—a less pleasing family relationship: a relationship involving slick exchanges of talk, a resolute avoidance of domestic chores, and a general 'doing down of mother'. But of course, we are not expected to take it as other than a piece of humorous writing. How does it fare as that? Poorly, I think. And I suggest that if we find ourselves regarding it as 'all the same, rather clever'—if we find ourselves deriving more pleasure from it than from the less pretentious but more honest first extract, we should seriously ask ourselves whether we know good writing when we see it.

From 'family' topics the teacher can move on to topics involving people outside the family circle—relatives, neighbours, and friends; and from these, where the widening scope of the writers' lives permits it, to the more complex experiences which result from their venturing out of their own district—out into the town, or the countryside, or into unfamiliar regions. But whatever the writing, the things to look for are the same: evidence of strong feeling, interest, and involvement; sincerity and lack of affectation; a 'right' selection of details; and a complete self-forgetfulness in the face of the absorbing task of recording an experience faithfully. At the end of this chapter I give some further examples of children's work; my reader may like to decide for himself on what grounds they should, or should not, be approved of.

At the beginning of each of the first two chapters of this book, when discussing two other kinds of writing, I thought it worth while to ask the questions, 'What incentive is there to do this work?' and 'What value has it for the doer?' If I had to give brief answers to these questions in relation to the writing of 'experiences', I would say that the incentive lies in the peculiar satisfaction which comes of 'making something new', and that the value lies in a getting to closer grips with the realities of living. In other words, in writing of the matters nearest his heart the child knows something of an artist's sense of achievement; while by making them into external things, by giving them the body and form of words, he helps himself to understand and enjoy them, or to master and accept them. Added to this, there must sometimes be the relief which comes of a disemburdening: I have seen examples of children's work which are in effect an intimate communication between child and teacher. For the teacher, a reward undoubtedly; for the child, a possible step towards maturity.

OTHER EXAMPLES

(20) *The Child Next Door*

Believe it or not, before that child had lived next door more than a week, he had become a human money-box by swallowing a sixpence. Then a month or so later he drove a needle into his foot.

His mother was sewing one evening, and he was sitting by the fire having a warm before going to bed. When his mother said it was time for bed, he showed off, jumped up on to the settee, and landed on a darning needle. His mother, who is a frail timid woman, came round to my mother asking her what she should do. Eventually he was dumped into a pram and rushed to the nearby doctor. The needle had broken off and the point was stuck right into his foot.

The next incident which happened was the chimney catching fire. The boy, Colin, and his little brother, Ivan, were fighting over a magazine. Ivan, getting frantic, threw it across the room and into the fire. It flared up, and the draught in the chimney sucked the blazing mass into the stack. Again his mother came dashing round to my mother, shouting 'Come quickly, my chimney is on fire!' My mother tried throwing salt up the chimney, but that didn't work, so they called the fire brigade.

Ivan, seeing that his brother was always in trouble, was not to be outdone, so he scalded himself with hot raspberry jelly. He was burned quite badly, and some difficulty arose in getting the jelly off him.

Perhaps the most alarming incident was the one which I am now going to relate. Colin had climbed on to the garage roof, which was of asbestos. He jumped up and down, and then with a splintering sound the sheet of asbestos gave way. Luckily the car inside was not damaged at all. Colin could not stand up for a while, but soon he had forgotten all about it and was dashing around as madly as ever.

Last summer, when the gardening had to be done, these two young experts settled peacefully down to work. During the course of the afternoon, Colin began to tease Ivan, who, getting furious, stabbed at him with a hand garden-fork. It gave him a nasty gash, and that evening, when Colin's father came home, he took him in a taxi to have anti-tetanus injections, to stop the chances of a disease commonly known as lockjaw.

Towards the end of the summer their father built a fish-pond at the end of the garden, and to get his revenge on Ivan, Colin seized the chance to throw his brother headlong into the pond. Indeed, it sounded as though someone was being murdered.

Believe it or not, that young lad now wants to pass his exam and go to the Grammar School for Boys.

(Second Year)

Duty Visiting

Duty visiting to some more distant relatives is an annual event. One day
mother receives a letter and announces that the whole family is going, next
Saturday afternoon, to visit Aunt Maud in Reading. The other members of
the family mentally cancel the radio and television programmes and football
matches that they were going to see and hear. We know that it is no use
arguing.

'After all, we do owe it to her,' is one of the many stock replies.

And who is Aunt Maud at Reading, anyway?

When we arrive at the house, after a long and uncomfortable bus ride,
Aunt Maud does not at first recognize us, but then we introduce ourselves
and Aunt Maud says:

'Why, of course! So silly of me, I'm sure! After all, it's been such a long
time, hasn't it, and haven't they grown!'

Mother replies in the same vein, and it is not until five minutes later that
she and Aunt Maud realize that they are standing on the doorstep and that we
others are standing, half frozen, halfway up the path. Whereupon we are all
ushered into a tiny room, which is just as cold as the garden. The reason?

'Well, you see we're having the builders in, and they've taken the door off
so that they can mend the hot-water pipes in the bathroom!'

'But, Aunt Maud,' I say; 'surely, if . . .'

'I see you haven't yet taught your boy that silence is golden and that little
boys must be seen and not heard, Elizabeth!'

Mother hastily interrupts and says, wouldn't it be better if the two boys
could go in the other room and read?

It is no warmer in this room, since the workmen have taken out the
mantelpiece and grate to get at the fuse-box (according to Aunt Maud).

The books we are given are in one of two categories—those with titles such
as *The Seventeenth Book of Latvian Fairy Tales and Nursery Rhymes*, and those
with titles like *Decline and Fall of the Roman Empire*.

After an hour of Caesars and Latvians with unpronounceable names, tea
comes as a welcome break—but soon we are wishing we could have stayed
with the Latvian fairy tales (which seem to be all identical save for the hero's
name). After brown bread with an almost transparent covering of margarine
('I find butter a little too rich, you know') and half a glass of milk ('So good
for growing lads'), Aunt Maud brings in the two luxury items: a huge plate
containing six tiny plain biscuits and a tiny plate on which stands a monstrous
slab of that anathema to all children—seed-cake.

Aunt Maud looks at it with pride, we with horror. However, we force
ourselves to eat it, surreptitiously removing odd seeds. After the first slab we
all, save Aunt Maud, say that we have had enough, that the tea was very nice,
especially the cake, but that we must be going now or else we'll be late home.

As soon as we are out of sight, we run to the bus-stop, with three thoughts in our minds: that we have done a good deed and are very righteous people; that we will never, never, visit another relation; and that we shall do more than justice to our supper when we get home.

(*Third Year*)

(21) *A Duty Visit*

Luckily for me, I do not see her very often.

In fact, the last time I saw her was in the summer holidays, and at the beginning of those, too. Angela is my only cousin, and is therefore somewhat spoilt by my mother, whose sister is Angela's mother. Since the rest of the family cannot stand Angela, she is not invited to our house very often.

We (my brother and I) watch from the bridge as the train slowly stops at the platform beneath us, and our cousin Angela steps out slowly from next to the guard's van (although she is twelve now), and slouches slowly along the platform to where we are waiting gloomily for her arrival. I politely say 'Hello' to her but receive no answer. She only turns her expressionless face towards me, looks at me for the first time, and then looks back at the ground again, her head keeping that position all the way to our house. The journey of silence is made—that is, silence except for my repeated attempts to start a conversation going. When we knock on the front door, my mother invariably opens it and exclaims, 'Hello, Angela dear!', shuts the door after we have trooped in, and then says, 'Did you have a nice journey, Angela? How is Auntie Kathleen?' To the first question the answer is, 'Auntie Kathleen told me to give you this,' and Angela extracts a pot of home-made lemon curd from under her comic in the basket and hands it to my mother, who then says, 'Thank you, Angela, and thank your Mummy for me, will you? And now, I've got work to do, so run along with the boys, who I'm sure will amuse you till dinner.'

We sit around for the next half-hour doing nothing except for me asking, 'What would you like to do? . . . What would you like to play? . . . Have a look at the *Radio Times* and see if there is anything on the wireless you would like to hear . . . Would you like to play cricket? . . . tennis? . . . rugger? . . . football? . . . Well, *what would you like to play then?*' and I almost add a swear word on the end, for, to every suggestion or question the answer has been, 'I don't know!' or 'No!' or 'I don't care!' or 'I don't mind!' On hearing this last answer I receive a glimmer of hope, but when we have played what she doesn't mind doing for a few minutes she takes a backward part in the game—if she has to run, only dawdling, and eventually not running at all. So the barrage of questions is restarted until I say, 'Here's an old annual of my sister's. Read this!' and she settles down quietly to do so till dinner. After dinner it is the same, and after tea it is still the same; and at last she goes, her longest sentence having been *eight* words in length! Next time she comes we (except my mother) have decided to go on a nice long walk, taking sandwiches, and not returning home till our cousin, Angela, has disappeared until the next few months have passed!

(*Third Year*)

Cycling in Early Summer

We started out on a beautiful morning with a bright sky above us and a cooling south wind. Nature was in her full glory, the air smelt sweet, birds were singing loudly, squirrels scampered up trees at our approach and rabbits' tails disappeared down burrows at our presence. Lambs jumped around friskily tormenting their mothers for nourishment. Cows lay lazily chewing their cud among the buttercups. A little foal galloped alongside her mother on its spindly legs. In another field a ploughman plodded along behind his horses furrowing the field. Butterflies flitted from flower to flower.

And so we went on in the presence of Nature's glory. Oh, what a wonderful thing to be alive!

At Langham we refuelled ourselves and continued our journey.

(*Third Year*)

(22) Cycling in Early Summer

Turning the last bend, we came to a halt by the river. The village at this time of the year is so unfrequented. Even so, a number of small boys were dipping jam pots into the river to catch minnows. One had caught a crayfish. We propped our bicycles by the buttress at one end of the bridge, and turned round to look at the memorial cross cut in the hill. Then riding on up the opposite side of the valley, we noticed a flock of house-martins wheeling in clusters above a farmhouse. They could not have been in England long, even though most summer visitors arrived early this year. Underneath the overhang of the farmhouse roof a row of mud nests could be seen. Some hung down limp and useless; others were inhabited by sparrows; but a few remained in a fit state for the martins. The slope from then on grew steep— so much so that we stopped for a moment at one bend and rested our bikes on the bank. We were now high above the village, and even the conspicuous white rumps of the martins could hardly be seen. Where the hill was too steep for farmland, Scots pines were growing. On the move again we emerged from amongst them into the sunlight at the top of the hill.

(*Third Year*)

CHAPTER 4

'IMPROVING THEIR WORK'

Correcting exercise-books—Correcting compositions—Handing back corrected work—Pupils' criticisms of one another's work—Passages for 'group correction'—The preliminary discussion—Some examples of corrected work—The need for 'self-consciousness' in all writers

THE CORRECTING of exercise-books is one of the biggest of the unpaid social services, a quaint survival, in an age when overtime is paid at 'time-and-a-half', of the formerly more general practice of giving generously in a good cause without counting either the hours or the cost. The amount of correcting done by most teachers is remarkable, far exceeding that 'decent minimum' which custom and convenience require; and a great deal of it is done in the teacher's own time. Perhaps, though, if I were pressed for the whole truth, I should have to admit that it is not always only a desire to serve the children which impels a teacher; it is sometimes also the feeling that here, in the marked exercise-books, are to be seen the real fruits of his labours—that the exercise-books are, in fact, a teacher's shop-window. For when all has been said about inspectors' reports, the efficiency of a teacher is often enough judged by other things—by the neatness of his registers, by the silence of his classes, or by the quantity of the red ink disfiguring the exercise-books which he displays on the Staff-Room table. So long as this is the case, there need be no fear that the marking of books will die; even if it did not serve—as it does—other social and psychological needs. After all, marking can also provide a means of escape from domestic cares and domestic chores, a barrier against loneliness, and a relief to feelings of guilt and insufficiency.

The plight of the teacher of English is a particular one. If his pupils are to make good progress in English, they *must* write compositions, and for the first three years in the secondary school they must occasionally write long ones; yet no pupils are going to write compositions week after week unless their teachers are prepared to correct them, or at all events to read them. Unluckily the children's need to write far exceeds the teacher's capacity to read; and many a teacher regretfully sets less written work than he ought, only because he knows it is beyond his powers to correct so much. There are, of course, some exceptional teachers—probably a good many—who make themselves slaves to marking. I remember being told by a young and ambitious teacher, who taught English in several large classes, that he let no week pass without demanding a substantial composition from each of his pupils, and that he never failed to return it corrected in the following week. I admired him for this; but he did not stay more than a year or two in classroom teaching. What the ordinary teacher needs is a marking plan which will last him for a teaching lifetime.

I cannot suggest a way out of this dilemma. One of these days, enlightened authorities will make it a practice to give teachers of English lighter teaching timetables, and the correcting of numerous compositions will then become a timetabled duty. Until that time, the teacher must compromise as best he can. He can compromise first by making compositions the chief, if not the only work which he corrects with his own hand, and secondly by being sometimes content merely to read each composition, and to offer a written comment at the end of it. For with regard to the other kinds of written work—the punctuation passages, and the grammar and language exercises—no teacher should waste his time on these if he has compositions to read and mark. English exercises are of comparatively small importance anyway, and there are not many kinds which the children cannot, under guidance, mark for themselves. This leaves the teacher free to devote such spare time as he has to the work that matters.

And what attention should he give to the 'work that matters'? What kinds of correction are the most useful? I suggest that, as a minimum, he should try to judge each composition as a whole, and offer a comment on it at the end. A good rule is, 'Praise if you can, and make it clear what you are praising, and why.' Children who are accustomed to seeing their pages covered with emendations and censorious remarks have learnt not to expect much from their teachers —a few words of commendation go a long way. And writing is one of those activities upon which a few words of praise or censure can have an extraordinary effect: once a child has been told that he has written a 'lively story' he will often be ready to attempt another one. On the other hand, if the work is bad, and if that badness is believed to be due to haste, indifference, or lack of effort, there is no point in withholding blame only for fear that the child will be discouraged; such work should be condemned, and better work asked for.

What else can the teacher do? I leave until a later chapter a discussion of the correcting of misspelt words; but what about the other errors—the ungrammatical expressions, the errors of judgement and taste, the ambiguities, the muddled constructions, the illogicalities, the misused words? What are we to do about sentences such as the following?—

(*i*) At six o'clock this morning I was awakened by the milkman I help throwing stones against my window; so I got up and told him so.

(*ii*) The tide is now just pinning me against the cliff edge.

(*iii*) I was dismissed from my job for being late at the age of nineteen.

(*iv*) The noise must have come from a car, or something like that.

(*v*) This electric blanket has a safety arrangement which, if it didn't have it, you might give yourself an electric shock.

(*vi*) Jim nearly passed out, and I got a thorough ticking off for the way I treated him.

(*vii*) My father is a teacher, and I know that teachers fear the inspectors as much as the boys.

I need not give a long list of faulty sentences such as these, for all teachers will have met with similar ones. The question is, what are we to do about them? Should we—as some do—invent a little marking code ('g' means 'grammar faulty'; 'c' means 'bad construction'; 'n.s.' means 'non sequitur', and so on) and indicate the errors by writing these code letters against them? But having done that, what can we reasonably expect our pupils to do? First they will have to interpret the code; then discover the faults; and then rewrite the sentences, after which it is our own turn again—to check the 'corrections' against the original errors, making sure that no errors have been overlooked, and after that to correct the 'corrections' themselves. By the time all this has been done, we may well feel that it would have been more satisfactory if we had put right a few of the worst errors ourselves. That is what I and many others do.

Actually, there are sometimes advantages in having this kind of work done by the class *as a group*; and the teacher will save himself time if, when reading the compositions, he puts a star against any faulty sentence (or passage) which can advantageously provide material for 'group correction'. At the same time he puts a star in his mark-book against the name of the child whose work is to be corrected. Then, when the 'handing-back' lesson comes round, he knows in whose books the faulty sentences are to be found.

Before I describe the process of 'group correction', I should like to give an account of the first part of the 'handing-back' lesson—the part in which some of the compositions are read aloud and discussed. In a class of young children there can usually be found some half-dozen who are willing to read their work to the others, more especially if it has been awarded high marks. When each reading is finished, the teacher may, if he wishes, utter a few words of comment or com-mendation; or if he prefers it he may allow the class to offer their own criticisms. In such cases, those offering criticisms should be asked to raise their hands, so that the writer of the composition can choose from amongst them, can hear each criticism, can answer it, and can defend himself if necessary. The teacher soon notices two things about the criticisms which children offer of a class-mate's work: one, that they are more interested in the matter than in the manner of his writing; the other, that unless prompted to do otherwise they will confine themselves almost entirely to adverse criticism. It is a good idea to write up on the board a few questions which will act as a guide to the critics. Thus:

(*i*) Were there any parts of the composition which you liked especially, or which seemed especially well done? Which were they? What was good about them?

(*ii*) Were there any parts which seemed tedious, which didn't hold your attention, or which could have been left out? Which were they?

(*iii*) Did the opening sentences arouse your interest? Was the com-position rounded off well?

(*iv*) Were there parts which seemed original or unusual? Did some parts seem to be 'out of a book'?

(*v*) Did the writer handle conversation well? Did he always have the right words ready to hand?

(*vi*) Was the course of events clear? Could you have wished for further information at any point?

(*vii*) Did you find yourself wishing you could write like that? If so, why?

I have set out some of the questions which can be asked if the composition is a story; other kinds of composition call for somewhat different questions. Incidentally, I confess that I usually write the questions up in shortened form. It saves time.

At this point I ought perhaps to speak of a difficulty which sometimes arises when children are allowed to read out their work, and especially when they are allowed to volunteer. The day comes when a child finds that what he has written amuses the class, and thereafter he directs all his energies towards 'writing for laughs'. Good sense and moderation quickly depart, and the child who was once, perhaps, the class's best writer becomes its silliest. Meanwhile, stirred by his success, others emulate him: their work too becomes full of facetiousness, of exaggerations and falsifications. There is but one remedy for this—to give up the practice of having compositions read aloud, or at all events to bar the offenders from taking part.

The reading out and discussion of the best compositions is usually pleasant and profitable, but it is not work for an entire lesson. Some written work may well be included, and this is where the 'starred sentences' and 'starred passages' which I mentioned earlier come in. The teacher writes these on the board, and discussion of them follows as a prelude to their being rewritten. Suppose that the teacher has written up the following passage, which is taken from a boy's account of a day trip to the coast:

> As usual, the journey was interesting, but not in the exciting way. Indeed, the scenery was very pretty indeed, but our minds were taken off this by the aches and pains, as our car, a Ford Popular, has no independent springing. I may have magnified or exaggerated the effects twofold, but I am a restless soul and do not take kindly to sitting in one place all the time.
>
> The run down, to put it commonly, took three hours, quite good really. Camber itself was very nice, the huge beach, the biggest I've seen, was very nice. The only factor against it being the very fine sand which whipped our legs unmercifully. Luckily there are several dunes breaking the wind, but we had to use the car as a break nevertheless. Due to this, only a minute fraction of the sand came through.

Obviously it would be possible to put this passage, or another like it, before the class and say, 'This description has some faults of vocabulary and expression. Rewrite it in a more correct form', and then leave the rest to them. But there is much advantage to be gained from having a discussion of the passage beforehand; without it, the class may easily find 'mistakes' which are not there, or make further mistakes while correcting those which are. The drawback of such discussions is that at first it is difficult to prevent the children from offering their amendments orally; until they fully realize what is required of them, they need to be occasionally reminded that the purpose of the discussion is diagnosis, not cure. It is sufficient, for example, if, with the teacher's prompting, they come to realize that 'in the exciting way' is unnecessarily wordy, that 'taken off this' is not what is meant, that there are redundancies in the third sentence, that 'quite good really' is too conversational for its context, that 'nice' sounds feeble, that 'factor', 'whipped', 'minute', and 'fraction' are the wrong words—and so on. After a little practice, the children find means of pointing to the faults without blurting out their own alternatives. Once it is agreed between teacher and class that such-and-such a word or expression is incorrect, the teacher underlines it on the board, as a reminder that this particular part of the passage needs attention. Only after such a preparatory discussion should the children be allowed to write their own versions; and with that amount of preparation, the chances are that many of the 'improved versions' will be good ones.

I would like to illustrate this more fully by giving another faulty passage. It describes a walk which the writer took along a beach beneath the cliffs, and relates the difficulty which he had in reaching the stairs before the rising sea cut him off. Here is a part of this account as it was written on the blackboard:

Walking Along the Beach

Ahead of me is an arch of sandstone which is now in the water. To get home I have to go under this arch. The tide hasn't far to go now. The arch is just in front of me and, as usual, there are pieces of wood and tins and a few whole bulbs. These all collect here because the tide goes out, and comes in, the latest here. The steps that lead to my house are only a few yards away, now that I have gone under the arch. The tide is now just pinning me against the cliff edge, so the stairs are just in time. I look back over the ground I have covered to see that it is completely covered.

The account was read aloud, and discussion followed. Without actually mentioning improvements, members of the class were able to suggest that 'arch in the water' was obscure; that 'get home' was inaccurate; that 'hasn't far to go' prompted one to ask 'Where?'; that 'there are . . . a few whole bulbs' raised the questions 'Where are they?' and 'What sort of bulb?'—and so on. When all the criticisms had been made and been accepted as legitimate, the children set to work to write their 'better versions'. The following version was the work of the pupil who had written the original one:

Ahead of me, with one of the two feet in the sea, lies an arch made of sand-stone. In order to get to my house I have to go through this arch. The arch is now just in front of me, but the tide has almost reached the foot of the cliff. As usual, there is a collection of light bulbs, tins, and pieces of wood, because this spot is the high water mark. Now that I have gone through the arch I can see that the steps that lead to my house are only a little way away. The tide is almost right up to the cliff bottom, so I have arrived at the steps just in time. As I look back across the bay I see that the whole beach is now under water.

It will be seen that the writer has improved considerably on his first version: referring back in his own mind to the original scene, he has been able to recreate it afresh. In some respects his revised version is better than this, the work of another pupil in the same class, who was not always sure what the original writer intended, and who had to 'interpret' accordingly. This account has less spontaneity than the other—but it has its own rather painstaking accuracy:

Ahead of me is an arch of sandstone around the foot of which the water has risen. To get home I first have to go under this arch. It will not be long now before the tide reaches its highest point. I am just in front of the arch now, and I see that as usual some tins, electric light bulbs and pieces of wood have been deposited at the foot of the arch. They collect here because high tide comes later at this place than anywhere else on the coast. Now that I have gone under the arch I am only a few yards away from the steps that lead to my house. The height of the tide is forcing me to walk close to the foot of the cliff, so I reach the steps just in time to avoid getting wet. I look back over the ground I have traversed to see that it is completely covered with water.

So far I have spoken about the revision of pieces of writing which are not, to say the very least, competently done; but the procedure I have described can be extended—and sometimes should be, I feel—to pieces which are open to criticism on the grounds, not that they are incompetently written, but that they adopt an unsuitable style. Consider this account of a visit to a public library:

If any day dawns in a downcast manner, and gloomy rainclouds are to be seen hustling across the once blue now grey and foreboding sky, I often make my way towards that part of the Library, now become a bus shelter, where a large notice proclaims that you are now entering the Reference Section, or place of deposited children, shopping baskets, trundle baskets, and old ladies. Here silence is a thing not impressed on people, and the mounting noise is usually in the category of deafening. During any visit to this depot, little boys with large mouths and feet tramp around, each suitably

E

armed with a volume of the *Encyclopaedia Britannica* and wage war on the legs of the deposited terriers . . .

We have all, at one time or another, met examples of wordy and facetious writing of this kind—we are familiar with the periphrases ('in a downcast manner'), the 'literary' affectations ('the once blue now grey and foreboding sky'), the wit ('now become a bus shelter'), and the exaggerations ('each armed with the *Encyclopaedia Britannica*). The whole thing needs gentle discussion phrase by phrase, and then a 'straight rewrite'. One pupil offered this alternative version.

> On wet days, I often make my way to the Reference Section of the Library, which is being temporarily used as a shelter from the rain, and is occupied by deposited children, shopping baskets, trundle baskets and old ladies. Here silence is not imposed, and the noise is deafening. Little boys with large mouths and feet run around, and annoy the deposited terriers by striking their feet with library books.

Here is another piece of writing, again without faults of grammar or construction, but written in an extremely formal way, as if dressed up for publication (as indeed it was). Again, the redundancies and pomposities were discussed by the class, and the amended versions emerged.

An Incident at School

> One of the most amusing episodes of the last year was indirectly caused by a row of lockers. A certain third-former, whilst awaiting a German lesson, was standing in an alcove formed by the end of these lockers and a fire extinguisher on a wooden stand. He suddenly became aware of the presence of a master and darted out of the alcove to where he should have been standing. In so doing he accidentally tripped over the fire extinguisher which fell heavily on to the floor and began putting out a non-existent fire. So great was the force of the rapidly-discharged liquid that the extinguisher rolled about in a decidedly drunken manner, until the master picked it up and aimed it out of the window. So it was that many boys wondered as to the whereabouts of an apparent fire that day.

Amended Version

> One of the many amusing incidents of last year was to do with a fire extinguisher. A third-former, while waiting for a German lesson, was standing in an alcove between a row of lockers and a fire extinguisher. He suddenly noticed that a master was standing near by, so he darted out to join his form-mates. In doing so he tripped over the fire extinguisher, which fell on

the floor, discharging its contents. The force of the escaping fluid was so great that the container was rolling about drunkenly, until the master picked it up and aimed it out of the window. That is why many boys thought there had been a fire that day.

I ought not to leave the subject of children correcting one another's work without mentioning a difficulty which sometimes arises when they do so. It occasionally, though by no means regularly, happens that children are embarrassed that their work should be exposed for criticism. Of course, if the teacher has taken his own copy of the faulty work before the lesson begins, he can write it up without using the pupil's exercise-book, and in this way can avoid revealing his identity; but for all that, his identity often appears, either because of evidence in the writing itself, or because the writer voluntarily betrays the fact that this is his own work which is under review. Gentle and tactful treatment of the work, with some indication of where its good qualities lie, will sometimes soften the offence; but if this does not serve, and if the teacher discovers from experience that the use of the class's own work is likely to be met by hostility, he must perforce use the work of another class instead, still keeping the identity of the writers a secret.

So, by reconsidering and revising one another's work, the children learn to turn a critical eye on their writing, to realize that 'first words' are not necessarily the best words, and to recognize dressed-up language in its various manifestations. Yet the procedure I have outlined here, although the best I know of for its purpose, is far from ideal. It is far from ideal because the children are asked to criticize the work of others, rather than their own work; and real improvement cannot begin until we realize that we ourselves, we also, can be guilty of the inaccuracies, obscurities, and ambiguities we observe in the writing of other people.

There is a circumstance in my own life which illustrates this. Many years ago, soon after I had taken up my first teaching appointment, I was given a fourth-year class to teach, and the work prescribed for me was 'the correction of sentences'. I greatly enjoyed this work: the sentences in the text-book were well chosen, if difficult, and I prided myself on the ease with which I spied faults which the pupils could not, and the skill with which I helped them to write better versions. But in those days, school work did not so much engross me that I had no spare time in the evenings; and several of my evenings each week were spent on a new and absorbing kind of work, the writing of stories for an educational publisher. These were in due course submitted to the scrutiny of the publisher's editor; and it was with no small surprise and vexation, when my work was returned to me, that I found myself accused of awkwardnesses, ambiguities, the omission of essential words, and several other of the most elementary mistakes. It seemed to me incredible that one who spent his days in so successfully discovering the blunders of other writers should spend his evenings in making similar blunders himself; yet such was in fact the case; and I learned then, and in the most painful way, that an eye for the faults of other writers is not necessarily also an eye for one's own.

The trouble is that a writer always labours under this disadvantage: he knows even before he writes what meaning he intends his words to have. When the boy wrote 'My father is a teacher, and I know that teachers fear the inspectors as much as the boys', he meant 'My father is a teacher, and I know that teachers fear the inspectors as much as the boys do'—and it did not occur to him that his words could be interpreted in any other way. Yet the reader who brings an open mind to this sentence may well attach a different meaning to it.

A writer, whether pupil or teacher or anyone else, makes a big advance on the day when he says, with a shock of self-discovery, 'I also am capable of making elementary mistakes and gross errors, and can be guilty of obscurities and ambiguities.' After that he becomes a self-conscious writer, and in this self-consciousness lie the possibilities of amelioration. From the classroom point of view, the ideal situation exists when the teacher has an occasional chance of sitting down with each pupil in turn, of privately working over a page of his writing with him, and of discussing how he can improve it. But how long will it be before conditions enable the teacher of English to do that?

CHAPTER 5

THE EXAMINATION ESSAY—I

*The two pre-examination years—The changed atmosphere—
Essay topics in the first public examination—New influences at
work in children's writing—The influence of* Three Men in a
Boat—*The 'essay manner'—Story-writing again—Accounts
and reports—'Experiences'—Descriptions of Places*

IN MY final two chapters on children's writing I should like to talk
about the work of the two years which precede the first public
examination (by which I mean the examination for the G.C.E. at
Ordinary Level or for the Certificate of Secondary Education).
For many children, who have lived until now in a world of gentle
dilatoriness, the move into the fourth year is also a move into a new
atmosphere—an atmosphere of preparation for, and preoccupation
with, the world of the examination-room. It is indeed a new atmosphere: the change is felt in all subjects, but in none so much as English,
and in nothing so much as the topics for English composition. Yesterday the pupils could wander at their will in space-suits, or be the
carefree heroines of gipsy romances; today they are confronted with
the need to discuss world disarmament, the banning of atomic weapons,
gambling, or capital punishment, or to write dispiritedly about 'Shadows', 'Envy', 'Dreams', 'Pageantry', or 'Castles in the Air'. Of course,
if this transition turns out to be in fact so uncomfortable, we must often
lay part of the blame on our own clumsiness: with too zealous an eye
to the future, we set about demanding from our fourteen-year-olds
what the public examiner only demands from the sixteens. The rest
of the blame we may fairly lay on the public examiner, who ought
never to have given us a lead by prescribing such topics in the first
place. (Not all of them do so.) One of the purposes of this chapter is to
suggest some ways of making gradual transitions from juvenile to
more grown-up writing; but before I do that, let me, like the over-
anxious teacher, look ahead and see what the 'end-products' are
expected to be.

By 'end-products' I mean, of course, the examination compositions which the children will ultimately write, and I am going to attempt to classify the topics according to kind. I do not promise that every topic to be found in past examination papers will fall into one or another of my categories, but I think that many of them are bound to do. Here are the categories:

(*i*) *Stories*. Examiners do in fact rarely ask for children's own fictions —for the probable reason that few children write good stories, and that if examiners tempt them to try it, they usually bring out the worst in the children, not the best. Examiners have been known to ask for a story and add a caution ('confining yourself to incidents within the range of your experience'). Sometimes they have set what are meant to be general essay topics (such as 'The Horse') and have got stories instead. In such cases, my sympathy has been with the candidates.

(*ii*) *Accounts*. The accounts required are usually of the kinds discussed in Chapter 2: accounts of 'how to make it' or 'how to do it', descriptions of processes observed, accounts of a more general kind (such as accounts of hobbies), and eye-witness reports.

(*iii*) *Personal and Family 'Experiences'*. Again, the kinds in question are those already discussed and illustrated in an earlier chapter ('The time when I was in hospital'; 'My family first thing in the morning'; 'Washing Day').

(*iv*) *Descriptions of Places*. 'Places' is here used to include rooms, buildings, gardens, streets, parks, towns, cities, villages, countries, hills and mountains, rivers, and resorts.

(*v*) *'Impressions'*. I use the word in an arbitrary sense. By 'impression' I mean a description of a place which the writer has 'felt' with all the novelty and excitement of a personal experience.

(*vi*) *Descriptions of People*. Accounts of people's appearance, dress, habits, and ways of life.

(*vii*) *Points of View*. Statements of 'views on'; 'defences of'; and 'attacks upon'.

(*viii*) *Discussions*—involving more or less reasoned argument, or at all events the statement of more than one point of view ('What are the advantages and what are the disadvantages for the children in a family if both their parents go out to work?').

(*ix*) *'One-Word' Topics*. Topics purporting to invite the formal 'literary' essay; often in fact invitations to the writing of half-hearted whimsicalities, unconnected observations, or space-filling inanities;

such topics as those I mentioned earlier ('Shadows', 'Envy', 'Dreams', 'Pageantry') or others only a little less abstract, such as 'Walls', 'Windows', 'Wings', and 'Wheels'.

In addition to these, there are sometimes requests for short pieces of writing of the more formal kinds: letters of business, formal letters, debating speeches, speeches of introduction, and votes of thanks.

There, then, is a rough survey of the ground. I intend to discuss each category in turn; but first I must digress a little in order to discuss, not the new topics, but what, in a loose sense of the word, may be termed the 'new' children. It is no part of my task to describe the changes which occur in children's behaviour with the onset of adolescence—nor, of course, do I imply that these changes occur suddenly, mysteriously, between the end of the third and the beginning of the fourth year; but taken in general, fourth-year children *are* changed—less naïve, less spontaneous in their responses, less confident, more reserved, more on the defensive, more 'conscious' in everything they do. And as may be supposed, these changes are strongly reflected in their writing; for it is only in rare cases—possibly under the influence of what Conrad calls 'a rare internal gift of simplicity of heart and rectitude of soul'—that children manage to carry into and beyond their adolescent years all the directness and candour of childhood. Directness and candour become indeed out of fashion; and called upon to write on a topic as personal as, say, 'Bath Night', they shrink from such unself-conscious statements as that printed on page 37, and, in the act of recoil, present us with conscious falsifications offered in the name of 'humorous writing'; as it might be this:

'Go up and bath at once, Ian,' says my mother, and I depart upstairs, groaning inwardly at this torture which is to be inflicted on me in a mistaken desire for cleanliness. Once in the bathroom I put in the bath-plug and turn on the hot water tap.

Hastily I undress, taking off my tie, jacket and shirt. With a wild swing of the arm I cast my shirt aside, only to find it has fallen in the bath. I pull it out quickly, and proceed to scald myself by wringing the boiling water from it. After a big pool has appeared on the floor, I discover I could easily have wrung the shirt out in the bath.

Now I sit down on the floor, carefully avoiding the pool. I try to pull off my trousers, only to find they won't be tugged over my shoes, for I have forgotten to take them off. There I sit with my trousers inside out hanging from my feet. With much tearing of cloth and losing of temper I get them off somehow.

Next I dip a foot into the bath. Ouch! I withdraw the foot hastily, and look at the red and blistered toe. I turn on the cold tap, and let the cold water run freely. It takes me a long time looking in the medicine-box to find some anti-burn lotion for my scalded toe. When I have put it on, I put the other toe into the bath. Br-r-r-r! I pull it out hastily, and look again in the medicine-box for a remedy for frost-bite.

Who are all these people who pretend to *like* having a bath?

Now to be sure, writing like the above is liable to emerge in any year after the first, but it is in fourth- and fifth-year children that it becomes a serious danger. If I am not mistaken, much of this kind of writing has its ancestor in Jerome K. Jerome's *Three Men in a Boat*, a book of which its author himself said, 'Its pages form the record of events that really happened. All that has been done is to colour them, and for this no extra charge has been made.' But there was only one Jerome, and there is only one *Three Men in a Boat*; and the influence of Jerome's delightful book on other writers, even at second hand, can be disastrous; on school-boys especially, who are able to adopt the manner, the exaggerations, the 'colouring', without either the accompanying humour or any underlying truth. Ultimately, as I have already indicated, this sort of writing involves a retreat from experience, and it often involves, too, a sort of exhibitionism, seen most clearly when the pupil reads it aloud to his admiring class-fellows. I do not suggest that a teacher should deal other than gently with this sort of thing; but I do think he may sometimes find it possible to show, by a side-by-side comparison, that an account such as that on page 37 is a piece of writing of much greater worth. After all, if a child is given a sufficient number of composition topics to choose from, he is at liberty to avoid all 'intimate' subjects if he wants to.

During the two years under discussion, there is another 'literary' influence which is sometimes seen to be at work, and which may play havoc with the honesty, directness, and simplicity of children's writing —I mean the influence of the popular essay, that kind of 'loose sally of the mind', as it has been termed, which urbane literary gentlemen used to contribute to the pages of certain weeklies and Saturday dailies. Such essays are still to be found bound up in book form, or collected into anthologies of miscellaneous writing. Often they were the work of men who in other spheres distinguished themselves; their essays, on the other hand, made up of reminiscences, whimsical wonderings, cosy anecdotes, tiny boasts, affected modesties, and small confidences flatteringly imparted to the reader—their essays could only at their best have been called 'loose sallies of the mind'; 'loose sallies of the mind-less' would often have been a better description. I do not think the 'Saturday essay' is any longer a form of adult entertainment; but, as I have already said, it is still to be met with in collections, and its echoes are still to be heard in the pages of school magazines. In the following example its influence is clearly seen on the work of an 'adult' student, who was called upon to write about 'A Visit to the Hairdresser':

> I sit down, with my pipe, by the fire, confronted with a task that must be done: to write an essay on the above subject. Upon learning what I had to write about I shuddered and started to rack my brains for ideas. What should I do? Should I pun about the barbarous prices some barbers are known to charge; should I over-dramatize, carefully explaining how to avoid these gentlemen; should I be serious?
>
> No, serious I could not be, for in truth what really happens when I visit a hairdresser is shortly written. When I see that if I waited any longer I'd have to move to Chelsea, I go into the shop, read a magazine until it's my turn, exchange platitudes about the weather, pay reluctantly and go out.
>
> But to be humorous? I have always been warned about the dangers and difficulties of humorous writing. I well remember being warned against it. Could I take such risks?
>
> I was baffled. Perhaps I should take advice. I asked my friends.
>
> 'Sorry, old man,' they said. 'Got enough to do without helping you.' I cried in despair to my mother. 'Well, dear, I suppose they set subjects like that to test your ingenuity.'
>
> So here I sit with my mind empty—can anyone help me?

Although this is not a school essay, I print it because it shows, in miniature, some of the worst characteristics of its forebears: the lack of substance, the small hopeful witticisms, the air of condescension. Yet many younger writers have found the same subject of absorbing interest—have evoked the sights and smells of the hairdresser's shop, the person and presence of the hairdresser, and their own feelings as their hair is being cut. Bad writing such as that I have just quoted begins when a writer is lazy and unobservant, believes himself to be 'above' his subject, and is concerned to impress his readers with his own personality rather than with his observations and sensations.

Here is another example, this one from the schoolroom. It was written by a pupil in his fifth year, and although it makes no attempt at humour, in other respects it shows as close acquaintance as the preceding example with the 'essay manner'. The subject is 'The Road to the Sea',

The Road to the Sea

There are two roads to the sea: the Highway and the Byway.

The Highway is usually regarded as being the most important. It is marked on every map. It has an important-sounding number. It takes pride in going 'straight there and back'. On every fine week-end in summer, its three or four broad traffic lanes are crowded almost to a standstill with brightly-coloured motor-cars filled with happy trippers anticipating a 'nice day at the seaside'. But how much sadder and wiser these same trippers look when they return in the evening! Do they smile gaily as the rows of stationary engines begin to heat up? Do they laugh and wave when, if they ever move, there is an accident? No. They sit in their cars and shout at the driver in front. They complain in forceful tones about the roads of Britain. Nobody admires the broad Highway at such times. Nobody looks at its smooth surface or its large signs.

I do not like the Highway. My friend is the Byway. The Byway is a tiny road, and is not ashamed of it. The Byway does not overreach itself, like the Highway. Admittedly, the Byway does not have crowds of travellers on it, but this is its greatest asset. And for those who do use the Byway, it holds many surprises.

You drive along a narrow country lane with high hedges and trees almost forming an archway over it, when suddenly the road opens out, and you find that you are at the top of a small hill with a vista of the surrounding country-side. Or you may suddenly come across a historic inn, or a charming little village. The Byway is full of surprises, and although some of its jokes, such as suddenly presenting you with a hump-backed bridge or a railway level crossing, may seem a little 'sick', at least they are interesting, and fun to negotiate.

When I go to the coast, I always go along the Byway. I love it like a friend I have known for many years. I know its every whim and fancy. When I travel on it, it is rather like a playful contest between friends. Each side takes a delight in scoring over the other. When I guess what is coming and say 'Slow down—there's a sharp corner round this bend', I smile to myself at another little victory . . .

I choose the Byway because it is almost human with its funny ways and little jokes—it has a personality of its own, which I find enjoyable to under-stand.

(Fifth Year)

There are passages here which would surely have met with the approval of the newspaper essayists; particularly appealing would have been the description of the Byway as a friend, capable of its own little surprises and jokes, and prepared to engage in a playful contest with its friend the traveller. This is whimsy of the true 'essay' kind. Yet all this playful chatter does not conceal the fact that the writer tells us nothing of interest about any road to the sea, either highway or byway; there is no evidence that he has even travelled along such a road. The writer who really cares about his subject will not be content with such evasive generalities; he will make it quite clear, by the particularity of his details, that the road really lives in his mind, and that he would have it live in his reader's. The essay printed above should be contrasted with another on the same subject which appears in the next chapter.

It is now time for me to return to my essay topics, of which, it may be remembered, I distinguished nine categories. To children entering on their fourth year, the first three categories, *Stories*, *Accounts*, and *Personal and Family 'Experiences'* will already be familiar; and at first it is probably best to go once again over the familiar ground, rather than to embark immediately on topics which are obviously more difficult or more challenging.

But it should hardly be necessary to do much about *Stories*, because children in their fourth year have often lost interest in story-writing altogether. If they do still want to write stories, it is no bad idea to insist on a greater verisimilitude than one did when they were younger, and this can be done in several ways. One way is to demand that the story has a recognizable setting—a building or a locality with which the writer is familiar—and that this background plays a significant part in the story. I have read stories which have shown their writers' familiarity with the Eiffel Tower, a North Wales Slate Mines Railway (I think it was), a bell-ringers' loft, and the docks at Southampton. Or there is the possibility of 'research first' topics, where the children have to do some reference-book work before embarking on their story. For example: 'What is a caisson? Find out how one is used, and what dangers are associated with it; and then make up a story in which a caisson figures.' (A caisson is a large water-tight case used in laying foundations under water.) Many popular types of story can be improved as the result of preliminary research; there is enough encyclopaedia and reference-book material available in most school libraries to make (for example) 'Landing on a Tropical Coast' into a lively and original piece of writing. Or again, there is the challenge of the conventionally 'exciting' title, such as 'Strange Happenings on a Lonely Shore', when prescribed with the proviso that caves, jewels, smugglers, wreckers, and thieves be banned from the story. One boy met this particular challenge by relating incidents in the life of a hermit crab—and did it quite interestingly too.

But by the beginning of the fourth year, stories have pretty well had their day. Not so *Accounts* of the kind I described in my second chapter; children can hardly have too much practice in the orderly presentation of material of whatever kind; and all the earlier topics can be worked over again. Accounts always run the risk of seeming dull pieces of writing; but they need not be; the most common fault is that, if they are on (say) historical or scientific subjects, they take on the character of mere 'history answers' or 'science answers'. What we look for in these less formal kinds of account is a personal touch —the sort of touch which I think is revealed in the following. The topic is an everyday topic enough, but the writer shows that treatment of it need not be dull.

(23) *My Hobby*

I remember being interested in history for many years before I gave my exclusive allegiance to the Pharaohs. The past has always fascinated me, especially the remote past, but it was really by accident that I discovered the fascination of Ancient Egypt. It was on a school party when I was about eleven, to the British Museum, that I became inspired. I cannot remember anything about that visit now, except a vivid impression of a speckled granite head of the Pharaoh, Tuthmosis III.

It has been five years since then, during which period I have often been disloyal to Pharaoh, my imagination deserting him for the Inca, the Roman Emperor and the Assyrian, but I have always returned to him in the end. In the course of those five years, I have conducted considerable research into the Ancient Egyptians' hieroglyphics, all of which was unfortunately rendered redundant by the gift of a hieroglyphic grammar from a kind relative. This notable work informs me that there are seven hundred separate characters to learn.

However, the main part of my spare time has been spent in learning to draw, in the Ancient Egyptian style. This is more difficult than it may seem at first, since one must forget perspective which they did not understand; one must learn instead to draw the twisted round version of the human body as they saw it. Also, plants, foliage, birds and all the characteristics of their lives have to be learnt as the Egyptians would have drawn them; and the decorative effect of the hieroglyphics. But most of all, one has to get the feeling which motivated their works of art: that desire to perpetuate. Only a few are able to acquire this. The casual copyist merely reproduces work without feeling, not in the spirit of the past. I count myself able to do this.

Only recently did I try to create Egyptian statuary in the round. Here again you meet the same quality, and I have confined myself to animals, one of which, a jackal, I managed to sell.

However, my latest and greatest work was a scroll, eight and a half inches wide and sixty feet long, which portrays the life of a typical king of Egypt of the New Empire (*c.* 1500 B.C.). I confess to little pride in this achievement which took eight weeks to complete. The purpose? None but self-amusement and self-glorification. This work led me to give two lectures on Ancient Egyptian Art to the Art Society, which were very favourably attended indeed.

What exactly inspires me to go on learning and reading about the Ancient Egyptians I do not really know. Perhaps it is their personal charm and their *joie de vie* which led them to perpetuate it for ever.

(Fifth Year)

There is not a great deal of help or advice which one can give to a fourth- or a fifth-year pupil when he comes to attempt a subject such as this, though it may be useful to advise him to 'stand outside' his hobby, taking neither it nor himself too seriously. The account appears to me to have a slight detachment and to be not without humour ('gave my exclusive allegiance'; 'I have often been disloyal to the Pharaoh'; 'research . . . unfortunately rendered redundant'); yet there is a core of earnestness too, evidenced in the writer's insistence on the 'feeling which motivated their works of art: the desire to perpetuate'. Above all, the particularity of the details shows the writer's strong *interest* in what he is writing about—and where the writer is interested, there is a good chance that the reader will become so too.

As for the *Personal and Family 'Experiences'* about which I wrote in Chapter 3, there need be no time of a school-child's life when these are not the subject of good writing, especially if the writing is preceded by the sort of informal preparatory discussion which I described on page 33. It has already been mentioned that, by the time they reach the age of fifteen, many children are too reserved or too sophisticated to write frankly about their own feelings and relationships; but it is sometimes possible for their teachers to overcome this reserve, and the task of doing so is made easier if the school has a long tradition of such writing, published regularly (if necessary anonymously) in the school magazine as examples of children's work. What the magazine holds up as examples the children will take as models; and teachers who print with apparent approval articles which are pompous, or sententious, or weakly facetious, must not be surprised if those qualities appear in the children's routine work. There should be a place in the school magazine for any writing which is fresh and unaffected—it is always easy to print such work under the general title 'Recent Writing' —and children who see that this is the sort of writing which is approved will soon be writing in the same vein. Here is the work of a fifth-year pupil, already almost a young man, who, after a suitable preparatory lesson, wrote about the 'youngest member of his family':

(24) *The Youngest Member of My Family*

I think that I myself, and most other boys, don't really like little babies generally, but this baby is an exception. I think that Andrew really is the most wonderful little baby I have ever seen. He is really lovely, with big brown eyes and a thick layer of black hair. When you hold him and stroke his cheeks he gurgles, and tries to smile, and dribbles. I have never heard him cry, which is perhaps the best thing about him.

Maybe I'm biased in my opinions about Andrew because I've been able to hold him, but he feels wonderful to touch, and his body is complete with tiny nails and fingers. Everything is perfectly formed, but soft and in miniature, almost pliable and rubbery.

The first time that I held the little chap was when we called on our way to a dinner. I asked Margaret if I could hold him. She tentatively agreed, if I wouldn't bounce him, and no sooner had I picked him up than he had dribbled all down my dinner jacket. I suppose that there was a bond sealing us then, but there has always remained a trace of a dribble on my dinner jacket collar.

Last time I visited Andrew he had reached the stage of being able to crawl around, and doing so if given the chance. That very afternoon Margaret had caught him attempting to stick a screwdriver in an electric socket in the wall. She also caught him drawing all over their newly-papered dining-room wall with lipstick. Maybe I'm getting old, but I certainly like this baby much more than any other I've known.

(Fifth Year)

A comparison of this essay with one on the same subject by a younger pupil (page 38) shows the differences we should expect: this writer is more detached, and he has the greater self-awareness and powers of observation which go with his age (notice especially his description of the baby's body); but there is the same delight in the fact of babyhood, expressed with the same freedom from reserve. The writer is not ashamed to speak of 'the most wonderful baby I have ever seen'; any more than the writer of the following—an account of 'the most disappointing day of my life'—is ashamed to admit to the bitter tears he once shed. I will offer no further comment on this next essay, except to point out how strongly the experience is relived—how the up-welling of powerful feeling brings with it keen memories of the original scene ('a thin trace of frost . . . still fringed the tufts of grass'). The writing is not without its conventionalities and formalities, but I think at its best it evokes both the occasion and the emotions which went with it.

(25) *The Most Disappointing Day of My Life*

How long ago it seems that I used to attend a large junior school at Grays in Essex. How strange and remote, too, are the interests that filled my life in those far-off days. Yet one interest remains today, and, I think, will never cease to satisfy the desires of my thoughts and body. That lingering interest is sport; especially the sport of football. I will never forget the day that we boys first played football during the games period at school and were told to memorize the various positions on the football field.

Ever since that day I acquired the burning longing to play in the school football team. Then, one day, when I had come of age to be eligible for the team, it was announced in assembly that the following week, after school, a practice match was to be held on the school field to choose new members for the team.

The day arrived, but the hours passed by slowly, oh so slowly, as if time was bent on destroying the enthusiasm that was burning inside me. But at last the bell went for the end of school and I immediately rushed to the changing-room with my friend. There we proudly put on our new boots and trotted out on to the football field. However, to our dismay, we found a very large group of similarly eager boys, all hoping to gain a place in the team, and so the master in charge had no alternative but to select boys at random to play in the trial match. As my friend and I were the smallest boys present, we were told that we could not play at that time, but if we wanted to wait we could watch from the end of the field. Although our hopes were initially dampened, we still held on to the hope that after a while we would be able to play.

That day the wind was biting cold and a thin trace of frost from the morning still fringed the tufts of grass. We waited with numbed fingers and watched gloomily the scene before us. Every so often a spark would fly from the boot of one of the young players as a stud struck forcibly on a protruding stone. As minute by minute ticked by, we began to edge forward on to the football pitch in the hope that the master would be encouraged to allow us to play. But he seemed to have forgotten all about us, and the seal was set on our inexpressible disappointment when he blew his whistle and the boys began to file off the field. Then he turned to us with a faint smile and said that he was sorry he could not let us play, and finished by advising us to run round the field several times to warm up before getting dressed. So, trying desperately to hide our disappointment, we jogged round the edge of the field together.

It would have been a disgrace for either of us to have expressed our feelings by bursting into tears. But that was what I felt like doing, and all the way home I fought a battle with my eyes, trying to hide the increasing moisture that was developing around them. On arriving home I threw the boots on the floor with a despairing cry which I managed to reduce to a mere sob, and ran up to my bedroom to let my tears flow in private.

Such were my desires in those days. It seems rather silly and sometimes even amusing to think back on that long cold wait on the football field, ended by those thoughtless words from the master. But when I finally did make the grade and entered the school team, I appreciated the privilege much more than I would had I succeeded on that first day.

(Fifth Year)

One of the kinds of writing which can be introduced in the fourth year, or even earlier, is the writing of *Descriptions of Places*. The sort most difficult to write is the description of a more or less unchanging scene, presented in great detail; and it is certainly not the best sort to begin with. 'Describe the view seen from the top of a high hill or a mountain'—it is difficult enough to present such a description in an orderly way so that each observation contributes to a realized whole; and it is even more difficult to sustain the description without becoming tedious. With beginners, it is better to ask for two-part or three-part descriptions: 'A Room with a View', 'An Old House and its Garden', 'Our Playing Field and its Pavilion', 'A Church and its Churchyard', (I will come to three-part descriptions later). The pupil is not forced to go into excessive detail: he can pass easily from the room to the view, or from the house to the garden. An incidental advantage is that for most children such subjects are likely to have personal, or at all events human, associations, which the 'View from a Mountain' has not.

What actual help can the teacher give his pupils beforehand when they are to write on 'A Room with a View'? First, he can advise them to choose a room which they are fond of—or perhaps, alternatively, one which has aroused in them feelings of fear and distaste. Secondly, he can advise them to describe the room as seen from one place within it—from the window-seat, say; so that when they have finished with the room they have merely to turn round to describe the view. Thirdly, he can advise them not to describe everything they see—only those things which strike them most, or which seem to be interestingly related to one another and to the room's owner (grandmother's

furniture and ornaments, for example). Lastly, he can talk to them
about a room-with-a-view which at one time or another has impressed
him personally. I cannot for the moment lay my hands on an entirely
satisfactory example from a pupil—the best examples I have read have
been descriptions of rooms in holiday homes or hotels, with outlooks
on to striking or much-loved scenery; the one I give here begins well,
but the writer's interest in the room (which is associated in his mind
with his feelings about his brother) does not extend to the view, which
he dismisses summarily.

(26) *A Room with a View*

It is cool in the hot summer, and bleak in the winter, and it faces north. It is
my bedroom, and I spend about twelve hours in it every day throughout the
twelve months of a year. In the winter I bring out the electric fire, and in the
summer I open more windows, so a reasonable temperature is kept during
the whole year. I say that it is my bedroom. It would be more correct to say
that half of it is mine, for I share it with my younger brother who has just
reached the train-spotting stage.

Along one side of the room is Robert's bed, with a large flat-topped chest
at the head. Except on the days when my mother cleans up, both the bed and
the chest are strewn with train booklets, lists, pictures of trains, and several
parts of a Wolf Cub uniform; though sometimes these have slipped off the
blue bed-spread on to the floor. My brother also claims a large revolving
office-chair—which our neighbours gave him several months ago, but
which, as far as I know, he has not used yet except for making himself giddy
—and the clock, which he refuses to have put in a place where we can both
see it from our beds. It is a clockwork one, and *Made in Scotland* is inscribed
rather conspicuously on the face. He has had it barely a year, and already the
alarm mechanism has broken down.

Between Robert's half of the room and mine is the wardrobe, leaning on
the back of which is his scratchy dilapidated model railway, which he brings
out only as a last concession to his friends' boredom. The aging rails run
around the boards eternally, and when the stuttering engines move, their
noise comes in convulsions of electrical interference over the radio.

To me, my half of the room is of much more interest. Over my bed is my
bookcase, still unpainted and showing a selection of woods, touched up with
Polycel. From one corner leads the wire connecting my reading-light, which
is invariably surrounded by stacks of ship photographs and boxes containing
even more. Any dirty clothes are usually slung here.

The windows are also in a state of disrepair, for one half of each handle is
missing, and there are areas of rust showing through the light green paint.

F

Beyond the windows is Sidcup, or part of it, and, on clear days, part of Bexley.

(Fifth Year)

'An Old House and its Garden' can be approached in a similar way —the writer passes from house to garden, or from garden to house, and mentions those things which make house and garden 'belong together'. As for 'A Church and its Churchyard', children who are not already familiar with one can be encouraged to spend some time in a church, and then in its churchyard, making no notes but looking quietly around, and subsequently writing about the things which have most impressed them. Here is 'An Old House and its Garden':

(27) *An Old House and its Garden*

During my childhood there were many old houses on which I left my mark, but there was one in particular which always held my interest, partly because of the fascination of the house itself, and partly because of the risk I ran getting into it.

It had been built as the lodge to a mansion, but to me it was a mansion itself. It had a high glass-topped wall around it, but this was merely the culminating obstacle. I had to cross War Department property, a Sports ground, and several private lawns before I stood in front of the wall—which was really rather an anticlimax because I discovered an iron grill through which I could squeeze easily.

Once inside, I was in a heaven on earth. The previous owner had been a keen gardener, and the whole garden was filled with apple trees, pear trees, all sorts of berries, and even a vine, the fruits of which always made me a little sick—a feeling counteracted by the unusual sense of luxury at eating such an exotic fruit free.

The orchard part of the garden was equally, if not more, delightful, for here the fruits were really delicious; and I often sat on a branch spitting apple-pips into the overgrown grass, which was ideal for wrestling or hide-and-seek, or the grimmer but more exciting game of avoiding-the-adult. In the blackberry and raspberry patches, hours of quiet contentment could be guaranteed, and I certainly never had a stomach-ache—except perhaps after eating grapes—from any of the fruits grown there.

The house presented a challenge which could not long go unanswered, and I soon found that the delights of the garden extended to the house as well. The doors and windows, of course, were all boarded up, but this merely emphasized the challenge rather than deterred me. The entrance was tricky, but fun. I would start in the remains of the greenhouse in which grew the vine, and mounting a dangerously shaky wall would walk along, rising at intervals, until I reached the sloping roof of the actual house. This I would mount until I reached a small window, inset into the roof, which had been left open. Once through here, I was in.

The house was large, dark, and terrifying; and with this terror it held the greatest fascination for me, and I would creep up the booming stairs, and peep round the ominous doors, and my heart would rattle round my body at every rustle and creak.

I was always glad to get out of the house; yet I always went in next time I came, and luckily I was never caught.

(Fifth Year)

CHAPTER 6

THE EXAMINATION ESSAY—II

Descriptions of places (contd)—'Impressions'—Descriptions of people—Points of View—Discussions—Essays with 'one-word' titles

IN THE account of composition writing contained in the foregoing chapters, I have touched once or twice on what seems to me the unique importance of the preparatory lesson. The exact form which that lesson takes will vary with the topic discussed in it; but its most characteristic form is probably that described in Chapter 3—a free exchange, between teacher and class, of anecdotes or other relevant matter, in the course of which the topic is 'aired' and its possibilities explored. The contributions of the older pupils to classroom discussions are likely to be more impersonal and less naïve than those of the younger; but as the lesson itself is always basically the same, I shall not trouble to make much further reference to it. In this chapter I shall confine myself largely to remarks on the choosing of topics, and shall give a few final examples of children's work.

In the previous chapter, when speaking of *Descriptions of Places*, I mentioned what I call a 'three-part description'. What I have in mind is three linked pieces of writing under such a title as 'Morning—Noon —Night', where the same locality is described thrice, but as seen at different times of the day. Here, as with the two-part descriptions, the division into parts means that no one part need be unduly drawn out— it is the long descriptions which children find particularly difficult to manage. The place chosen ought obviously to be one which the writer knows well and which appeals to his imagination; and that is why, within the limits imposed by the title, the children should be allowed freedom of choice. When Certificate examiners ask their candidates to attempt such tasks as 'describing the room in which you are taking this examination', it apparently does not occur to them that the room will probably be one about which the children have no strong feelings, and that because of this, any attempt to describe it will be perfunctory and half-hearted. Yet strong feelings can make all the difference; and such a subject as 'Morning—Noon—Night' allows the children to choose a place which appeals to them, and gives scope for variety and contrast. I have read a good many interesting descriptions with this title; the one I give below is of a holiday resort, described (I think) with real affection. It is of Bembridge Beach, on the Isle of Wight.

(28) *Morning—Noon—Night*

Bembridge Beach early on an August morning is a beautiful place. The sun is low, and long shadows cast themselves on the flat beach. Off the rocks are the lobster-men lifting their pots, their boats chugging in the quiet still morning. Out to sea, against the sun, is the silhouette of an American tramp-ship making an early start.

The silence is broken by the howl of a dog, and around the bend of the beach comes a local gentleman, complete with walking stick and trilby, taking his Airedale on its daily exercise. Two long shadows move along the beach irregularly, finally disappearing behind the headland. Clink-clink! Someone runs across the pebbles for an early morning bathe, and the crunch of sea-boots heralds the arrival of the life-boat watchman. Then, drifting on the wind, comes the faint sound of a breakfast gong. All the beach is coloured by subtle shades of yellow and grey, and every sound is magnified, so even the doors on the end of the lifeboat pier can be heard opening. An old sailor walks down the promenade and sits on a plank. All is peaceful.

By twelve o'clock the tide has come in, and everybody is crowded into a three-yard strip of shadowed sand. Deck-chairs abound, and there is a constant stream of people from the ever-diminishing beach. Ice-creams are sucked and coffee cups clink, and, by the flagpole, a group of young people in gaudy hats and striped bathing costumes sit round a young guitarist. The housewife is knitting, the ship spotter is watching, the athlete is swimming, and the oarsman is rowing. Everybody does just what he likes, and everybody is happy. The sun is high, and dark shadows form under each deck-chair, and bodies become darker. The sea, a deep royal blue, is bespeckled with sails. White sails, blue sails, red sails, even striped sails abound. Women marvel at the *Queen Mary*, returning from New York, while men marvel at the exploits of Maigret, and boys and girls rave over the latest record. Young children, with buckets and spades, wait patiently for the tide to turn. The old sailor chats of his experiences and travels. All is far from peaceful.

Evening comes, the people have gone, and the sun has sunk behind the trees. The lobster-men are baiting their pots, the young couples are strolling in the shadow of the promenade, the dinner gong is heard, and the flapping sails can be heard as the last sailor brings in his yacht and pulls it up the shingle. The lights of Southsea, on the mainland, are reflected in the dark water, and three lights, two white and one green, chug down Spithead and to the Channel Islands. The old sailor lifts himself up. His day is over. All is peaceful again. (*Fifth Year*)

It will be noticed that the writer does not strain himself to make each part of his essay into a complete picture—he is content to present just those features of the scene to which memory and affection guide him. In the first paragraph, the insistence is more particularly on sounds—it is these which one would expect to strike an observer on a still morning. In the second paragraph, again as one would expect, the insistence is on colour and animation; in the third, with the approach of darkness, it is on lights and sounds.

There is one other kind of description which is well within the scope of children in their fourth or fifth year. It is the kind which requires the observer to be constantly on the move, and the scene to be constantly changing. It is suitable for children who find difficulty in describing a 'stationary' scene, but who are able to record their observations connectedly, in the order in which they occur. Two usable titles are 'A Trip Down a River' and 'The Road to the Sea'. I have already given one 'Road to the Sea' (page 62); here is a second one which, although in places not very competently managed, shows the greater success achievable by a pupil who is really interested in his subject. It is an odd fact that the road described here does not exist, nor had the writer ever set foot in the region he chose; he told me that he had made a study of maps and reference-books, and then described 'the kind of road he would have liked to walk down'. The result is a piece of writing born of affection. I like the balance and rhythm of one of the sentences: 'Sharp sea breezes whip across the rough uncultivated land, and the long yellow grass bends in the wind's path'; also the 'fresh' language in which he tells how the 'choppy sea comes up and down, rattling the rounded stones'.

(29) *The Road to the Sea*

In Northern Wales, a road on the way to Bangor is met by a small rough lane, leading off towards the coast opposite Beaumains in Anglesey. If you are interested in the lane and eager to get to the sea, which doesn't seem very far away, you leave the road and make your way down the lane.

After travelling about a hundred yards, the main Bangor road is hidden by a clump of trees, and all that can be seen behind you is an imposing headland towering above the trees, looking towards the Menai Straits as it has done for thousands of years . . . The land is flat and undeveloped, except for a few farms standing by the roadside, with their farmhouses and outhouses made of local stone. The lane has turned to a track made of hard mud, with grit and ash spread in places. Heather and odd weeds grow in the middle of the track, and tractor tyre marks can be seen where the mud is soft. Sharp sea breezes whip across the rough uncultivated land, and the long yellow grass bends in the wind's path.

Suddenly, after passing through a belt of small trees, your destination is there before you. The rough sea, on which a small yacht sails in the distance, is about ten minutes' walk ahead of you, and only a section of low woods have to be passed through to reach the sea. The vegetation is like that of Kent woodlands in spring . . . The track has dwindled to a footpath, and by the number of footprints, not many people use it.

Quite unexpectedly the woodland gives way to a short rocky beach, above which sea-birds hover, and the choppy sea comes up and down, rattling the rounded stones.

After the long walk, you may sit and stare at the sea, the coastline, the animals of the shore, and, across the Menai Straits, Anglesey in the distance.

(*Third Year*)

I give one other description of the same kind; this one shows greater maturity of approach, and is enriched by meditation and reminiscence:

(30) *A Walk by a River*

The river itself was small and muddy. It was of the type that can be found flowing through, or near, most recreation-grounds of any rural town. The little banks were steep, and strange pieces of wire and iron spikes occasionally protruded from the crumbling earth.

We walked along, my dog and I, slowly, without following any particular route or staying very near the river bank. As dogs do, he zigzagged through the grass before me, sometimes running on far ahead, or unexplicably, standing still until I passed him, and then running madly after me.

These shallow rivers are usually full of the most interesting things. Rusty but complete bicycles lie here and there along the river's stony bed; knives with one blade missing are always to be found. I wonder sometimes how they get there. Are they lost, these complete bicycles and handy pocket-knives? I think the fascinating sight of a solid object dropped, spinning, into the stream sometimes drives the little children to steal their best friends' most treasured possessions and hurl them with glee into the water.

I walked on slowly, the turf sinking under my feet at each step, and a brown ring of dirty water being left around the heel's imprints. My dog ran down the bank and buried his nose in the water. Then he waded out further into the river, holding himself stiffly back from the current. He had found a bicycle, or part of one. If it had been made of wood he would have undoubtedly tugged at it with his teeth, but after one sniff at the rusty and probably tasteless metal he continued wading up-stream parallel with me along the bank.

I have long wished to know the laws concerning these rivers. Does anyone own them? They are certainly fenced as though they were private property. Barbed wire fences cross them every hundred yards or so, driving unfortunate waders to the banks. I remember when I was a very little boy I used to trespass on to a farmer's cow-field and play football with some other boys of my age. It was my stubborn belief that if ever the farmer made an appearance we could always pick up the ball and wade out into the stream that bounded the field, so becoming 'in bounds' again. Nobody, we thought, owned the water.

That little stream had been very different from this one, running so slowly and silently through this town, half hidden under bridges and buildings. But it was pleasant enough to walk along its banks, to feel the springy grass under my feet, to forget for a short time that I lived in a town, and only to remember the days when the rivers I knew ran through woods and meadows, and were a sanctuary for young footballers.

(*Fourth Year*)

The elegiac note (if I may so describe it) observable in the last composition leads me to digress on to the subject of young people's writing as it relates to their own childhood, or to children generally. It may have been noticed that several of the examples of work quoted (Nos. 24, 25, 27 and 30) are concerned with childhood; amongst adolescents there is often a reasonable readiness, providing it is clearly understood that they are children no longer, to write feelingly about their own past. But the whole matter needs handling with tact and care, for the proviso is an important one. Some months ago, I found in the essay paper of a public examination the subject 'Childhood Fears', and thought it likely to evoke some lively writing; but when I put it, with alternatives, before my own pupils, they left it severely alone. This set me wondering what, in effect, the title meant to these pupils. Did it mean 'Write about some of the fears which you had when a child,' (which is, I hope, what the examiner intended)? Or did it mean 'Write about some of the fears which you, as a child, now have'? A little enquiry brought out the fact that the pupils interpreted it in the second way. Some time later I set the topic again, but worded it differently—'Childhood Fears Recalled'; and this time, merely by making it clear that I regarded my pupils as no longer children, I evoked an eager and interested response. (Incidentally, the pupil who brings himself to write about childhood matters will frequently off-set this indulgence by giving special evidence of his own adult status—the writer of No. 24 mentions his 'dinner' and 'dinner jacket'; the writer of No. 25 employs 'learned' phraseology—but this, in the circumstances, is understandable and excusable.)

In the previous chapter, I spoke of the writing of *Impressions*, a subject to which I now turn. These impressions I somewhat arbitrarily defined as 'descriptions of places which the writer has "felt" with all the novelty and excitement of personal experiences'. But 'impressions' are in fact more than descriptions of places: they take their origin in places, but necessarily embrace people and incidents as well. I have in mind such pieces as David Copperfield's descriptions of his first view of Yarmouth, or Marlow's description (in Conrad's *Youth*) of his first view of the East. Either of these makes a suitable introduction to the kind of writing I am speaking of, and by reading it to the class the teacher immediately gives them an idea of what is being aimed at. Here is part of the Conrad passage. It may be remembered that Marlow was second mate on board the barque *Judea*, that it caught fire and foundered, and that Marlow sailed from it in an open boat to a Javan port, arriving at night and falling asleep after he had made his boat fast to the jetty.

> When I opened my eyes again the silence was as complete as though it had never been broken. I was lying in a flood of light, and the sky had never looked so far, so high, before. I opened my eyes and lay without moving.
>
> And then I saw the men of the East—they were looking at me. The whole length of the jetty was full of people. I saw brown, bronze, yellow faces, the black eyes, the glitter, the colour of an Eastern crowd. And all these beings stared without a murmur, without a sigh, without a movement. They stared down at the boats, at the sleeping men who at night had come to them from the sea. Nothing moved. The fronds of palms stood still against the sky. Not a branch stirred along the shore, and the brown roofs of hidden houses peeped through the green foliage, through the big leaves that hung shining and still like leaves forged of heavy metal . . . I see it now—the wide sweep of the bay, the glittering sands, the wealth of green infinite and varied, the sea blue like the sea of a dream, the crowd of attentive faces, the blaze of vivid colour—the water reflecting it all, the curve of the shore, the jetty, the high-sterned outlandish craft floating still, and the three boats with the tired men from the West sleeping, unconscious of the land and the people and of the violence of the sunshine.

Here we have the glowing excited writing of one upon whom the East broke as a new experience. After reading it to our pupils we encourage them to search their own past for experiences of a similar character, and perhaps to talk a little about them. The experiences will almost certainly be humbler ones, but that does not matter provided they are recalled with something of the original sense of delight and novelty. I have read some interesting impressions of France, Switzerland, Italy, Spain, and Majorca, as well as some 'domestic' impressions—of a first view of the Royal Festival Hall in London, for instance. I give an extract from a boy's long outpouring about his holiday in the Hautes Alpes—an essay in which he recorded one vivid impression after another. The extract is an account of an open-air 'church' service amongst the mountains.

(31) *The Service Among the Mountains*

... After lunch we washed up with water from the village stream, and then lazed about on the bank while the minister finished writing his sermon indoors. Then, at half-past two, we set off down the slope, while I wondered where the church or chapel was. We arrived at the dingy wall of a large chalet, to find a group of people seated on the rough grass in the shade of the building. We sat down and joined them, while more people were arriving every minute in twos and threes. M. Cadier chatted for a few minutes, and greeted the new arrivals; then, at a little after three o'clock, when about forty or fifty people had assembled and there were no signs of any more arrivals, Monsieur moved a short way in front of the group, the quiet chatting died down and away, and except for one small boy, aged about two, the congregation became reverently silent.

Our pastor was still wearing his black sweater, corduroy trousers, thick white socks and climbing boots. The light wind played with his greying hair as he began the service.

The motley congregation joined in the hymns—none of which I knew—and listened while the priest of the mountain valley prayed for 'those of this valley and those who come from distant places', and while he gave his sermon. In about the middle of the service, a psalm, in three verses, was sung by a group of girls (who afterwards came up to the chalet to drink coffee from aluminium bowls). Of all that I heard in those mountains, there are two sounds that I would like to bring back to England and keep close at hand. One is the sound of hundreds of cowbells echoing from one slope to another; the other is the sound of those girls praising gloriously, and in song, the God who made the ground on which they stood and the mountains around them. The singing must have been very soothing, for it sent to sleep the boy of two, who stopped bawling during the second verse, and slumbered in a sprawl across his mother's outstretched legs.

After the final blessing the reverent air gradually departed. For a while it was as if no one quite knew whether he was still in church. The spell was soon broken, however, and the conversation rose to the pitch usual with the peasants of those mountains.

(Fourth Year)

I must not leave the subject of 'impressions' without recommending teachers to explore the possibilities of any local or national event which has colour or individuality in it. I am thinking of such an event as a carnival or a circus visit or, when good fortune brings it along, a royal procession, a royal wedding, or a coronation. The coronation in 1953 of Queen Elizabeth of England stirred up amongst school children a fever of excitement which sometimes put words into the mouths of even the inarticulate. The writer of the following was a boy of no exceptional gifts—yet the strong feelings engendered by the occasion (a visit to London on the evening of the day after Coronation Day) gave him fluency, and one or two sentences of his long account seem to me to have real eloquence.

(32) *London at Coronation Time*

... We reached London and met Jim and Noreen as arranged, and came out of the station into the dense crowds and heavy traffic.

It took us about five minutes to cross the first road, and it grew worse as we got into the centre of the West End. I am rather hazy as to which route we took, but I think that we turned right along the Strand and then through various streets, all the time dragging the girls past dress shops and letting them drag us past men's clothes, until we came out into Trafalgar Square. The traffic here was even worse, and coaches were at a standstill, only moving feet at a time. We dodged through the traffic on to the Square itself.

Here also the crowds were thick, although there was more space to breathe in. We went close up to the fountains, and were soaked by fine spray when a strong gust of wind blew over. The thing which struck me was the uniforms which surrounded me: I couldn't go five yards without bumping into soldiers and airmen of all colours and countries, a lot of them being Americans. . . . Then we went up to Haymarket and into Piccadilly Circus. Eros was in his golden cage, which looked very strange to me, for I had seen him many times in his natural state. The advertising signs were brilliant in their reds and blues, and car-drivers were having quite a difficult job missing people looking up and around them, and not looking to themselves. Here I found myself with my arm round Noreen's waist and we continued on our way together.

The Mall was really breath-taking. The triumphal arches were illuminated and were really beautiful, the delicate network picked out in gold against the sky. A great crown was suspended beneath each of the four arches. We had difficulty in making our way along, for the crowds and traffic were amazing. On we went, until at last the massive bulk of the Victoria Memorial was before us, and behind it was the palace, transformed to a golden palace by floodlights. The balcony was spotlighted, though empty. Emotion was high, for it was only the night after the Coronation, and one had only to wave an umbrella and cheer amongst the tremendous crowd to have the whole forty thousand cheering.

We stayed there for about an hour, hoping for the Queen to appear, but at last we left the Mall and went through St James's Park, which was beautifully dark and calm after the shouting and the lights of the Mall. We came out along Birdcage Walk, up Whitehall and back to Charing Cross. We were in time to catch the last train home.

On the way back, Noreen went to sleep on my shoulder and I went to sleep with my face buried in her hair; and so ended a wonderful evening.

(*Fourth Year*)

Writing *Descriptions of People* is a good deal more difficult than writing descriptions of places, and the uninviting topics so often prescribed in public examinations ('Write a character sketch of an old soldier or an old sailor') do little to encourage children to try their hand at this work. One thing is certain—such descriptions can never be successfully written according to a set plan (describing in turn the subject's physique, clothes, habits, and so on). The writer needs to visualize his person as a complete being, moving in his customary environment, and the account of him needs to be selective rather than exhaustive. It is no bad idea to start with topics which involve places as well as people. 'A Shop and Its Owners'—'A Bus and Its Crew'— 'My Friend's House and His Family'—those are the sort of topic I mean. I have read some excellent accounts of 'My Friend's House and His Family'. The description of the house provides an introductory setting, so that the writer does not start 'from cold'; he makes an easy transition to his friend's mother and father, and so to the brothers and sisters, and he is not faced with the necessity of writing exhaustively upon any one individual.

Later on, when an essay-length description of a single person is desired, the writer should be given freedom to choose his subject, and it should be remembered that he will write best about someone who has affected him personally—therefore usually not a fictional or an historical figure. I give here a topic which—especially if it is set in the extended form suggested later—often calls up some lively writing: 'Describe a person, other than a relative, who has impressed you as having a very strong character.' A colleague remarked to me that, outside a child's family circle, the people who usually make the strongest impression on him are his teachers. Here is a boy's account of the head teacher of his former school:

(33) *A Man of Strong Character*

Mr Barking was indeed a very self-willed and strong individual, and being headmaster of a school in a small Midland town, he had ample opportunity to display his forcefulness to his pupils, whether in a peaceful or a violent manner. He was a very stout person and full of charm and personality, his large red face accentuating the smallness of his round blue eyes, and his small spectacles creating an atmosphere of pleasance and warmth wherever he went. He had a large shining bald patch on the top of his head, and a small bright nose to match, which, although he religiously abstained from drinking, indicated a merry, joyful life.

But it was not drink and high life that tinged his shiny face that rosy pink hue and creased a smile on his large cheeks; no, it was his love of the outdoor life and the tang of the open air in his nostrils that made him the man he was. Every English period he would stride merrily into the form room, his large gown flowing behind him and his large waistcoat, adorned with a gilt watch chain, protruding before him. Then he would climb into his large chair, place his large red hands flat on the old desk, and proceed to tell us of his wanderings, while the fascinated class listened intently about the moors of Devon, the coast of Cornwall, and the highlands of Scotland. He would tell stories of the times when, while he was a junior master at the school, he formed a rambling club for his pupils. With rucksacks on their backs, and the lust for adventure pounding through their veins, this happy band would set out on a Saturday morning to tramp the roads and fields around.

He strongly convinced us that those were the best days for viewing the countryside, before man had encroached upon its beauty, and before the accursed motor-car had carried its complements of city dwellers to litter and crowd the fields. 'There are still a few places left untouched,' he would say; but he always refused to tell us where; 'because,' he said, 'next time I go, I will find a whole horde of tourists driving their heavy cars over it, lighting fires on it, and leaving nasty bits of paper lying around.' He was quite content to visit any country district of England, however dull, provided that there were no cars, people, or litter to bother him.

Often this wonderful man would show us some sketches he had made in the highlands of Scotland. They were none of them works of art, but his tiny nostrils twitched with excitement as he explained to us the story of each drawing. One day he even brought along a few photographs to show us, but he refused to tell us where he had taken them, and I can quite understand his attitude.

Although he spent a large part of his lesson carried away with his stories, nevertheless he was an excellent teacher. Somehow he managed to indoctrinate in us a good knowledge of English literature, and, as can be expected, he was very strict. However, the boys were very fond of him, and were sorry to see him make way for a younger man. I met him a few weeks ago; he was about to take a long walk up to an old ruined castle to draw a picture of the marvellous view obtainable there. After we had said hello and discussed school life, I watched his large figure toil slowly but determinedly up the long road until he was out of sight. There was a happy man.

(Fifth Year)

It will have been noticed that this account of Mr Barking is in places rather conventionally phrased (the writer uses such expressions as 'religiously abstained', 'full of charm and personality', 'tang of the open air', and 'happy band')—yet it seems to me to have some commendable features too. First, there is the writer's strong interest in his subject, evidenced by the careful details and by the fact that his own thoughts and feelings have clearly been influenced by those of his teacher. Then there is the way in which he has introduced descriptions of his subject's personal appearance—not only a general description, but also descriptions of him as seen on memorable occasions (when entering the classroom or when talking about his drawings). Again, there is the bringing in of snatches of conversation and references to particular incidents. Observing these things, we may think it helpful to give more detailed instructions to pupils attempting this topic. As, 'Describe a person, other than a relative, who has impressed you as having a very strong character. Give some account of his appearance as you recall it on the most memorable occasions of your meeting with him, and introduce some of his most characteristic sayings and doings.'

And now, what of the *Points of View* and the *Discussions* which are invariably to be found amongst the kinds of writing demanded by examination essay papers? On an earlier page I expressed the view that such topics as 'World Disarmament' and 'Gambling' were unsuitable for children taking their first public examination. In saying this I do not wish to imply that children of fifteen are too young to take an interest in public matters or in subjects of current controversy—only that their views, when written down, are likely to have little that is original or personal about them. We come up against the question of the good and the bad chief examiner (an examiner's competence is shown by nothing so much as by the topics in his essay paper); if he chooses discussion topics which demand familiarity with the 'major controversies of the day', he puts many of his candidates, and perhaps not the worst of them, at a serious disadvantage. Admittedly, he has the support of a good many foolish parents—and perhaps a few foolish teachers too—for whom a prematurely-acquired body of opinion on current affairs and on major social and moral problems is the mark of the well-informed teenager. But it is a fact that these 'well-informed' teenagers are not always found to be the most gifted ones; often enough they are mere mediocrities, whose desperate cultivation of the passing hour, carried out at a time when their more gifted contemporaries are still grappling with ordinary adolescent preoccupations, reveals only a pitiful and limited precocity.

However that may be, it remains a truth that the topics on which the younger teenager writes with the greatest competence and feeling are those which concern his own world, with himself as its centre—those which involve him not as a member of society but as a private person. That 'world with himself as its centre' is certainly large enough—it embraces his home, his parents, his brothers and sisters, and every subject of domestic controversy; his clothes and personal appearance; his school and his associates, together with all the differences of opinion which school and social life generate; his teachers and club leaders; his occupations beyond the home (clubs, church-going, pastimes, dances, games, expeditions); his own developing mind and body; his studies, with his notions of their usefulness or uselessness; his groping into his own past, his sense of the future, and his speculations regarding employment, marriage, success, childhood, old age, and death. On all these matters which affect him so nearly he is constantly forming and revising opinions, and it is on these that he is most likely to express views which are 'felt', personal to himself, and suitable to a child of his age.

When first we introduce work of this rather exacting kind, it is a good practice to demand from the children, not complete lengthy essays, but mere informal pieces of writing which need be no longer than the writer chooses. As many as three or four should be set as a single homework assignment. I have in mind such subjects as these: (*i*) Discuss 'suitable shoes'; (*ii*) Give your views on funerals; (*iii*) 'Dancing is a waste of time.'—Do you agree? (*iv*) Write about the hair styles you approve of. (*v*) What do you consider to have been the good things about your own upbringing? (*vi*) 'A big house, a big car, and a handsome wife (or husband).'—What else do you want out of life?

—And other topics. There should be at least a dozen for the children to choose from, and they should be allowed, if they wish, to write as little as one short paragraph of random observations. Later on, when they have had practice and have acquired confidence, they can be encouraged to attempt topics which give scope for the expression of more than one point of view, and which consequently invite a more extended layout. I am thinking of two-part topics, such as ' "Everybody has a good side and a bad side."—Show how this is true of you'; and three-part topics, such as this: 'Give, in three well-defined sections of your essay, three different points of view on a subject which has recently caused argument in your family or amongst your friends.'

Below I give a brief essay expressing the writer's views on 'The Ideal Woman', a topic I discovered in an essay paper of one of the more enterprising Examination Boards. Set before the pupils in an 'extended' form, the topic was worded like this: 'Write about "The Ideal Woman", mentioning and illustrating what you think to be her distinguishing qualities. Do not give too much space to describing her person, but give some thought to the older teenager, the wife-and-mother, and the woman in her middle or later years.' The classroom discussion which preceded the writing was brisk, for the topic, once it had been set out as above, was seen to give scope for full-length treatment; and of the various essays on it I particularly liked this one, written by a serious boy of some sensibility.

(34) *The Ideal Woman*

Although 'looks are not all-important' it must be admitted that they play a large part in one's opinions. Before marriage, I shall not expect the girl in question to be too serious or too worried about how much I spend on her, for instance when I take her out. When I do take her out, I shall not mind what my friends think of her; I hold different standards from those of my friends. My opinion of the beauty of some of the supposed 'dream girls' is a poor one; I like light, perhaps golden hair (with a girl of course), cut short in a feminine sort of way, and (without wanting to turn this into a list) a smooth-complexioned face, not hidden by locks of hair, with a smile always ready to show. Although a slim waist is nice, I should prefer her *not* to have a figure like an eight. I should like her to allow me to spend money on her without her telling anyone; her associations with my friends, however, I should leave to her—if she doesn't like them she needn't meet them. I should expect her to be understanding, and at times serious—though only when necessary. A final clause: she should not rely too much on make-up. 'If she were *meant* to have long eyelashes and blue eyelids she would have been given them . . .'

Assuming I were to find this practically non-existent woman, and we were to get married, she would still have certain requirements to fill. My wife would not need to be above a reasonable intelligence—as I'm not myself—but she would have to be a little more serious when she had a house to run, and children to look after. Much of my money would still be spent on her, and most of the rest on our children, and I hope she wouldn't object to my spending some money on myself. She could buy anything in reason . . . this does, of course, draw the line at most of the hats on the market. She would be a pleasant hostess, and would make sure that she (and I) looked nice when we went out. Perhaps I can be excused these rather idealistic unrealistic views; I feel that one should spend money on one's wife. The title is 'The Ideal Woman', and a few five-year-old's views left over until one is fifteen still seem to take priority.

When we reach old age, I hope that we don't simply live a life of nothing-ness—but old age *is* a problem and one which it is difficult to solve. I hope that we shall take an interest in life around us and keep up with the times. One fervent hope is that we won't pay *too* much attention to the 'trouble with the young people today' and that we won't fuss *too* much over the way our grandchildren are brought up. But this depends largely on my wife.

(Fifth Year)

To this account of 'The Ideal Woman' I add, without further in-troduction, one two-part essay—on 'The Drawbacks and Joys of Being Young'. Both essays seem to have the personal approach, the modesty, the informality and the sincerity which one looks for in writing of this kind.

(35) *The Drawbacks and Joys of Being Young*

I consider that youth has many joys to offer, but it also has several almost intangible drawbacks. Firstly, most young people live with their parents, and are thus little concerned about income tax, rates and the other financial bothers which seem to accumulate around one as one becomes older. Today, in Britain at least, people have never been so prosperous, and consequently young people are mostly well fed and clothed, and many are afforded luxuries which were beyond the reach of their parents. This prosperity does breed happiness to a certain extent, but behind this brave, happy, carefree exterior, I think all young people who ever stop to think about themselves, and where they are going, feel a kind of poignant and somewhat apprehensive anticipa-tion of the future.

However needless this apprehension may seem to people who have sur-vived a world war and the hardship that followed, it is very real in my mind,

G

and I am sure it is present to varying degrees in other young people. Some young people are either so active that they have no time to think, or they prefer not to, but for me the inexperience of my youth presents many different problems. One problem is that of employment: I ask myself what job could I possibly do with my knowledge. I can prepare crystals of copper sulphate from copper oxide and sulphuric acid, and I can conjugate *être* in at least four tenses, but what sort of job can I do with these qualifications? Another troubling thought is that, with the rather fast rate of exchange of girl friends, how will I know when to get married, or indeed whether to get married at all? Such thoughts often run throughout the young mind in more sober moments, but one must not imagine that the inexperience felt by most teenagers causes continual depression.

One of the most delightful things about being young and growing up is that one is learning new things and having fresh experiences nearly every day. I do not think that any boy would ever forget his first 'date', his first illicit cigarette, his first chance of driving a powered vehicle. Experiences like this are what add to the pleasure and interest of being young. The first time a boy puts on a pair of long trousers, and the first time a girl wears a pair of stockings, they feel that they really are growing up, and this is a welcome feeling to most young people. In the stage of fastest development, most boys at least feel a great comradeship with their contemporaries, and take great delight in the virility and spirit which is a feature of healthy youth. I cannot speak for all youths in this respect, but I find that life comes in spasms of depression and longer periods of real bursting happiness. As it is said that happiness can only be felt after the experience of sadness, I think that the brief periods of depression which are probably a feature of most boys' adolescence are quite justified.

(Fifth Year)

In the previous chapter, I gave some space to condemning the so-called literary essay, especially the degenerate form of it which, as a 'loose sally of the mind', has often been an acceptable feature of certain periodicals and daily newspapers. It is presumably this kind of writing which is looked for from our pupils by those examiners who set such '*One Word*' *Topics* as 'Shadows', 'Dreams', 'Walls', 'Envy', and the rest of them. Indeed, a friend of mine who marks essays for one of the Examination Boards tells me that such writing as 'The Road to the Sea' (page 62) is thought highly of by his chief examiners. I give below the worthiest example I can find of this sort of essay—an essay on 'Shadows'. In it the writer applies all his misused ingenuity to the task of proving something he does not really believe —that 'shadows are in the whole of our life'; and it must be granted that he achieves a sort of bleak triumph when he manages to work in 'the shadow of death' at the end. Yet when we know that the writer of 'Shadows' is also the writer of 'The Service Among the Mountains' (No. 31); when we are told that the two pieces of writing were written within a fortnight of each other; when we compare the hesitancy and the contrivance of the former with the assurance and naturalness of the latter; then we cannot help wondering if it is worth while asking young writers to waste their time on 'one-word' topics at all. The two essays are a sad illustration of a difference which often distinguishes bad from good writing—the difference between 'having to say something' and 'having something to say'. It is the pupil who has something to say whose writing will interest us most, and if we properly understand our jobs as teachers and examiners, we shall direct our efforts towards giving him as many chances as possible of saying it.

Shadows

When we think of a shadow, what image is conjured up in our minds. Possibly our first conception is the shadow of some person or some object which holds a special place in our memory.

A shadow is one of the most dramatic of all phenomena, and being so, it makes such an impression on our minds that many of our memories are influenced by, if not composed of, shadows. It is the shadowy surroundings which make a café under the trees so enchanting; the shadow is the essence of our recollections of mountain evenings, or even of the long summer evenings at home. Few beautiful spectacles or pleasant experiences take place in bright sunshine. For his pleasure man seeks shadow: he reclines in the shade of a sturdy elm-tree; he enjoys the flicker of shadows in candle-light; the scenes nearest his heart are enhanced by wavering shadows.

There is almost nothing so prominent in our lives which is as truly negative as a shadow. A shadow is simply an absence of light; that is certainly entirely negative. Darkness is one continuous shadow; and even in daylight the shadows lose their individuality when an unthinking cloud crosses the path of our light, and casts one universal shadow. While we have daylight, shadows do, in fact, give us a complete chronicle of the sun's behaviour? Each shadow has a message which can be deciphered.

Shadows are particularly evident in certain circumstances. We see them formed in duplicate when the spotlight falls on the star performer of an ice-show. The film director makes free use of this device: we see the villain's shadow before we see the villain himself. The shadow on the blind is a favourite last resort of the detective-fiction writer. The painter gives us his interpretation of the phantasm of shadows.

For many people, films are the chief entertainment; yet do they realize that their pastime is nothing but shadows—that these latter are the very fundaments of the black-and-white picture? 'Ah,' you may say, 'but what about the sound?' Shadows enter even here: the sound is created by a 'stripe' along the edge of the film, a 'stripe' which consists of light and shade.

Indeed, shadows are in our whole life. They are everywhere: at work, we see the shadows of our hands on our books, our controls, or whatever human contrivances we work at; in town, we are always in or near shadow except when the street we are in points towards the sun; in the country we enjoy the shade of a convenient tree, of a cottage wall. These patches of darkness are so evident in our lives that several common sayings contain the word 'shadow'. Shadows are with us all the time, even until we eventually confront the very shadow of death itself.

(Fourth Year)

CHAPTER 7

THE CLASS READER

The class reader—Reading aloud and reading to oneself—
Testing their memories—'Teaching tests'—Studying the
characters—The story as a whole—The writer's 'style'

'CLASS READER' is of course the term ordinarily applied to a prose work chosen for reading and study in class. In the early part of this century the class Reader was usually a book of extracts from longer works, from novels particularly; nowadays it is more often a long continuous story—a novel, a romance, or a mere yarn. In any school where numerous story-books are available, either as ordinary stock or as part of class or school libraries, the class reader will very likely be only one of the several books which a boy or a girl will read during a school term. There will be others which will be read more casually— romped through or even skipped through; and this reading will be done at home, or in spare moments at school, or in 'silent reading' periods. The class reader differs from these in that it is chosen by the teacher as deserving closer attention, and some parts of it will usually be read aloud in the classroom.

During the years of this century which preceded the First World War, and even during the war itself and for a time after it, the value of reading aloud was never questioned, for the Victorian practice of 'parlour reading' during the long winter evenings had died slowly, and reading aloud was still considered a social accomplishment. In school it was considered more than an accomplishment—it was considered a necessity; for the supply of classroom readers was meagre and here was the most obvious means of making a book last for a long time. The value of reading aloud was not seriously questioned, I fancy, till the late nineteen-twenties, when people began to deplore the amount of classroom time given to it, pointing out that the majority of adult reading was done silently, and arguing that it was in silent reading, not in reading aloud, that children needed practice at school. The argument was one which it was difficult to controvert; the only reasonable objection to it was that it was too uncompromising; and it might have had the effect of killing reading aloud altogether if that practice had not been far too convenient a one for teachers to abandon so lightly.

What, nowadays, is there to be said in favour of it? Obviously, it ensures that the book is read completely, if not attentively; it also ensures that all the pupils reach the same spot at the same time (very desirable if a test or some other kind of written work is to follow). In cases where the book is an ambitious choice—shall we say a story of Lawrence or of Conrad in which there are puzzling allusions, implications, cross-references, or overtones of meaning—there is much advantage in having the words read aloud: the teacher then can, without much disturbing the flow of the narrative, interject a rapid word from time to time, and so make sure that an essential point is not missed. Then in cases where a long story has already been read silently (read for homework or preparation, perhaps), it is often desirable to have parts of it read aloud in class—parts which illustrate the theme, maybe, or merely parts which are especially enjoyable, and which are the more enjoyable on this second reading, when the pleasure can be shared with others. And one more thing: if a long novel has to be rapidly revised before an examination, it is no bad practice for the class to read to one another a selection of the 'highlights'—a selection so arranged that, with the help of linking matter improvised and spoken by the teacher, they form a connected narrative.

Thus much can be said in favour of reading aloud; nevertheless, the case against it remains very strong, particularly when it is the only reading the children ever do. If children are to make headway with their general education, they must early develop the capacity to read on their own. Moreover, if the story or novel is a long but absorbing one—as it might be *Lorna Doone* or *The Cloister and the Hearth*—it suffers much from being taken at a slow pace; the pupils need to be allowed to rollick through it on their own, and then come back to parts of it for classroom gloating. (I can recall in my first year at school reading Stevenson's *The Black Arrow*, and being strongly impressed by scenes and incidents in it; but the slow pace at which we were forced to go prevented me from seeing these parts as a connected story—and indeed, we never finished it.) Above all, in cases where the novel is one which has been prescribed for a public examination, the reading of it aloud—the whole novel, from cover to cover—must surely be a waste of that time which ought rather to be spent in the detailed study of it.

To these remarks I should like to add one suggestion. In these days when many more readers can be come by than was formerly the case, it is not a bad idea to have one prose book per term especially reserved for reading aloud. It can be used for filling in odd gaps of time—for example, at the beginning of a lesson, while the teacher is writing up a lengthy extract on the board. Reasonably well-ordered children can be trained to organize this reading amongst themselves, and to begin it before their teacher comes into the room. Exceptionally well-ordered children will read thus in the absence of the teacher with as few interruptions as if he were present.

Whichever method of reading is adopted, most teachers occasionally give tests on the reading which has been done. 'Read those chapters for homework, and I will give you a test in class.' It can be instructive to watch children preparing themselves for such a test, for from the kind of preparation they make we can often judge the usefulness of our teaching. Do they commit to memory a list of persons, places, and distances? Do they record inkily on desk-lids, or miserably on bits of blotting-paper, the meanings of all the 'hard words'? If these are the things they try to memorize, then clearly these are the things they expect to be asked about; yet are not some of them the things which we ourselves would think of least importance, and take no shame in forgetting? And when, at the end of the term, we congratulate ourselves with the thought that *Treasure Island* has been 'thoroughly done and tested', have we really done anything useful beyond ensuring that thirty young unfortunates have not dodged their homework? A classroom test which concerns itself solely with memorized names, facts, and definitions will often hinder study rather than promote it: it treats a novel as if it were a book of science, or, much worse, a mere source of unappetizing information, and not as a source of pleasure or as a means of enlivening the mind. Still, tests of the kind I am referring to—essentially tests of the memory—will no doubt continue to be given; if we do give them, let us make sure that they are not utterly purposeless and worthless.

The most popular of all memory tests is the 'slip test', where the children are given slips of paper, and are required to jot down brief answers in numbered order, after which they are allowed to mark the work themselves. There are several kinds of 'slip-test' of varying usefulness; the least useful is probably the test requiring 'one-word answers and no alternatives'. It is easy to understand what a strong appeal such a test has for the inexperienced teacher. The work can be marked rapidly and without disputes: the giving of each answer calls forth no display of importunate hands, no outcry of importunate voices offering ingenious alternatives; there are none of those private wrangles which waste time and make for a restive class. The only disadvantage of such a test is that it usually cannot be made to test anything worth testing; the limit imposed on the length of the answers is bound to have a limiting effect on the questions. If one is to give a memory test, is it not better to ask only a few questions, and to direct them towards matters which a careful and thoughtful reader ought to have remembered and understood? The answers will turn out longer, certainly, but the marking of them by the children themselves need not cause too much confusion. When the time for marking comes, the teacher calls out each answer, and accepts or rejects some of the alternatives offered by the pupils; then, if there are pupils still unsatisfied, he tells them to put large question-marks against the answers about which they are in doubt. This means that the teacher must collect the papers and look over the queries, but this does not usually take him very long, and it saves time and avoids controversy in the classroom, while allowing the test-questions to be more varied and useful.

In my view, the most valuable of all tests of reading is what may be called a 'teaching test'—the kind of test which sets out to teach in the actual process of testing, and which aims at transforming a superficial reading into a thoughtful one. Here, the teacher is not only trying to find out how deep understanding has gone—he is also trying to deepen it further; and he is concerned less with the child's ability to memorize facts than with his power to perceive implications and the inner significance of situations. And because his object is not primarily to test his pupils' memories, he can allow them access to the printed book; indeed, for this kind of test to be successful, it is essential that the children have the text before them.

But, it may be objected at this point, if the children are to be allowed to have the book open before them when they do the test, in what sense can it be called a test on work previously done? If the test is upon the previous night's homework, say, and the children know the conditions under which it is to be administered, will they bother to do the homework at all? In point of fact, neglect of the homework will soon show itself plainly: the majority of the questions will not be rapidly or confidently answered unless the pupil has the support of a previous reading. So, when testing a reading of Chapter 1 of *Treasure Island* (I choose a well-known book and take the first chapter of it) the teacher does not ask what a capstan-bar is, nor require the meanings of 'handspike' and 'connoisseur' and 'diabolical', nor does he ask for a memorized list of the captain's articles of clothing. To demand such things is to misunderstand the whole purpose of reading literature. But the teacher *can* with profit ask questions such as the following: (*i*) How do we know from page 16 that the captain has been a sailor for a large part of his life (page 16 of the 'King's Treasuries' edition)? (*ii*) Which words on page 16 show that he looks upon the luggage-barrow as a sort of boat? (*iii*) How would you explain Jim's unreasonable fear of a 'man with one leg' whom he has never seen (page 17)? (*iv*) Why is Jim less afraid of the captain than anyone else is (page 18)? And so on, through the chapter. The virtue of such questions is that they compel the reader to reconsider the story, and usually to find more in it than he did before. On reading question (*i*), for example, he is led to ponder the implications of 'voice . . . tuned and broken at the capstan bars'; question (*ii*) makes him observe the consistently nautical flavour of the captain's conversation (he tells the man with the barrow to 'bring up alongside'); question (*iii*) makes him see that Jim's dread of the one-legged man is born of the fact that even the formidable captain is terrified of him; while question (*iv*) shows the reader that it is Jim's knowledge of the captain's weakness which lessens his fear of him. All the while he is answering these questions, the pupil is making fresh discoveries. Of course, there is no need to apply to such a chapter as this the concentrated technique of the textbook 'comprehension test' (twenty questions per short paragraph); ten questions on the whole chapter should be plenty, provided they help towards a more complete reading, and do not have recourse to irrelevancies. Naturally, there is no reason why the children should not look up the 'hard words' in their dictionaries if their teacher wants them to; but it is important to realize that less may be lost through ignorance of the meaning of a word than through failure to scrutinize the sentence in which it occurs. In helping children to read we should encourage them to keep their eyes on the context of any difficult word; the word will then, often enough, look after itself.

Before leaving the subject of the 'teaching test' I should like to give examples of ten questions which might cover an entire chapter of the same book (*Treasure Island*). The chapter I have chosen is Chapter VIII ('At the Sign of the Spy-Glass'); in it, Jim Hawkins is sent with a message to the inn kept by John Silver, who later is discovered to be the leader of the mutineers. Here are the questions, and their answers, without further comment from me:

Q. We are told on page 65 that Silver 'seemed in the most cheerful of spirits'. Can you suggest why this should be?

A. He is looking forward to going to Treasure Island and getting the treasure for himself.

Q. When he addresses Jim as 'our cabin-boy' he speaks *quite loud*. Why does he speak loudly?

A. To warn Black Dog to leave the inn before Jim sees him.

Q. On page 66, Silver enquires, 'Who did you say he was? Black what?' Why does he make out that he has not caught Black Dog's name?

A. He does not want Jim to think that Black Dog is one of his (Silver's) friends.

Q. Talking to Morgan, Silver tells him sharply that he has never seen Black Dog before. Why does Silver *tell* him he hasn't—not just *ask* him if he has?

A. Silver wants Morgan to agree that he hasn't.

Q. Silver tells Jim that Morgan is an 'honest man'. Why is it important for Jim to think so?

A. Morgan is to be one of the crew of the *Hispaniola*.

Q. Silver says, 'Ben is a good runner.' Then why doesn't Ben catch up with Black Dog?

A. He doesn't try to.

Q. On page 68, Silver flatters Jim, saying he's 'as smart as paint'. What is his object in doing this?

A. To get Jim on his side when he makes his report to Mr Trelawney.

Q. Why, on page 68, does Silver return to the subject of his 'unpaid score'? What is he trying to suggest about Black Dog?

A. That Black Dog has run off to avoid paying for his rum, and not for any other reason.

Q. Silver says, 'I shall be rated ship's boy.' What does he mean by that?

A. Jim will have to take his orders from Silver.

Q. On page 69, how does Stevenson make it clear that Silver has the power to deceive even a very shrewd man?

A. Even Dr Livesey says, 'John Silver suits me.'

So much for the 'teaching test'. I think of it as a useful technique of wide application—usable with children and students of most ages, and applicable to poetry and drama as well as to prose. For this reason I shall mention it again later.

It will be seen that most of the sample questions given above relate to a proper understanding of the story *as* a story. But how about the characters of the story—should we not encourage the closer study of the characters also? Should we not give them individual attention as if they were real persons, and allow our pupils to write little sketches of them? Is not the writing of such sketches in fact the whole end of the study of a novel? From an examination of the practice of some teachers one would certainly conclude so. Even the little first-year children are sometimes made to write down from dictation short studies of the persons in their stories—of Jacob Armitage or of Oswald Partridge, it may be, in *The Children of the New Forest*. Yet it is difficult to see what purpose is served by this sort of note-making. Its persistence may spring from a belief—a belief long since discredited—that the chief business of a novelist is to assemble a portrait-gallery of 'really true-to-life persons'; or it may spring from an assumption—a false assumption, in fact—that since the children will be required to write 'character-studies' for their school-leaving examination, they cannot begin practising it too early. But in point of fact, at this early stage no such close examination of character is needed. The most we want the children to do is to observe those things about the characters which affect the development of the plot and its outcome; we want them to see the characters in relation to the story, and not to 'reconstruct' them as if they were living persons. With beginners the whole question of character is best approached lightly and tentatively, if it is approached at all—in informal discussion, perhaps, or perhaps through a study, along the following lines, of 'characteristic utterances' or 'characteristic actions'.

Let us suppose that a novel, *Northanger Abbey*, has been given a first reading by a class of fourteen-year-old girls (boys would not come to it till much later) and that they are now ready to give a little thought to the people in it. The teacher writes on the board a list (List A) of fifteen characters, using some of the names twice so as to make up the full number. She then writes up a second list (List B) consisting of short 'characteristic utterances', one for each of the fifteen names in List A. None of the utterances contains an obvious clue to the name of its speaker. Of course, the order of the two lists is not the same; and the pupils' task is to write down List A in an order corresponding to that of List B. This is done without reference to the book, and it is work which children enjoy doing. The test is then marked, and there follows a discussion of the way in which each utterance is characteristic of its speaker. The discussion is the more interesting because some of the children will have attributed utterances to the wrong speakers, and there arises the question of how far, if at all, such wrong attributions can be justified. In a later lesson, the children can be allowed to look out some 'characteristic utterances' for themselves, and in due course there will emerge a few of the most significant facts about the chief persons. For example, it will be observed that John Thorpe is given to gross exaggeration, and to contradicting an earlier statement by a later one. Now comes the question—have these characteristics of John Thorpe any bearing on the general development of the novel? They most decidedly have: a whole unexpected turn of the plot in Chapter 30 depends on them. It is out of such simple probings as this that a child's interest in the presentation of character is aroused; he is encouraged to see character as something studied not for itself, but rather for its bearing on the plot, or perhaps even on the theme of the novel. The characters do not exist to make pretty pictures; they exist to 'serve the novel'. To discover this is to spend profitably the time which otherwise might have been wasted in making full-length studies, or, worse, in drawing up lists of 'good and bad qualities'.

'Characteristic actions' are studied in much the same way as 'characteristic utterances', but they must be looked for in novels which are primarily novels of action.

And now, what about the novel or the story *as a whole*? I intend to say so much more about this in Chapter 9, where I shall try to discuss the themes of several novels, that I need touch on it only very briefly here; and indeed, the question of 'the novel as a whole' does not often arise with lower-school books. There is no theme in *Treasure Island*, nor any obvious intention behind it beyond that of telling a jolly good yarn and making it seem as 'real' as possible; nor is there any theme in J. Meade Falkner's *Moonfleet*—though there *is* an insistence on the sober realities of life, and also a pervading compassion and humanity which make it worth while to read parts of it aloud in class. (It is a better book than *Treasure Island*, I think.) On the other hand, no one will deny the presence of a theme in another popular lower-school book, *Animal Farm*; even the younger pupils are prepared to read it at more than 'story' level. But when I speak of considering the novel *as a whole* I do not necessarily have in mind novels with a 'message'; I think also of novels such as Jack London's *The Call of the Wild*, where the novelist's intention is in no sense didactic, and yet to miss that intention is to miss the point of the book. Perhaps in this case the loss is not serious; even without seeing the implications of the title, children can get pleasure from the book as an adventure story. For see the implications they usually don't—not till those implications are pointed out. Ask a class of children who have finished reading the novel—ask them why it is called *The Call of the Wild*, and they will tell you that it is because the book is about 'the lure of the open spaces', or because it is about 'how Buck, a tame dog, is called by the Wild', or at the most because it 'tells how Buck goes back to the life his ancestors lived'. But the book itself is much more explicit: it sets out to show how Buck rediscovers the life of his wolfish forefathers, stored as forgotten 'memories' within his brain and blood; and each stage of his discovery takes him farther away from the life of civilized man. If to show this is the writer's intention, it is surely part of the teacher's job to make the intention clear.

How is this best done? Here is one way of doing it. After the children have read the book, the teacher initiates a discussion with the object of uncovering the book's theme and making a tentative statement of it; after which the children review the book chapter by chapter, looking out the 'supporting evidence' for themselves. In *The Call of the Wild* (Heinemann's 'New Windmill' edition) they will find such things as these: Buck's inherited fear of being shut in a trap (page 30); Buck's first thefts (page 36); Buck's other 'retrogressions' (pages 37, 38, and 39)—the increasing keenness of his sight and scent, his mimicry of the behaviour of his ancestors, and his wolf-howling to the stars at night; his pride in 'heading the pack' (pages 61 and 62); his wolf-fight to the death with Spitz (page 64), felt by Buck to be a 'familiar thing'; his instinct-prompted refusal to cross the White River (page 111); his increasing association with wolves; and his final departure, after the death of John Thornton, to become the leader of a pack of timber-wolves. These passages, as I have said, can be looked out by the children themselves; and these, incidentally, are some of the passages which one might choose to read aloud.

Many children's books have slighter themes even than this: there is Frances Hodgson Burnett's *The Secret Garden*, for example, with its gentle though indirect insistence on the power of a garden to revitalize the mind and being. I am not urging that we should risk spoiling the book by dwelling too much on abstractions such as these; on the other hand, I do feel that the book will make a more lasting impression, and be read again with more enjoyment, if we make some reference to what, *as a whole*, it is trying to say.

So much for the subject-matter—the story, plot, characters, and themes—of the children's novel or other reader. Apart from the subject-matter, what else can we profitably study? The 'art of the novelist' perhaps? Hardly yet; not in general; nor indeed, perhaps, for many a long day. Yet there is one aspect of his art which we can sometimes study, if the writing is worth it: we can study his 'style'. If there is real pleasure and profit to be gained out of it, we cannot begin to study his 'style' too soon.

But, it may at once be objected, surely any close study of a writer's style is extraordinarily difficult at this early stage, and quite inappropriate to it. So indeed, it would be if I were using the word 'style' in its widest sense; but the sorts of simple study I have in mind are in fact neither inappropriate nor difficult. When I write of style, I am not thinking, at the one extreme, of any qualities of structure, balance or harmony (intangibles which young children are unlikely to perceive, let alone be able to describe), nor, at the other extreme, of figurative devices, or of contrived and patched-on elegancies of expression. I am thinking of the various simple means by which writing for children is made vivid and alive. For the study of such writing there is a simple technique which any teacher can apply, and which makes an agreeable and, I think, profitable lesson.

Let me give an example. Here is a passage from a little novel called *Chang*, a story of life in the Siamese jungle, written with first-hand knowledge by Elizabeth Morse (it is published in Dent's 'King's Treasuries' Series). The passage comes from Chapter 2, and is part of an old man's account of a fight with a tiger.

(*i*)

I staggered back a pace, and with a growl like thunder, he sprang upon me. I lowered my head to his attack; then he bore me to the ground, where I lay pinned under his great body. I was almost suffocated by the fur and the stench of him; but, realizing I was not quite dead yet, I managed to get my hands around his windpipe. His hind legs clawed at my body—the scars I bear to this day—and all the while I clung to his throat, pressing harder and harder with my hands . . . like a steel trap they were, pressing on his gullet. How long the struggle lasted I do not know. It seemed a lifetime to me. But just as my strength was exhausted, his body suddenly went limp and he toppled over on his side, releasing me.

We will suppose that the teacher, in the course of his own reading of the book, has looked with approval on this passage—it has vigour and immediacy, and is likely to appeal to children. The teacher sees that the effect of it depends a good deal on the choice of single words— words like 'pinned' which suggest vigorous action, or words like 'clawed' or 'stench' or 'steel' which make an appeal to the senses. This passage, then, for his purposes displays good 'style'; and it is this passage that he chooses for closer study.

The method is this:

(*i*) The pupils read the whole chapter in the usual manner.

(*ii*) They are then told to turn back and study pages 29 and 30, within the limits of which the chosen passage is contained.

(*iii*) The pupils are allowed a few minutes to do this, and then they are asked to close their books.

(*iv*) The teacher writes on the board a modified version of the chosen passage. In composing the modified version, he removes from the original that quality which most contributes to its effect as a piece of writing—that is to say, he removes the most forceful and telling words, replacing them by words or phrases which, while conveying the general sense, lack the original vitality. These substituted words and phrases he underlines. Here is a modified version of the passage from *Chang*:

(*ii*)

I *stepped* back a *little*, and with a *sound* like thunder, he sprang upon me. I lowered my head to his *approach*; then he *pushed* me to the ground, where I lay *fixed* under his *big* body. I was almost *made breathless* by the fur and the *smell* of him; but, realizing I was not quite dead yet, I managed to get my hands around his *neck*. His hind legs *scratched* my body—the *marks* I *have* to this day—and all the while I *held* to his throat, pressing harder and harder with my hands . . . like a *metal* trap they were, pressing on his *throat*. How long the struggle lasted I do not know. It seemed a *long time* to me. But just as my strength was *running out*, his body went *still* and he *fell* over on his side, releasing me.

(*v*) The teacher now explains to the class that the original passage has such-and-such qualities which the modified version lacks. He asks the class to 'restore' the original from memory, substituting for each italicized word or phrase the single word contained in the printed book.

(*vi*) The children write the original from memory, having regard all the while to the clues provided by the modified version. They then check their work, using the printed book.

(*vii*) Working over it point by point, teacher and class discuss the original in relation to the modified version. In what way is the original better? Where the children's memories have failed, and they have inserted alternative words, are those alternatives as good? Are they better still? (It sometimes happens that they are.)

(*viii*) The lesson closes with one or more re-readings of the original passage.

I ought perhaps to add that the work outlined above takes a full lesson, and it is necessary to keep everything on the move—otherwise the most important part, which is of course the discussion at the end, is likely to be scamped. Not too much time should be allowed for the class's (first silent) reading of the pages in the book. It would be possible to restrict this reading to the single paragraph which was to be modified; but then there would be danger of the class learning it by heart.

What is the value of this kind of work? I would say, first, that the children are forced by such exercises to consider language more closely, and that itself is worth doing. Secondly, they are made to see for themselves in what ways particular effects are achieved, and the insight gained can be put to use, if the teacher wishes, in 'follow up' composition work (the children writing their own descriptions of a man's combat with a wild animal, or of one wild animal with another). Thirdly—and this seems to me not unimportant—the children are helped to come as near as anyone can to the experience of 'creating' the original passage; they do in effect re-create it. It is a matter for great satisfaction and triumph for the child when he manages to restore the original exactly, as sometimes he does.

As the method outlined above has a number of slightly different applications, I should like to consider it in relation to extracts from other books.

Here is an extract from a short story by H. G. Wells, *The Red Room*, which is sometimes studied by third-year children:

(*i*)

I bruised myself on the thigh against the table, I sent a chair headlong, I stumbled and fell and whisked the cloth from the table in my fall. My candle rolled away from me, and I snatched another as I rose. Abruptly this was blown out, as I swung it off the table, by the wind of my sudden movement, and immediately the two remaining candles followed. But there was still light in the room, a red light which staved off the shadows from me. The fire! Of course, I could thrust my candle between the bars and relight it.

The passage, which describes the efforts of a frightened man to fight off panic in a dark room, owes some of its urgency to Wells's choice of verbs, most of which imply quick and vigorous action. Observing this, the teacher makes his modified version by altering ten of the verbs, as in the version which follows:

(ii)

I knocked myself on the thigh against the table, I sent a chair headlong, I tripped and fell and pulled the cloth from the table in my fall. My candle went away from me, and I took another as I rose. Abruptly this was put out, as I lifted it off the table, by the wind of my sudden movement, and immediately the two remaining candles followed. But there was still light in the room, a red light which kept off the shadows from me. The fire! Of course I could insert my candle between the bars and re-illuminate it.

The class is told that the two versions are identical except that ten one-word verbs of the original have been replaced by ten other one-word verbs in the modified version; the class's task, as always with this kind of work, is to restore the original from memory. If this exercise is thought to be too difficult as it stands, the ten inferior verbs in (ii) may be underlined by the teacher before the class begins to write.

Here is another variant of the same procedure. This time the passage is part of the description of a scene from Conrad's *Youth*, already quoted in Chapter 6; one of its characteristics is the nice choice and placing of the adjectives:

(i)

Not a branch stirred along the shore, and the brown roofs of hidden houses peeped through the green foliage, through the big leaves that hung shining and still like leaves forged of heavy metal. This was the East of the ancient navigators . . . I see it now—the wide sweep of the bay, the glittering sands, the wealth of green infinite and varied, the sea blue like the sea of a dream, the crowd of attentive faces, the blaze of vivid colour—the water reflecting it all, the curve of the shore, the jetty, the high-sterned outlandish craft floating still, and the three boats with the tired men from the West sleeping, unconscious of the land and the people and the violence of the sunshine.

H

When writing up the 'modified version' the teacher omits fifteen of the adjectives, but sets them out separately in a list at the end:

(ii)

Not a branch stirred along the shore, and the roofs of houses peeped through the foliage, through the leaves that hung shining and still like leaves forged of metal . . . I see it now—the sweep of the bay, the sands, the wealth of green infinite and varied, the sea like the sea of a dream, the crowd of faces, the blaze of colour—the water reflecting it all, the curve of the shore, the jetty, the craft floating still, and the boats with the men from the West sleeping, unconscious of the land and the people and the violence of the sunshine.

List: vivid, ancient, three, heavy, attentive, tired, brown, high-sterned, big, glittering, hidden, outlandish, green, wide, blue.

Obviously, the instructions given to the children are that they are to insert the fifteen adjectives in their right places, and check the work by reference to the printed book.

I would now like to describe another and different method of modifying a well-written passage—a method which is not bound up with the insertion or the omission of single words. It is suitable for use when the class are studying a passage which narrates a series of rapid movements or actions. Here is such a passage, from Chapter 2 of A. E. W. Mason's *The Four Feathers*:

(i)

Ethne had stopped at a door on that steep hill leading down to the river, and the horse which she was driving took fright at the mere clatter of a pail and bolted. The reins were lying loose at the moment; they fell on the ground before Ethne could seize them. She was thus seated helpless in the dog-cart, and the horse was tearing down to where the road curves sharply over the bridge. The thing which she did, she did quite coolly. She climbed over the front of the dog-cart as it pitched and raced down the hill, and balancing herself along the shafts, reached the reins at the horse's neck, and brought the horse to a stop ten yards from the curve.

The writing here is economical: no more information is given than is necessary for the reader to follow the course of the brief exciting narrative. The version which the teacher writes up includes all the words of the original, but the whole pace and fire of the thing are destroyed by insertions—as it might be like this:

(*ii*)

Young Ethne had stopped her dog-cart at a cottage door on that steep hill leading down to the river at the foot of it, and the horse which she was driving took it into his head to take fright at the mere clatter of a farmyard pail near by, and as a consequence it bolted off. The horse's reins were lying loose at the moment when this happened; they slipped and fell on the ground before Ethne, poor girl, could seize hold of them. She was thus seated absolutely helpless in the green dog-cart, and the horse in its panic was tearing down to where the road curves sharply in making its way over the bridge. The remarkable thing which she (Ethne, not the horse) then did, she did quite coolly. She climbed without the slightest difficulty over the front part of the dog-cart as it pitched up and down and raced at quite incredible speed down the sunny hill, and after balancing herself along the dog-cart's shafts, she without difficulty reached the reins which were situated at the horse's neck, and to her great relief brought the horse to a decided stop, ten yards more or less from the curve in the road.

The class are told that all the original words are there, but that some words and phrases have been added; their task is to omit the superfluous matter, and restore the original as nearly as possible. It will be seen that there are one or two utter absurdities in (*ii*)—the 'green dog-cart' and the 'sunny hill', for example—but these are used to point out how, on occasions, a descriptive adjective can be out of place, and a blemish on the whole piece of writing. This is no bad lesson to learn, for children who fancy themselves as descriptive writers are apt to use adjectives too freely. After studying the passage from *The Four Feathers*, the children can try their hands at describing a 'scene of action' like it.

There, then, are some of the different uses of modified versions as part of the study of good writing. My extracts were chosen with no special care: there are hundreds such in the books of the authors most commonly used in school—Stevenson, Buchan, Masefield, Mark Twain, Wells, and Jack London—as well as the more recent authors whose books are nowadays available in school bindings. Nor is the preparation of a modified version an especially difficult matter: the teacher merely decides what quality makes the chosen passage a success, and then prepares a version which takes that quality away. This can usually be done on the spot, in the classroom, without previous preparation. But there is one thing which must be constantly borne in mind: a modified version is a bad piece of writing, and should be used only to show up the merits of a good piece. As I said earlier, the teacher should come back to the original version, and the lesson should close with a reading of it. It will then be the author who has the final word.

CHAPTER 8

POETRY AND PLAYS

Presenting poetry—Reading and discussing a poem—Some examples—Learning poetry by heart. Dearth of good plays for children—Children conducting their own drama periods—The use of the school stage—Drama in the classroom—Closer scrutiny of a Shakespeare text

A STORY was told me many years ago of a teacher who, being faced with the task of giving a demonstration lesson before a student, took a daffodil to school and put it in a jam jar on his desk. The lesson was Poetry, and the poem was Wordsworth's *I wandered lonely as a cloud*; when the teacher came to the words 'Fluttering and dancing in the breeze' he took a sheet of pink blotting-paper and wafted it over the daffodil so that it fluttered unsteadily to and fro. When asked by the student whether this demonstration was a necessary part of the lesson, the teacher replied that it was not, but that it was a useful device for 'making the whole experience more vivid to the pupils'. Certainly, according to the account I heard, the pupils were extraordinarily attentive; the more so because, previously, in an idle moment, the teacher had drawn a 'funny face' on the pink blotting-paper.

This story, though perhaps not a true one, illustrates a particular method of teaching poetry—'teaching by demonstration'; but it also illustrates the risk we run when we introduce into a poetry lesson any sort of activity, or even discussion, which leaves impressions other than those the poet intended. For in future what was that poem to mean to the children? Was it to mean Wordsworth's coming upon the daffodils and his subsequent 'involuntary evocation' of them?—or a teacher waving a piece of pink blotting-paper (with a 'funny face' on it) over a flower in a glass jar? And do we not run the same risk when we attempt to promote appreciation of a poem by any other indirect means—by asking the children to illustrate or act it, or by putting it on as a choral 'turn' at a school concert?

Consider some of the implications. Jenny's and John's drawings for Tennyson's *Break, break, break* will be impressive as pictures of the sea and ships, and will do credit to them and to their art teacher; but how far will they go towards expressing, even for the young artists themselves, the feelings which are the real subject of the poem? And then there is acting: Roger and five of his form mates will have rollicking fun acting *How They Brought the Good News* (three boys on their hands and knees 'being horses', three others mounted on their backs, and the rest of the class taking turns to read the narrative); a notable climax will be achieved when the roan rolls over and lies 'dead as a stone'; and the ending of the poem, when the horse Roland is rewarded with a 'last measure of wine', will be enlivened by a liberal up-tipping of the largest bottle of ink; but afterwards, when the wood-splinter has been taken out of Roger's knee, and the ink mopped off the classroom floor, will the memory of the lesson be anything more than the memory of a joyful riot? And as for choral verse-speaking: when we indulge in it, are we certain that we are not also indulging a mere desire to secure 'good speech' as such—or even, if we conduct our choir, indulging a long-repressed desire to appear in the rôle of a *maestro*? I once saw and heard a choir of children reciting *The Key of the Kingdom*. The fact that the front row of the choir held between them a long and large key constructed from wood and painted cardboard ('This is the Key of the Kingdom') did not suggest that they or their teacher had much idea of what the poem was about.

What wonder, then, if for the careful teacher there are only two acceptable ways of handling a poem in class—one, reading it (or having it read) without any kind of comment; the other, trying, with the help of question and answer, to interpret the poem in *words* (the stuff of which poetry is made), and wherever possible in words taken from the poem itself.

The danger of all other methods is, in short, the danger of introducing irrelevancies and incongruities. Yet even when the teacher deals entirely in terms of question and answer, the introduction of irrelevancies and incongruities is not necessarily avoided; this is particularly so when the poem is used as a basis for questions which lead one further from, and not closer to, the poet's own thought and experience. One sometimes comes upon text-books which, out of passages like this (from Southey's *The Inchcape Rock*):

> Down sank the bell with a gurgling sound;
> The bubbles rose and burst around;
> Quoth Sir Ralph, 'The next who comes to the rock
> Won't bless the Abbot of Aberbrothok.'

develop 'questions' such as these: (*i*) Can you explain the difference between 'gurgling' and 'gargling'? (*ii*) Describe two methods of making bubbles—(*a*) with a clay pipe, (*b*) with a metal ring. (*iii*) The word 'rock' here means a large stone. Can you think of any other meanings of 'rock'? Find out about the manufacturing process which enables seaside rock to have the 'name right through' . . . And so on. If the reader objects that my invented examples are impossibly absurd, I can only assure him that they are hardly less so than some of the examples which, out of consideration for their authors, I have refrained from quoting here.

Before I come to speak of the poetry lesson, I would like to say a word about the atmosphere which ought to prevail in the classroom when poetry is read or discussed. Obviously, the atmosphere should be the 'right one'—but let me add quickly that by the right atmosphere I do not mean an atmosphere of hush and sanctity, such as would be appropriate to a 'worshipping at the shrine'. No, I mean an atmosphere which is friendly, informal, and relaxed—an atmosphere not always easy to achieve, and only achievable at all where the children are prepared to give their fullest co-operation. For after all, the things of poetry are civilized things, and the reading and discussion of it can hardly be expected to go hand in hand with the need to impose classroom order. One can amuse oneself by picturing a schoolmaster of the old type teaching *The Ancient Mariner* to a recalcitrant class ('He prayeth best who loveth best All things both great and small'), and constantly interrupting the lesson to call forward and whack the offenders; but is not the incongruity which such a picture suggests to some extent present in all poetry lessons which treat the subject as a *lesson*? A friendly, informal, and relaxed atmosphere—no questions pressed too hard or too long—a casual discussion of the poem, with occasional probing attempts to get to the heart of it. How hard, often enough, even to achieve such an atmosphere—doubly hard to conduct a poetry discussion within it! No wonder many of us feel that a good proportion of our poetry lessons are failures.

Some poems demand no classroom discussion at all: the mere reading of them several times is all that is necessary for enjoyment. Most junior anthologies contain a fair number of such poems—simple, direct, vigorous statements, the probing of which would be superfluous, tedious, and even harmful. I shall pass over these and come directly to poems of more difficult substance. Here is a poem which might be studied by children in their first or second year:

The Hut

Whatever place is poor and small
The Hut was poorer still,
Stuck, like a snail upon a wall,
On what we called a hill.

It leaned upon an apple-tree   5
Whose laden branches lay
On the hot roof voluptuously,
And murmured all the day.

One hand-broad window, full of boughs,
Mirrored the flaming hearth   10
As if a Dryad warmed her house
With fire from under earth;

And one the livid lasting-pea
And staring marigold,
The knotty oak and elder-tree   15
Showed in the morning cold.

The sapling ash had mined the floor,
The chimney flew the bine;
The doorway was without a door,
But flaunted eglantine.   20

The swallow built upon the beam,
The rat was much at home;
And there one foolish child would dream
Where sorrow could not come.

RUTH PITTER

This is a poem which I think should appeal to most children; both boys and girls like the thought of a 'house of their own'. But what are we to do with it after the preliminary readings? In the case of a more complex poem we might begin by asking what the poem as a whole is about; or, if the nature of the poem demanded it, we might set ourselves to follow the thread of the thought or argument. But neither of these procedures is appropriate here; the poem merely describes a hut, inviting us to visualize it clearly, and then rounds off the description by the poignant statement of the last two lines. So what is there in fact to discuss?

Well, there are the 'hard words'. But we do not really want to direct the children's attention to the hard words—we want the children to look through them, and fasten their minds on the things behind the words. So we ask our questions not about the words but about the hut. What was it like? How did it appear on the outside? (It was 'poor and small'.) We know that it was not a very firm structure. Which words tell us so? ('Stuck'—'like a snail'—'leaned upon an apple tree'.) And about the boughs on the roof—had they apples on them or not? (Yes, they were 'laden'.) We are told that the branches 'lay voluptuously'. 'Voluptuously' means 'with enjoyment'. What did the apples enjoy? (The hot sun.) And the laden branches 'murmured'—what caused the murmuring sound? (Probably the movement of boughs and apples on the roof when the wind blew.)

That is the way. What, essentially, we are trying to do is to make the children more aware of the 'things of the poem'. And it is so with the inside of the hut. We do not waste time in asking the children what a Dryad is—we tell them she is a tree-nymph. But we want them to see the 'hand-broad window' as the child in the poem saw it. What should they see? The boughs outside and the reflection of the flaming hearth against it. And as for lines 11-12, which at first sight are not quite clear, we have only to ask 'What, exactly, *was* the Dryad's house?' for the meaning to be plain. (The Dryad's house was the tree outside, through the boughs of which the reflected fire appeared to be rising.)

The next stanza presents a difficult construction, but a small amount of discussion will sort it out. ('And in the cold morning, one window showed the livid lasting-pea and staring marigold, the knotty oak and elder-tree.') And the stanza which follows raises an interesting question: Is the 'sapling ash' a little ash-tree growing in the earthen floor of the hut? Or is it an ash-tree outside the hut—with its roots coming up through the floor inside?

And so to the last stanza. After we have asked a question about the rat who was 'much at home' (Does it mean he didn't leave the house often?), we arrive at the last two lines:

> And there one foolish child would dream
> Where sorrow could not come.

To these lines, children will respond variously, according to their intelligence and sensibility. We cannot ask them much about the feelings expressed here; yet we can ask questions which may help to establish those feelings in the children's minds. What sort of dream did the child in the poem dream? (Probably a dream about the future—about a home of her own, perhaps.) Why does the poet speak of the child as foolish?

(Perhaps because she now realizes that those dreams were extravagant.) And why was the hut a place where sorrow could not come? (Probably because it was cut off from the adult world and its problems.)

Now all this may look rather formal and forbidding when written out as it is above; but if the questions are asked tentatively, and the children are not pressed or puzzled too much, the discussion will prove profitable. Even so, discussion of a poem like *The Hut* should not be allowed to take too long; if too much attention is given to details, the poem easily disintegrates—the pupils' sense of its unity is lost. To help in preventing this, the poem may be re-read once or twice during the discussion, and some last readings of it should close the lesson.

Here is a different approach to a poem—an approach which emphasizes the importance of the preliminary readings. It is suitable for use with poems more closely composed than *The Hut*, especially such poems as follow a line of thought, meditation, or argument. The following poem by Edward Thomas is the sort of poem I mean:

Birds' Nests

The summer nests uncovered by autumn wind,
Some torn, others dislodged, all dark,
Everyone sees them: low or high in tree,
Or hedge, or single bush, they hang like a mark.

Since there's no need of eyes to see them with   5
I cannot help a little shame
That I missed most, even at eye's level, till
The leaves blew off and made the seeing no game.

'Tis a light pang. I like to see the nests
Still in their places, now first known,   10
At home and by far roads. Boys knew them not,
Whatever jays and squirrels may have done.

And most I like the winter nests deep-hid
That leaves and berries fall into:
Once a dormouse dined there on hazel-nuts,   15
And grass and goose-grass seeds found soil and grew.

EDWARD THOMAS

With a poem like this, it is an advantage to give more time than one ordinarily would to the mere reading of it. Let us suppose that the teacher starts by asking two or three of the children to read it in turn, explaining that he wants them to read it as if they really understood it. Only an exceptional child will give a completely intelligent first reading; the majority of children will here and there reveal, by false inflections, that they do not properly follow the line of thought. One reader, possibly, will treat 'uncovered' (line 1) as a finite verb; after hearing him to the end, the teacher will ask for other readings of lines 1–4, and will not rest until someone has made it clear that 'uncovered by autumn wind' is a phrase qualifying 'nests'. Another reader may show that he considers 'no game' (line 8) as the object of 'seeing'; another that he reads 'most' in line 7 as an adverb (as it is in line 13). Naturally, in discussing these readings, the teacher does not need to make use of grammatical terms; his question is only 'How ought he to have read that line?', and by persistent trial he finds a pupil who reads the line aright.

The question of how a particular line ought to be read can indeed be a fundamental one; the interpretation of a considerable part of the poem can depend on it. For example, are we to read—

> And most I like the *winter* nests deep-hid

or

> And most I like the winter nests *deep-hid*?

There is a good deal of difference. If we emphasize 'winter' we show that we think of these 'winter nests' as being preferred by the poet to the 'summer nests' of line 1; but if we emphasize 'deep-hid' the suggestion is rather that these deep-hid nests are preferred to others not so tucked away. A little consideration makes it clear that it is the second of these alternatives which is the right one: the 'summer nests' of line 1 are the same thing as the 'winter nests' of line 13 (the summer nests surviving in the winter). When the children have learned to read this and other lines aright, they have already made a big advance in coming to terms with the poem.

Now it will be remembered that I suggested of the poem *The Hut* that, after it had been read once or twice, the class might go on to a discussion which essentially tried to answer the question 'What things are mentioned in the poem and what were they like?' That is well enough for a poem which is largely descriptive, but it is not really sufficient for a poem which follows a line of thought or argument. In the case of a poem such as *Birds' Nests* it is better, before any discussion of details, for the teacher to elicit from the children a short statement of what the poem as a whole says. For when one is studying a poem, or indeed a play or a novel, it frequently pays to start from the complete work—to discover first what, as a whole, the work is driving at—and only afterwards to examine the details. The opposite procedure—to examine the details one by one, and try gradually to build up a 'composite picture'—is liable to lead to confusion; only a comprehensive act of the mind will see the constituent parts as a unity.

A simple statement, then, which the children, if questioned, will themselves supply. 'It is a poem about birds' nests. When autumn comes, everyone can see the nests which have been hidden during the summer. The poet feels rather ashamed to think he has never spied them before, but the pleasure of discovery is still there. And of all these "winter nests" he most likes those which till now have been deeply hidden away.'

With this summary as a sort of 'background of reference', any discussion of details runs no risk of seeming unrelated—though indeed, not much discussion of details should be necessary. As with *The Hut*, the teacher's task is to direct the children's attention to what is already there—to pick up the things of the poem, so to speak, and put them down again. Most of the questions will be simple ones, just enough to enforce a second thought or a closer scrutiny. As, for example, how do the nests come to be uncovered? And these 'torn' and 'dislodged' nests (line 2), what do they look like? And they're all 'dark'—what makes them look so dark? (The teacher tries to suggest the appearance of the nests seen amongst leafless boughs, and against the sky.) Then they 'hang like a mark'—what kind of a mark? And a mark for what? (A target for the eyes.) A difficulty may arise, too, in the next line, over 'no need of eyes'—what sort of eyes is there no need of? (Sharp eyes.) Then there are the implications of 'even at eye's level'. And what about 'made the seeing no game'?—when *was* seeing nests a game? And why a *game*?

Now stanza 3: exactly *what* is felt to be a 'light pang'? (The teacher refers back to lines 6-7.) And 'now first known'—this may call for a paraphrase, such as 'now discovered for the first time'. Line 12 may also call for a paraphrase: 'Even if jays and squirrels knew them.' And why jays and squirrels particularly? (Predatory birds; ubiquitous animals.)

Finally, stanza 4: one general question may be found more useful here than a number of particular questions. Of all these winter nests, why does the poet most like the deeply-hidden ones? There is more than one possible answer to this, and the children should be encouraged to find words of the poem to support their opinions. The special charm of these nests seems to lie in the finding of something secret and uninvestigated by humans—something, too, which has survived for new uses (a bowl for leaves and berries, a dining-room for a dormouse, a garden for seeds of goose-grass). There is a fascination in the discovery that wild life has its own secret goings-on, and this fascination is dwelt on at the conclusion of the poem.

As with the poem *The Hut*, some final readings should close the lesson; and it will be an advantage if, after a week or so, the poem can be returned to and re-read without comment. It is then that the reader reaps the reward of the attention bestowed on it in the first place: the poem which perhaps meant little at first sight has grown familiar during the interval, and has lost some of its complexities. Thereafter it may even be liked and committed to memory.

Before leaving poetry, I would like to say one or two words about the learning of poems by heart. No one can ever have discussed this subject with adults, teachers especially, without encountering the widely-held belief that many of the poems which we learn unwillingly at school are valued in later life for the spiritual support they provide in moments of crisis. Jane Austen must have been aware of the existence of this belief; she makes a reference to it in *Northanger Abbey*, where she remarks of young Catherine Morland that 'she read all such works as heroines must read to supply their memories with those quotations which are so serviceable and so soothing in the vicissitudes of their eventful lives'. Jane Austen is of course treating the belief as the absurdity she knew it to be; though probably even Jane Austen, if questioned on the matter, would have admitted that to the mind of an educated adult there will sometimes occur a fragment of a poem which seems to him a comment on the situation he faces or on the predicament in which he finds himself. Unluckily, those educated adults are not people who have learned poetry unwillingly; they are people who have never intentionally learned poetry at all—they have absorbed it almost as if it had been the air they breathed. As a general thing it may be said that if poetry really matters to a child, he learns it with little effort or with none at all; if it does not matter to him, he learns it under pressure and forgets it as soon as he can.

So that to learn poetry in the mere hope that it will supply spiritual comfort on some future day is to learn it with an insufficient motive; and an even less sufficient motive is to learn it in the belief that to know many poems is the 'mark of an educated person'. Yet I suspect that this is in fact sometimes done—that there are schools where the pupils are prepared for their future in educated or half-educated society by being equipped in just this way. This seems to me a pity. Poetry may have some value as a social acquirement, but that is far from being the principal value which poetry-lovers would wish to see attributed to it.

No, let the children learn poetry if they like doing it (many do); and let the poems be those which they themselves take a fancy to and voluntarily choose. The reasons for their choices may sometimes appear to us not very good ones—'I chose this poem because it had shorter lines than the others'—but that is better than their learning the teacher's choice, being tested on it, and being punished with detention 'if they get under half marks'!

There should not be much to say about the study of the plays most commonly used with children of eleven to fourteen, simply because very few of these plays are worth studying. For the children in their fourth and fifth years, yes, there are plenty of plays: the Sheridans, Ibsens, Shaws, Barries, Galsworthys, and a dozen more recent writers whose work has enough merit for them to be taken seriously. But for the elevens to fourteens: if you count out oddities like *She Stoops to Conquer*, or disregard the too-few history plays or collections of mediaeval plays, what is there? Collections of between-the-wars one-act plays, which offer you one decent play per volume—the rest being class-conscious domestic comedies, cops-and-robber melodramatics, Boy-Scout-hero or schoolboy-hero extravagancies, with perhaps a piece of post-Barrie whimsy thrown in, and some such play as *The Thread of Scarlet* or *The Bishop's Candlesticks* to make up the weight! The duplication alone—the fact that an anthologist must often make his own collection largely from the collections of his predecessors—is a pointer to the shortage of good material. Yet with children in their first two years, unless they have developed sufficiently to tackle the shortened versions of the Shakespeare plays, there is usually little alternative—except, indeed, to make up plays of their own.

Often, then, it is one-act plays or nothing. If these plays are played out in the classroom, in a space which has been cleared for that purpose at the front or in the middle of the room, there is at first little that a teacher need do beyond supervising in the most general way. With a little training, the children will organize the lesson themselves, choosing their own 'producer', their own actors, their reader (where needed) of the descriptions of scenes, and their maker of sound-effects. The teacher can sit by, watching and listening, and counting it a fault in himself if he interrupts the play too frequently.

For there are kinds of lesson where a teacher should do as little as possible, and I think the junior drama lesson is sometimes one of them. I recall having a student-teacher observe me while I started off a third-year group on what was to have been a rapid first reading of *She Stoops to Conquer*; a week later, when the drama lesson came round again, I asked him to take over the class and continue with the play. Afterwards I asked him how he had fared; he replied that he had made no actual progress with the play-reading, but had spent the period 'selling *She Stoops to Conquer* to the pupils'. On another occasion another student-teacher, given similar work with a shortened version of *Julius Caesar*, spent so many lessons on extraneous matters—drawing diagrams of the modern and Elizabethan stages, filling in the historical background, and so on—that he did not achieve even a single reading of the play; although, had he set his mind to it, he might have gone through the play twice, and have made parts of the second reading into a polished piece of work.

Now both these students were well-intentioned, but what they were asked to do seemed to them too simple, too lacking in active *instruction*; the rôle assigned to the teacher seemed to them to be too unimportant a one. They made a mistake common enough amongst beginners (a mistake which a good Training College puts right, though), of sup-posing that a teacher must be a full-time performer, constantly 'on show'. At any moment, it seemed to them, a supervisor might come into the room and expect to see them in action. Some teachers never make any advance from the notion that teaching is essentially a con-tinuous one-man performance; if more teachers thought otherwise, there would be much less mere lecturing, much less dictation of notes, than there is. I spoke once to a woman teacher who had had a Ministry inspection at her school. 'And what did you do, Miss Jones, when the inspector came into your room?'—'Oh, Mr Walsh, I just read poetry to the children till he went out again.' Miss Jones read poetry well, and she had reason to be proud of her performance; yet I am not by any means sure that, so far as the inspector was concerned, she really did what was required of her.

Our first object with these lower forms should surely be to have the children read once through their plays as quickly as possible—more particularly the longer plays, those which take four or five lessons to complete; for what they need above all other things is to make some

sense of the plays as wholes. Any further work will be valueless if they
have not done that. Subsequently, the best of the one-act plays can be
worked over again—or the best scenes of the longer play, as the case
may be. It is here that the teacher steps in, helping to choose the cast,
and taking a larger part than he at first did in the production. Yet even
here he must keep the play constantly on the move, overlooking faults
rather than making continual interruptions.

Nowadays, most schools have a stage in the assembly hall; some
schools have a theatre even. When the chosen scenes have been per-
fected in the classroom it is often a good idea to play them over again
in the theatre. Student-teachers sometimes hesitate to use the theatre
because of the greater difficulty they experience in controlling the
children: while they themselves are on the stage, demonstrating a nice
point of technique to the players, one-third of the class are conducting
private fights in the auditorium, while another third are in the wings,
playing with the light switches and kicking over the pots of paint. But
if the teacher goes the right way about it, children using the stage will
be as orderly as children using the classroom. Before they go to the
theatre there should be some preparatory work done: the cast should
be chosen, the children assigned their places, and the meaning of certain
terms explained (the children need to know which is the right and
which is the left of the stage, and the meaning of the terms 'up stage'
and 'down stage'). When in the theatre the non-acting children should
occupy a single row of chairs immediately before the stage, while the
actors should form two groups, one on each side, and either sitting *on*
the stage or, better still, sitting on the steps which lead up from the
auditorium. The teacher should stand behind the row of non-acting
children, and should not often move far from this position; placed so,
he has the whole class under his eye. These may seem unnecessary
precautions, but it is a fact that normally orderly children become very
excited when first allowed to act on a stage. They are also sometimes
unexpectedly shy when it is their turn to speak; but they soon adapt
themselves to the greater amount of space, and learn to project their
voices and themselves in a manner which would not have been possible
in the classroom.

I would like to conclude these remarks on classroom drama by giving
some special thought to the children's first readings of Shakespeare.

In the foregoing account of the reading of plays, I have assumed that
the teacher will want to have the play acted out before spectators; but
in point of fact many teachers think it sufficient for children to read the

play while seated at their desks. There is, they argue, justification for this: the reading of an unfamiliar play is a task so exacting that the readers can hardly take their eyes off the book, let alone perform movements to match the words. Why, then, bother to place the readers in front of the class? There is sense in this argument; but the principal advantages of a reading in front of the class are not that the actors can then 'do the actions as well as say the words'; they are that the audience can *see* each speaker, thus identifying him by sight as well as by voice with the character he personates, and that the actors can *address one another*, thus helping the audience to envisage the dialogue as a series of meaningful personal exchanges. These are advantages which are very easily secured where there is space at the front of the classroom, and they often make so great a difference to the pupils' understanding of the play that it would not be sensible to forego them.

Let me illustrate this point with the help of the following passage from *As You Like It:*

> *Ros.* You are here followed by a faithful shepherd;
> Look upon him; love him; he worships you.
>
> *Phe.* Good shepherd, tell this youth what 'tis to love.
>
> *Sil.* It is to be all made of sighs and tears;
> And so am I for Phebe.
>
> *Phe.* And I for Ganymede.
>
> *Orl.* And I for Rosalind.
>
> *Ros.* And I for no woman.
>
> *Sil.* It is to be all made of faith and service;
> And so am I for Phebe.
>
> *Phe.* And I for Ganymede.
>
> *Orl.* And I for Rosalind.
>
> *Ros.* And I for no woman ...
>
> *Phe.* If this be so, why blame you me to love you?
>
> *Sil.* If this be so, why blame you me to love you?
>
> *Orl.* If this be so, why blame you me to love you?
>
> *Ros.* Who do you speak to, 'Why blame you me to love you?'
>
> *Orl.* To her that is not here, nor doth not hear.

I

Now it will be seen that the demands made by this passage upon the actors *as* actors are few, but that the grouping of the actors so that each remark is addressed to the right person can be of real value. It is important that Phebe's 'Good shepherd' should be addressed to Silvius (for Rosalind also is a shepherd); it is equally important that with the words 'this youth' Phebe should turn her eyes on Rosalind (for Orlando also is a youth). It matters, too, when it comes to the lines that follow, that Silvius should address Phebe and Phebe Rosalind, while Orlando and Rosalind should both of them address imaginary people (*i.e.* turn away from the people on the stage). And it is much the same with the questions 'Why blame you me to love you?' When once I introduced this passage to a class which had never seen it before, I asked the pupils to read it seated at their desks, and it was quite plain from the way they spoke the lines that they had very little idea of what was supposed to be going on. It is true that a little pondering over each line would have told them who was the person addressed or indicated; but such pondering requires just that extra imaginative effort which the average child does not easily make.

When the cast of a play is first read out, it is a good idea for the actors to stand up in turn and be identified with the parts they play. If there are any oddments of costume or property available (a dagger for Macbeth, a crown for Duncan), that makes it easier still.

I suggested earlier that we should take care, during the classroom performance of a play, not to constantly interrupt with our comments, suggestions, and explanations; but there is no reason why, once the children are again seated at their desks, we should not encourage some scrutiny of the actual words of a difficult text, especially if the text is Shakespeare. Unluckily, there are objections to the two most popular ways of doing this, which are (*i*) to work through a speech and, with the help of question and answer, provide a series of marginal notes which smooth away difficulties, and (*ii*) to select a suitable passage and ask the class to make a written paraphrase. The first of these is too dull, the second too exacting. A third way, more entertaining and not entirely without value, is one which can be conveniently referred to as 'Paraphrase Reversed'.

Let us suppose that the class have finished acting the first scene of *Scenes from Julius Caesar* (a shortened form of the play, edited by J. Dover Wilson and published by the Cambridge University Press). An exercise based on the opening pages would look something like this:

1. *Page* 6: 'Walked in shoes made by me' (4).
2. *Page* 6: 'make excuse for' (2).
3. *Page* 7: 'will surely be sent to punish' (4).
4. *Page* 7: 'go here and there' (1).
5. *Page* 7: 'do as other men do' (4).
6. *Page* 8: 'how the race goes' (5).

And so on. In each case the pupil is required to look on the page indicated and find the phrase of which the given words are a paraphrase. The number in brackets indicates the number of words in the phrase which is to be found. Thus, for 1, the pupil is required to find 'gone upon my handiwork'; for 2, 'cull out'; for 3, 'needs must light on'; for 4, 'about' (in 'I'll about'); for 5, 'fly an ordinary pitch'; and for 6, 'the order of the course'. No help in these is provided by the editor's footnotes. My usual way is to choose some ten to fifteen 'difficulties', spread over from five to eight pages of the scene just acted; the pupils are allowed to underline each phrase as they find it and write the paraphrase lightly in pencil against it. (Anything which later proves wrong is rubbed out.) It is important to allow plenty of time for this work; most children do it rather slowly, sometimes ranging over the pages several times and considering the meaning of various phrases before settling on the right ones. Indeed, it is a virtue of this kind of work that the children are forced to ponder many lines besides those which contain the right answers; and I should perhaps add that they do the work with some eagerness and will take considerable pains to search out the 'phrase which corresponds'.

The making of the little paraphrases by the teacher requires some thought, and the beginner will do best to prepare them beforehand. In particular, it is important that each paraphrase should be as different as possible in construction from the phrase which it represents. Where this is not the case, the pupils are able to spot the original by its formal similarity to the paraphrase, and the exercise defeats its purpose.

It is an old gibe against paraphrasing that it forces children to 'reduce first-rate verse to third-rate prose'. That is hardly an objection that can be made here, for here the pupils start with the third-rate prose and it is used as a means of directing their attention to the first-rate verse. If, for use with bright children, the exercise which I have just described seems unsubstantial or trivial, I would suggest an extension: each phrase, when found, should be compared in point of expression with the paraphrase which has been used to discover it. What a contrast between the flatness of 'do as other men do' and the appositeness of 'fly an ordinary pitch'! What a contrast, in all examples, between the periphrastic and generalized on the one hand and the concise and vivid on the other! Here is a simple but intelligent beginning to the study of Shakespeare's language.

CHAPTER 9

THE EXAMINATION NOVEL

*Choosing the examination novel—The first readings of the novel
—Note-making—Studying a novel is essentially a series of 'readings'—Reading for the story—Reading for the plot—Reading for
the theme—Reading for the characters—Reading for the narrative
method—Reading for the characterization—Concluding remarks*

IT HAS been said that 'There is no such thing as the novel; there are
only novels.' But even if there were such a thing as the novel, the
examination novel, and even if it were possible to characterize and treat
the examination novel in terms which would be seen to have wide
application, I should not expect such generalities as I should write to
do other than confuse or bore my reader. I am compelled here to take
the view that 'There is no such thing as the examination novel; there
are only examination novels'; and I have chosen for comment a half-
dozen of the novels which at various times have been prescribed by the
Examination Boards: Joseph Conrad's *The Rover*, Charles Dickens's
A Tale of Two Cities, George Eliot's *Silas Marner*, Jane Austen's *Pride
and Prejudice*, Thomas Hardy's *The Woodlanders*, and H. G. Wells's
The History of Mr Polly. I shall also make brief references to one or two
other novels. If my reader has recent acquaintance with some three or
four of my six, he will find the recommendations contained in this
chapter easier to understand.

But first, a word about choosing novels. The task of choosing the
novels which candidates are to study for their first public examination
is not primarily the teacher's but the examiner's, who provides a
list of titles from which the teacher chooses one, or perhaps more than
one. Since this is so, the question '*Which* novels?' is not one which
much concerns the teacher, whose main part is to grumble when the
choice has been made for him. Yet there is no harm in even the teacher
asking himself what ought to be the characteristics of a good examination novel; the answer will help him to exercise intelligently such

choice as he has, and will give directions to the studies which he subsequently devises for his pupils.

What do we want of an examination novel, then? I suggest three
things. We want it to give pleasure to the children who read it; we
want it to give them an imaginative pre-experience of some of the
complexities of actual living; and we want it to be challenging enough
to deserve the close study we customarily bestow on it. These three
requirements seem to me such as to call for no comment. For if the
children cannot find pleasure in their book, they are unlikely to find in
it anything else of value; if the book gives them no scope for new ways
of thinking and feeling, it fails to perform one of the expected functions
of literature; and if it does not provide any challenge which they cannot
meet at a first reading, it clearly does not need actual study at all. Any
proper study of a novel should be something undertaken by teacher
and children working together; it should be a process of 'guided
reading'; and provided the novel gives scope for that, and the 'guided
reading' brings enjoyment and a little increase of maturity, the choice
will be the right one.

The first thing the children must do with their book is to read it to
themselves, and then they must read it again; and then they must read
it yet again. No other work is profitable without that; and children
need to be reminded that, whatever other work is undertaken in class,
it is their own reading, their own private familiarity with the book,
which in the end will matter most. Very few children read their novel
thoroughly enough; yet teachers of school-children should be grateful
that in this matter their pupils are usually more amenable than adult
students taking the same examinations. The average adult student's
notion of studying a prescribed novel is to skim once lightly over the
pages, cast the book aside, and with all speed 'get down to the literary
criticism'. This consists of writing up the dictated notes of his lecturers
and summarizing the published critical commentaries. If the lecturer
makes a sudden reference to some matter of detail in the text, his
students look blank; if he presses a question they ask resentfully, 'But
do we *have* to know the book in this degree of detail?' When they
are told 'Yes, you do' they are even more resentful. By comparison, school-children are readier to accept guidance, and if the teacher
insists, they will often read the book several times and with reasonable
care.

Mention of the note-making habits of adult students reminds me to
say how frequently the mere writing of notes, in lieu of an intelligent

reading of the text, can mar the proper preparation of an examination novel. A Board of Examiners, reporting on the wartime work of candidates in an English literature examination, made a comment which is much to the point. 'The written answers' (they said in effect) 'were unusually good this year, and an exceptionally close knowledge of the text was shown. This was probably due to the fact that many of the children, having been evacuated from their homes to strange schools and surroundings, had less scope than usual for the taking down of dictated notes, and so had to fall back upon repeated readings of the text.' That was the gist of their comment, and the implied criticism of our methods of teaching literature was, I fear, completely justified. It is not that children should not be allowed to write notes; it is that they should not be allowed to write notes which they will subsequently read as a substitute for the text. Detailed summaries of the story and formal studies of the characters, however thoroughly committed to memory, are seldom of much use in the examination room; but the candidates do not know that, and they often give to these kinds of work an energy which, if directed elsewhere, would bring them closer to the novel and put them into a better state of readiness for anything the examiner might ask. It is very much a question of the right kind of note; and what I think to be the right kind is a number of 'indexes', which are an essential part of the study-method I am now going to describe.

This method involves, first, a series of readings—or to be more exact, *re*-readings, each from a different viewpoint: a reading for the story, a reading for the plot, a reading for the theme or themes, and a reading for the function of the characters (these readings more or less cover the *contents* of the novel); and subsequently, if the pupils are equal to it, readings for the narrative method and the method of presenting the characters. All these readings, considered together, may look like a stiff assignment, but in fact the readings I have in mind are not 'readings from cover to cover', but rather selective surveys concentrated on those matters which for the immediate purpose are relevant. With these readings goes the preparation of a series of reference-lists or 'indexes'— page-numbered lists of items, set down in the order in which they occur in the book (or, where circumstances make it preferable, in chronological order). The *story* 'index', for example, sets out, in not more than one sentence each, the chief events of the story, chronologically arranged. The list is not a summary: it means nothing to those who have not read the book. What it does is to enable the pupil to have the whole novel under his eye, to see it in its true proportions, and to have quick access to any part of it about which he wishes to refresh his memory. It should be made as short as possible—not more, in the ordinary case, than two or three pages long—and each item should be begun on a new line. Once made it should be *used*—for discussion or revision purposes, or for finding the material for written answers.

No attempt should be made to draw up a story 'index' until the novel has been read at least once; on a first reading the pupil does not know what to include and what to leave out. Besides, there is sometimes the confusion which comes of characters being introduced without their names being given. In the course of *Great Expectations*, for example, four different convicts, all unnamed, are introduced successively; it is only later on in the novel that the reader finds out who they are, and learns the names of some of them. A story 'index' made after a first or a second reading is more informed, and also is likely to be shorter and more to the point.

Sometimes the preparation of a story 'index' presents a special difficulty, as in the case of a novel where the incidents are not narrated in chronological order. Such a novel is Conrad's *The Rover*, which frequently departs from the chronological presentation of events in order to recall the past or anticipate the future. Conrad's purpose in adopting so involved a narrative-method is briefly discussed on a later page of this chapter; let me only remark here that, for the average pupil, understanding of the novel is much increased if, while taking into account the order in which the incidents are presented, he also lists them in the order in which they happened. On a first reading, many children are so bewildered by Conrad's digressions that they learn with surprise that the chief events of this novel extend over a comparatively short space of time—from Saturday night to the following Monday morning, in fact. It is these events that need to be noted down chronologically: from Bolt's landing from the *Amelia* on Saturday night, together with Symons's visit to the tartane and his imprisonment there —through a long and busy Sunday, during which Peyrol and Réal develop their plan for deceiving the English—to the escape of Symons on the Sunday night, the imprisonment of Scevola, and the departure of Peyrol, on Monday morning, to carry out his self-imposed mission. Once the young reader has sorted out these events, and can see them in their original sequence, he is in a much better position to relish the narrative as it actually stands.

So much for story and story 'indexes'; and I now pass on to a consideration of *plot* (keeping the distinction between the two made by

E. M. Forster in *Aspects of the Novel*). After the preliminary readings of the novel, and the preparation of the story 'index' as described above, it is wise to have another reading, in the course of which the intricacies of the plot are examined and sorted out. This need not be a very lengthy business, for the plots of most examination novels are straightforward enough; yet there may well be need for one or two unravellings which the children cannot (or have not bothered to) do for themselves. For example, when reading *The Rover*, young readers do not always perceive the extent of Scevola's participation in the events which lead to his imprisonment and subsequent death. (He is wildly jealous of Réal, and when the latter has left for Toulon, Scevola wrongly assumes that he is on board the tartane, and is plotting some treachery with Peyrol and the English. Going down to the tartane to investigate, he is himself imprisoned there, and is subsequently carried off by Peyrol, whose object is to leave the farm safe for Arlette and Réal.) To take a few more examples : *Pride and Prejudice*, a novel with a more straightforward plot, probably needs close scrutiny at only one point—the point at which Darcy, making use of his previous and painful knowledge of Wickham as a potential seducer, is enabled to discover Lydia and force Wickham to marry her. In *A Tale of Two Cities* a complicated situation arises when Carton accidentally acquires power over the two Old Bailey spies, Roger Cly and John Barsad, and uses that power to force them into helping him release Darnay from prison (all very contrived, this). In *Henry Esmond*, the part played by Esmond in attempting to restore the Stuart monarchy demands a close look; in *Jane Eyre*, the circumstances attending St John Rivers's discovery of Jane's identity. In some other novels, on the other hand, the windings of the plot are easy enough to follow without effort (in *Silas Marner*, for example, George Eliot is at great pains to make everything appear to come about in a natural manner); and in such cases there is no point in spending time on 'plot' as distinct from 'story'.

Two more readings are needed if we wish to make a complete survey of the novel's content: one a reading which will discover and trace the development of the writer's theme (if he has one); the other a reading which will examine the characters one by one and see in what way they 'serve' the novel. About *themes* we should be sensible: we should not expect to find themes in novels of mere entertainment, nor invent them if they are not there; nor should we condemn a novel as inferior if it has no discoverable theme; nor should we exalt to central importance a theme of small significance. All the same, some of the novels set for first public examinations do have themes which deserve at least a little attention if the novels are to be fully enjoyed and understood.

One of the novels I have already spoken of, *The Rover*, a novel of romantic adventure though it primarily is, also deals lightly with two themes—the theme of Brotherhood and the theme of Manhood. The first of these is worked out by a contrasting of the Brotherhood of the French Revolution with the Brotherhood of the Coast; the second by a measuring of the other men of the novel (Scevola, Réal, and the Cripple) against the Rover, whom Arlette describes as 'the man himself'. With the theme of Brotherhood goes that of patriotism, so that the questions which appear to be asked and answered are these: 'What, after all, is true brotherhood? How, ultimately, is love of country shown? In what characteristics of mind and body does true manhood reside?' I will say no more about these themes, except to remark that there is relevant matter on the following pages of the novel: 2, 5, 20, 22, 25–8, 32, 35, 40–4, 48, 67, 69–71, 74–7, 81, 86, 92, 93, 96–8, 107, 117–18, 133–4, 142, 146, 161–2, 166–71, 182–3, 206–14, 219–20, 224–5, 245–8, 275, 280, and 286 (in Dent's L.Y.T. edition). I would like to turn to a better known novel, *Silas Marner*, where the principal theme is more obviously a part of the novel's essential substance, and suggest a method of tracing it through the novel's pages.

This theme is unfolded as an essential of Marner's own history, which is in effect an account of the course of an ardent man's affections when they are denied normal expression. George Eliot sets out to show how the lonely and deprived man, desperate for love as a very necessity of existence, fastens and concentrates his affections on a heap of gold; how he suffers violent sorrow when the gold is lost; how good fortune brings another object of affection, which gradually loosens the hold money has on him; and how, in his later years, he is indifferent to his gold when it is brought back to him. This theme—of man's need for love, and the way it is related to a greed for money—is not beyond children's comprehension or outside the range of their interests; yet they may need their teacher's help (more here, perhaps, than with the other readings) in seeking out and recognizing the relevant passages.

The method I suggest of doing this—a method which applies to all novels, and not only to *Silas Marner*—is as follows. First, the teacher initiates a discussion, which ends in a provisional statement of the novel's theme. Then the children look out the relevant items for themselves, helped perhaps by a list of page-numbers which the teacher supplies. After all the material has been found, and written up as an 'index', the theme is discussed again, is reconsidered, and is perhaps re-stated. So, in reviewing *Silas Marner*, the pupils will remark quite early (page 13 in the 'King's Treasuries' edition) that Marner has a 'fervid nature', and that this 'fervour' finds ample outlet in the religious society of which he is a member—in his close David-and-Jonathan friendship with William Dane, in his love for the girl Sarah, in his discharge of social obligations towards the 'brothers' of his fellowship (page 17), and above all in his religious devotions, which have God for their centre. Marner's condemnation by the fellowship (page 20) effectively cuts him off from all these objects of his affections: he is renounced by the 'brothers', by William Dane and by Sarah, and also (as he thinks) by God, whom he condemns as a 'God of lies' (page 20); and in this loveless and forlorn condition he leaves Lantern Yard and makes his way to Raveloe.

Lonely as he is in his new life, he does not suddenly lose all capacity for loving; and this explains his queer outburst of grief when one day he breaks his much-valued pitcher (page 30). All his fervour is at last concentrated on his heap of gold; hence his utter desolation (page 60) when the gold is taken from him. That Eppie is destined to replace the gold in his affections is made clear at the moment when Marner, short-sightedly observing her shining hair in the firelight, believes it to be his money come back to him (page 151). After that it is important to notice that a growing love for Eppie involves him in a return to social life (pages 177–9), in the formation of new friendships (pages 191–5), and ultimately in a return to worship and to God (page 184). It is surely meant to be significant that when Marner is reintroduced after a space of sixteen years—Marner in his 'love-crowned age'—he is on the way home with Eppie from church, and carrying her Prayer-Book for her. Nor should we overlook the significance of Marner's remarks when, at the end, his gold is unexpectedly recovered: 'It takes no hold on me now, the money doesn't. I wonder if it ever could again—I doubt it might, if I lost you, Eppie.'

So the simple theme is traced through the novel, and in tracing it the children are made, in an elementary way, to ponder on 'man, the heart of man, and human life'—which is one of the things we want them to do.

Before leaving the subject of themes, I should like to show how my remarks apply to one or two other novels. In *Pride and Prejudice* there is of course the theme (or rather, constant preoccupation) which pervades all Jane Austen's novels—the theme of 'proper social conduct and right personal relationships'. It is as though these novels were asking such questions as these : 'In a society which sets such store by *formal* good behaviour, what should be genuine good behaviour? Which, in the end, are the attitudes and feelings which civilized and humane folk ought to practise and approve?' Jane Austen answers these questions, not directly or didactically, but by diffusing her sense of 'rightness' and 'goodness' through the words and the actions of those characters whom she loves and whom she invites her readers also to love. So, in *Pride and Prejudice*, when Charlotte Lucas tells Elizabeth Bennet how Jane Bennet ought to 'secure her man'—by making the most of every half-hour in which she can command Bingley's attention—Elizabeth is amused: 'You make me laugh, Charlotte, but it is not sound. You know it is not sound, and that you would never act in this way yourself.' Later on, Charlotte Lucas secures Mr Collins by employing just such a method. Astounded at first, Elizabeth then hastens to congratulate her friend; but thereafter 'Between Elizabeth and Charlotte there was a restraint which kept them mutually silent on the subject, and Elizabeth felt persuaded that no real confidence could ever subsist between them again.' In all this we are not conscious of being preached at; but a principle is established and an attitude made plain. If, in these novels, we allow our pupils to miss such pervading principles and attitudes, we leave them the poorer, I think. But whatever difficulties we may have with so general a theme, we can find in *Pride and Prejudice* another, a related but a simpler and more manageable one; for the novel also asks, and sets out to answer, another question: 'What, after all, is a true gentleman, a true gentlewoman?' In providing an answer to this, Jane Austen shows how little relevant are any considerations of rank or wealth; delicacy and good feeling are as likely to emerge in a Mr Gardiner as in a Darcy; they are as likely to be absent in a Lady Catherine de Bourgh as in a Mr Collins. Nor is it difficult to follow this theme through the novel; the children should give an especial eye to the words and the actions of Mr and Mrs Bennet, Darcy, Bingley's sisters, Lady Catherine, Mr Collins, Sir William Lucas, Mr and Mrs Gardiner, and of course Elizabeth.

Dickens himself claimed a sort of theme for *A Tale of Two Cities*—the theme of 'social retribution' which he derived from Carlyle. According to Carlyle's view of history, the French Revolution provided evidence of the way in which one kind of social 'excess' (here the excessive cruelty, hauteur, and indifference of the aristocrat) ultimately gives birth to another. Dickens sought to give form and body to this theory in his characteristically high-spirited way, but it is not a theme which need much trouble our pupils; *A Tale of Two Cities* remains primarily a novel of incident and melodrama. On the other hand, *The Woodlanders* develops one of the principal Hardy themes in some detail and with much seriousness—his theme of the incompatibility subsisting between, on the one part, rural persons without surface graces but with sterling worth of character, and, on the other part, town-bred people with education and refinement but without constancy or deep principles. On the one part we have Giles Winterbourne and Marty South; on the other, Fitzpiers and Mrs Charmond; while between them stands Grace Melbury, country-bred but city-educated, and so torn between two lives. The reader should notice the inbred good manners which go with Giles's apparent gracelessness; the fact that he and Marty are always in harmony with their surroundings (they are at home in the woodland at all seasons); Giles's sacrifice for Grace Melbury; and Marty's constancy to Giles's memory after Grace has left the neighbourhood; and by contrast the restlessness and instability of both Fitzpiers and Mrs Charmond, both of whom are driven melancholy-mad by the country life. Hardy handles this theme again in *The Mayor of Casterbridge*.

The novels of H. G. Wells abound in themes, some of them touched lightly upon, some of them developed at great length—for Wells was a man of views and opinions. *The History of Mr Polly* concerns itself amongst other themes with the growing ugliness of late-Victorian England and the way in which that ugliness afflicted the soul of the sensitive Polly. For Polly is shown as a man more than usually aware of the ugliness amid which he is condemned to pass his life; his whole attitude is a wordless protest against life's meanness and lovelessness. Moreover, being endowed with a 'facile sense of beauty', he is occasionally conscious that there are alternatives to ugliness. His history is primarily one of evasion, of refusal to face up to his circumstances, and of an occasional and pathetic reaching out towards beauty and romance. 'The great crime which the moneyed classes and promoters of industry committed in the palmy Victorian days was the condemnation of the workers to ugliness, ugliness, ugliness; meanness and formless and ugly surroundings, ugly ideals, ugly religion, ugly hope, ugly love, ugly clothes, ugly houses, ugly furniture, ugly relationships between workers and employers. The human soul needs actual beauty even more than bread.' The words are D. H. Lawrence's; but what Lawrence says there, Wells had already concretely asserted in his novel. The theme is so

essential to *Mr Polly* that it would be absurd to undertake any study of
the novel without taking it fully into account.

May I again suggest that, while finding themes where they certainly
are, we should beware of trying to find them where they are not—in
Jane Eyre, for example, where there is at the most an unconvincing
'Virtue Rewarded' theme which Charlotte Brontë derived, with much
else in the novel, from Richardson's *Pamela*; or in *Lorna Doone*, which
is a novel of entertainment pure and simple.

After giving some thought to the theme of our prescribed novel, we
can allow ourselves to turn our attention to some of the *characters*; and
the first thing to do is to prepare—or allow our pupils to prepare—an
'index' for each of the principal persons, showing in page-numbered
order his chief appearances in the novel. To know when and where
your character makes his chief appearances is the first step towards
being able to talk intelligently about him; and lists of this kind are a
very different thing from 'character-studies', the making of which used
to be such an important part of the pre-examination year's work. I
think that for some teachers it must be still; for I observe that quite
recent school editions of some of the standard classics devote part of
their Introductions to telling the story in outline, and the rest to
describing the characters one by one. This sort of practice at once pro-
vokes the despairing questions, 'Why on earth? What is the use? Where
is the point of it all?' For the characters of a novel are not displayed in
that novel as in a portrait-gallery, the end-products of the novelist's art,
posed for the reader's appraisal; they are in the novel in order to 'serve'
it—to assist the story, or the plot, or the theme, or all three, or perhaps
merely to provide entertainment or relaxation. So that the first question
to ask ourselves about any character is not 'What are his chief characteristics?' but 'What is he doing in the novel at all?' And in finding
out the answer to this question, we expect to acquire fresh insight into
the novel as a whole.

May I show what I mean by referring to some of the people in the
novels I have already discussed? I will avoid the major characters and
speak of some of the minor ones: Mr Gardiner in *Pride and Prejudice*,
for example. What is he doing in the novel? In what way does he
'serve' it? He certainly helps the story and the plot; for it is Mr and Mrs
Gardiner's taking Elizabeth on a tour of the Midlands which brings her
to Pemberley (the house of which she 'might have been mistress'), and
so unexpectedly brings about her reunion with Darcy. But Mr Gardiner
does more—he 'serves' one of the themes of the novel. A brother of one

of Elizabeth's 'vulgar' relations (her mother) of whom Darcy has already disapproved, a man in a respectable line of trade and with no pretensions to family or distinction, he is nevertheless one of Elizabeth's connections for whom she feels she need not blush; he enters at once into a pleasant association with Darcy, and it is made clear that their association is soon to ripen into friendship. Mr Gardiner helps to answer the unposed but implied question: 'What, after all, is a gentleman, a gentlewoman?' In different ways, as I said earlier, many of the other characters help to answer the same question. Even so minor a character as Sir William Lucas is interesting in this respect: a man without good breeding or real delicacy of feeling, he has been knighted as a consequence of the visit to his town of a Royal Personage during his mayoralty, and thereafter devotes all his energies to 'living the part' of a titled person.

Or consider one of the minor characters in *The Rover*—the Cripple who helps and advises Peyrol when he wishes to restore the derelict tartane, and who organizes the villagers of Madrague in the task of launching it. Here is a character apparently thrown in gratuitously, apparently necessary to neither story nor plot. Yet he reinforces Conrad's contentions regarding true manhood, as is shown by the way he earns Peyrol's grim approval. ' "There is no denying it—you are a man. I tell you," insisted the Rover roughly, and as if the insignificance of mortal envelopes had presented itself to him for the first time at the end of his roving life, "I tell you that there is that in you which would make a chum one would like to have alongside one in a tight place." ' That is the judgement on the Cripple made by 'the man himself'. By comparison, the other men fall short. About Réal, Peyrol is slightly disdainful—he is brave enough, but he has repressed all true feeling to the point where he is prepared to throw away his life in the mere line of duty. About Scevola—the 'blood-drinker', the harbourer of an intellectual hatred, the man who has slaughtered on principle—he is scornful to the point of contempt.

When we come to consider *The History of Mr Polly* we find—apart from the characters who are necessary to keep story and plot moving—a whole range of persons who are introduced for a while and then dropped again; these in their different ways help to develop the theme as it is outlined on page 129. Each character contributes something. Parsons, Polly's earliest friend, shows Polly the possibilities of, but does not succeed in providing, escape into the world of literature and art; the girl in the pink print dress, met early at an inn, provides for the

young apprentices their first revelation of feminine beauty; Polly's first
employer, and indeed some of the subsequent ones, (for example, the
employer who preferred to employ Baptists because of their capacity
for 'good all round business work'), show us something of the ugly
relationships between workers and employers; the pork butcher Rymer,
introduced as a passing character, shows us how and at what price commercial success is achieved; the clergyman officiating at Polly's wedding
gives us a glimpse of 'ugly religion'; Miriam provides, and Uncle
Pentstemon makes devastating comment on, 'ugly love'; and the terrifying Uncle Jim, a 'Reformatory Reformed Character', reveals himself
as the ugliest product of an ugly age. Against all these is set the brief
vision of the unattainable provided by Christabel, remembered afterwards as belonging to the time when 'beauty had called to him with so
imperious a voice'. So that this is a novel, perhaps more obviously than
most, where a full-length study of each character would be valueless
and misleading, so clearly do so many of them 'serve' the theme and
do little more.

So far, in writing of the ways in which we can study a novel's story,
its plot, its theme, and its characters, I have had an eye to only the
content of the novel; but what about the novelist's manner, the 'way
in which it is done', the 'art of the novelist'? Are such studies beyond
fifteen-year-old children? In any great detail I think they are; yet
examiners do sometimes ask simple questions about *narrative-method*
(about the use of coincidences, for example, or the contriving of
climaxes), or about the *characterization*. Unluckily, in such matters as
this, it is very difficult to suggest a single approach, for every novel is
different from every other, and each has to be considered as an individual case.

Let us first consider narrative-method—that is to say, the way in
which the events of the story are presented, and the means by which
the reader's interest is aroused and maintained. The narrative-method
of *A Tale of Two Cities* is a simple one, and a common enough one with
Dickens: it involves processes of alternate 'mystification' and 'clarifica-
tion'. In other words, Dickens first presents a situation mysterious
enough to arouse the reader's curiosity and make him want to read on,
and then clarifies that situation by providing an explanation; and this
process is repeated throughout the book. In order not to throw too
great a strain on the reader's memory and intelligence, Dickens does
not usually leave him mystified for long: such 'mysteries' as Mr Lorry's
message 'Recalled to life', Mme Lefarge's habit of knitting at all times

and in all places, the man hanging on beneath the marquis's coach, and Mr Cruncher's disappointment when he attempts to resurrect Cly, are none of them left long unexplained. There is only one major 'mystery' —only one which the reader must hold in mind through the space of many chapters: the reluctance which Manette shows in accepting Darnay as a son-in-law. An explanation of this is delayed till the climax of the novel, when it is revealed that the former persecutor of Manette was Darnay's uncle. This somewhat unsubtle narrative-method, suitable for a work first published in weekly instalments, naturally makes use of many contrived climaxes, and even coincidences are not disdained: at two points in the novel the course of events is decisively affected by the remarkable (and improbable) close facial resemblance of Darnay to Carton.

By contrast *The Rover*, written for the more intelligent and painstaking reader, makes use of Conrad's most involved method of narration— the method of *Lord Jim*, *Heart of Darkness*, and *Nostromo*. This method makes no attempt at strictly chronological presentation, and indeed, at its most characteristic, narrates the consequence of an incident before the incident itself has been disclosed. The effect of this 'jigsaw' method is to arouse curiosity to a high pitch; but it is a difficult method for children, who, in common with adult readers, must hold simultaneously in their minds the novel as it stands and the completed 'jigsaw' which, by a single comprehensive act, they are required to put together. Fuller pleasure comes with the second reading, when 'relations' begin to be more firmly established in the reader's mind. Taken in chronological order, the incidents of *The Rover* reveal little contrivance, except for the one remarkable coincidence of Peyrol having previously been acquainted with the English sailor Symons.

Just as no two novels exactly resemble each other in their narrative-method, so do no two adopt the same method of developing their characters. Conrad's, the most subtle, is a method of 'gradual revelation'—we are allowed only a gradual insight into the characters' motives and preoccupations. So, in *The Rover*, it is only little by little that Scevola, the 'blood-drinker', is explained to us: it is comparatively late in the story that we learn one of the most significant facts about him—that in pre-Revolution days he had been regarded as a comic and contemptible figure, the butt of all the village girls. The real origins of his fierce desire for 'equality' are thus disclosed. It is the same with Arlette: the experiences which made her what she was are withheld from us (we see only their effects) until late in the novel, when she

K

herself gives an account of her active part in the massacre at Toulon. Dickens's method in *The Tale of Two Cities* (where, however, the people are unusually lifeless for Dickens) is his most characteristic one: he provides each person with a formula (Mr Lorry, for example, is 'a man of business trying not to let his heart intrude'), and then, in that person's subsequent appearances, applies the formula by means of repetition and ferocious exaggeration. Hardy, in *The Woodlanders*, builds up his characters by laborious synthesis: having decided what sort of person Mrs Charmond is to be if she is properly to serve his theme, he introduces her as a play-actress; gives her false hair; presents her lying extended on a couch; makes her sing amatory songs, powder her face, and smoke cigarettes; furnishes her room with Versailles furniture; and sets her laughing out loud when a passing countryman falls from the top of a high bank near her house. He presents Fitzpiers by a similar means, and, though a little more subtly, Giles and Marty also. Jane Austen, in *Pride and Prejudice*, frequently gives a one-sentence or a two-sentence generalizing account of a person when he is first introduced, and then amplifies it in subsequent narrative and dialogue. Observe, for example, how true to himself is each member of the Bennet family when he or she comments on Mr Collins's letter (in Chapter 13 of the novel).

So what is to be our classroom treatment of the novelist's 'manner'? I think we ought first to read the novel attentively ourselves, to find out as much as we can about the novelist's narrative-method and his way of presenting and developing his characters, and subsequently to impart to our pupils such of our discoveries as we think they can profit by. Usually, something elementary can be done. The following terms will frequently be on our lips when we are discussing these matters, and if the children know what these and a few other terms mean (this is not an exhaustive list), they will probably possess the minimum of equipment for writing about a novel's workmanship: story, plot, chronology, mystification, suspense, coincidence, digression, climax, dénouement, narrative, description, dialogue, (im)probability, drama, melodrama, pathos, humour, 'flat' character, 'round' character, and caricature.

A last word about 'indexes'. As for the story, the plot, the theme, and the characters, so for the narrative-method and the characterization —short 'indexes' should be made, all with page-references to the text. These should be the only notes; and, as I said before, once made they should be *used*—to enable the pupil to look up a point rapidly when he is discussing the text in class, and to provide quick access to the raw material from which written answers are to be made. Always they should direct the pupil's attention back to the printed page—and provided they do that, they will be a blessing and not a curse.

CHAPTER 10

THE BOOK OF VERSE

Difficulties confronting pupil and teacher—Small value of ancillary studies—The study of metrics—The study of figurative language—A short poem examined—Another—Treatment of longer poems—Note-making—The poet's style—A good 'literature answer'—The problem of honesty

CHILDREN PREPARING for their first examination are usually expected to study a book of verse, either parts of it or all of it; sometimes it is a larger number of short poems which is prescribed, sometimes a smaller number of long ones. Almost invariably—if you allow that the study is to be spread over no more than three terms of a busy school year—the poems chosen by the examiners are too many or too long; and it is this fact more than any other which induces the sense of hopelessness with which the children so often face the examination, and explains why their examination answers reveal superficial knowledge or downright ignorance. There are some children who take eagerly to poetry—who read it voluntarily and commit it to memory without effort; but there are many more who are not brought to it except by a teacher's care and patience, and who need time to acquire the familiarity which must precede liking. For such children, a few carefully-chosen poems should be sufficient—two long narrative poems, say, or a dozen short poems at the most. The examiner of the future who prescribes in moderate quantities will have the right to expect in his candidates that close knowledge of the poems which the present-day examiner often looks for in vain.

In the meantime, we have to take things as they stand, and at present the task of the teacher is to help his pupils become familiar with a fair amount of poetry in a short space of time. The pupils must do more than that: they must be able to write intelligently about the poems—be able to prove their familiarity with them and give evidence of their enjoyment. So that the teacher's task is a double one. Small wonder if

136

he sometimes casts about him in despair, seeking for some settled procedure which will turn everything into plain sailing.

If only (for example) there were some fixed rules or laws, some 'framework of reference' by which a poem's characteristics could be discovered and its quality measured! When the fourth or the fifth year comes, the teacher, who until now has been content to let the children read and enjoy, sometimes feels the need to introduce certain ancillary studies as aids to criticism—the study of metrics, perhaps, or of figurative language, or even of a technical vocabulary. I wonder if my reader, turning the pages of a child's discarded exercise-book, has ever come across an entry like this:

Rhythm in Poetry

non-stress ∪   stress —

> Iambic ∪ —
> Trochaic — ∪
> Anapaestic ∪ ∪ —
> Dactylic — ∪ ∪

e.g. (1) Thĕ traīn | whĭch stānds | ăt plāt | fŏrm foūr |

e.g. (2) Chārlŏtte | hāvĭng | seēn hĭs | bōdў |

e.g. (3) Ănd thĕ wīnd's | ŏn thĕ heāth | ăt thĕ sēt | ŏf thĕ sūn

e.g. (4)

There, it would seem, the teacher's inspiration faded out. But the intention behind the entry is plain: it sets out to establish certain patterns which will act as the guide to a feeling for rhythm in poetry. Does it in fact do so? Is it about rhythm in poetry at all? Is it not just an attempt at a simple exposition of a system of metrics? This particular entry was not followed up by any application of the system to other and longer pieces of poetry (it appears to have been a small isolated study, the work of an idle moment); and that is just as well, for nothing but harm could have come of pursuing the work further. Admittedly, the scansion of English verse used to be a favourite classroom activity, second only to clause analysis: one beginner teacher told me that during his boyhood in South Wales—before the Second World War, admittedly—the whole of every Saturday morning was spent on Scansion. And it can be imagined that, once done, such work was not likely to be wasted; we may be sure that the examiners in public examinations were made to feel the full effects of it. Page upon page of memorized English verse, criss-crossed over with odd little markings—

and all in the name of 'the study of the poem's rhythm'! Let us hope that this strange practice has at length died out, and given place to more sensible employments.

Let us also be clear in our own minds what the facts really are. There is no system of metrics which is capable of recording the true rhythm of a poem—no way of setting down in symbols the exact way in which a line of poetry moves. To do so would involve being able to record not only stress but also degree of stress; not only stress but also length; not only length but also exact length; not only stress and length but also the closeness of syllables to each other. What our system of metrics does do is to enable us to express by symbols certain basic and inflexible patterns which are, as it were, the 'background music'—felt but unheard—against which the spoken words of the poem move in subtle and flexible variation. A sensitive reader is aware of both simultaneously—the metre which forms the 'background music', and the rhythmical succession of sounds as the human voice utters them; and from the relationship of these two proceeds some of the pleasure to be derived from poetry. But it is a pleasure which is not dependent on knowledge or introspection; and whatever interest the study of metrics may have for adults, it is a dangerous study for children, who have abused it too often in the past for us to wish for its revival. The examiner can do more than anyone to keep such studies dead; it is because of his (in general) resolute avoidance of references to them that they are dying out. But examiners must remain wary; for even a single slip (for example, a request for a discussion of 'some of the metrical effects in Browning's poetry') may send whole schools of children scurrying back to their little loops and dashes—and the whole sorry business will begin all over again.

Are we then to forego all consideration of the true rhythm of a poem —all reference to the exact way in which the lines move? By no means; but I think this can usually be done in terms of the poem itself—in terms of the sound of the lines when read aloud—rather than by means of a special notation. Let us take the example of a stanza from the ballad *Edward*—the stanza in which the mother of the distraught Edward asks him what he will leave to his wife and his children when he goes into exile:

> 'And what will ye leave to your bairns and your wife,
>   Edward, Edward?
> And what will ye leave to your bairns and your wife,
>   When ye gang owre the sea, O?'

'The warld's room. Let them beg through life,
        Mither, mither.
The warld's room. Let them beg through life,
        For them never mair will I see, O.'

The most interesting line rhythmically is the fifth one, where the falling together of the two long and heavy monosyllables ('warld's' and 'room') imparts to the words a remarkable spaciousness, and strongly reinforces not only the idea which they convey but also the feeling of desolation that goes with it. The obvious way of making this clear to young readers is to speak the lines and demonstrate the effect; and any further comment need involve no vocabulary more technical than such words as 'length', 'emphasis', 'spaciousness' and 'sonority'.

So that the secret of a 'successful study of the poem's rhythm' is a simple one. It is for the teacher to read the poem aloud; for the children to read it after him; for teacher and children to hear other people reading it; for the poem to be heard again and again, till the words ring in the ear and the mind, and the poem's music has become integrated with the rest of its meaning. But it takes time—all these readings take time. I refer my reader back to my claim, made in the first paragraph of this chapter, that a mere handful of carefully-selected poems are a sufficient prescription for a year's study.

Let us leave the question of rhythm and scansion then, and turn to the question of figurative language. Figures of speech—those devices of language whose strange names and definitions used to be memorized as so important a part of the fifth year's work! I can only hope that in most schools the study of these, too, is dying or dead, for the experience of teachers (and even more so of examiners) must have long since proved what a dangerous study it is to pursue. For you have only to teach your pupils to identify the various figures of speech, and they will conclude that to do so is the true end of all criticism—or worse, that the greater the number of figures, the better the poem! It is this misconception that, taking firm root in the pupil's mind, ultimately gives birth to 'poetic criticism' like the following:

The poem opens right away with a magnificent hyperbole. It then goes on to give us two similes in succession, and these are closely followed by a very lovely metaphor. Then, after only three lines of ordinary writing, we get a very fine example of onomatopoeia. It is so good it reminds us of that other fine example we get in Tennyson, about 'the moan of doves in immemorial elms and the murmuring of innumerable bees'. And what comes next? Only six lines further on we get a first class example of prolepsis, which is not a very common figure of speech, and so is the more welcome here. The poem ends up with a sort of mixture of a metonymy and a synecdoche, which forms a fitting conclusion to this very lovely poem.

The kind of criticism of which this is a parody does not stand up to examination. It tells us nothing of importance about the poem, and nothing about the extent of the critic's understanding and appreciation of it. It looks at the words on the page, but it does not even begin to look through the words to find what lies behind them. The examiner who wishes to discourage his candidates from writing in this way will do so by never himself employing technical terms—not even 'simile' and 'metaphor'. It is quite possible to ask questions about the comparisons, direct or implied, in a poem—or, indeed, about any other features of its style—without having to resort to technicalities. The fewer technical terms we put before our pupils, the more we force them to find other and more proper means of studying poetry.

And what are they, these 'other and more proper means'? In my view, methods of study should not differ much as between younger children and older ones, and therefore the method I described in Chapter 8 is appropriate here. This method is a combination of many readings of the poem with a discussion which attempts to penetrate the poem's words and discover the things and experiences behind them. 'Many readings' explains itself, and I have already written enough about it; but I should like to return to the question of discussing poetry and to illustrate my remarks by references to a selected poem—Thomas Hardy's poem *Afterwards*. I choose it deliberately because once, at a lecture, a teacher complained that 'there were so many poems which gave you nothing to talk about', and on my asking him to give an example, he mentioned this very poem. Here it is:

> When the Present has latched its postern behind my tremulous stay,
> And the May month flaps its glad green leaves like wings,
> Delicate-filmed as new-spun silk, will the neighbours say,
> 'He was a man who used to notice such things'?
>
> If it be in the dusk, when like an eyelid's soundless blink
> The dewfall-hawk comes crossing the shades to alight
> Upon the wind-warped upland thorn, a gazer may think,
> 'To him this must have been a familiar sight.'
>
> If I pass during some nocturnal blackness, mothy and warm,
> When the hedgehog travels furtively over the lawn,
> One may say, 'He strove that such innocent creatures should
>   come to no harm,
> But he could do little for them; and now he is gone.'

If, when hearing that I have been stilled at last, they stand at the door,
Watching the full-starred heavens that winter sees,
Will this thought rise on those who will meet my face no more,
'He was one who had an eye for such mysteries'?

And will any say when my bell of quittance is heard in the gloom,
And a crossing breeze cuts a pause in its outrollings,
Till they rise again, as they were a new bell's boom,
'He hears it not now, but used to notice such things'?

THOMAS HARDY

At a first glance, the poem certainly seems to present few difficulties and to offer little scope for discussion. Yet the experience embodied here—the thought which, in various guises, is repeated from stanza to stanza—is not particularly easy to grasp (the poem is something more than the list of 'things I have loved' which make up another anthology-piece, Rupert Brooke's *The Great Lover*). What Hardy essentially expresses is a sad man's wish to be remembered after his death—and to be remembered in relation to some of the things most personal to him. After the poem has been read several times in class, a start can be made with the fourth stanza, for this puts Hardy's recurring question more explicitly than the other stanzas do. When the general meaning of the stanza has been discussed, the children can be invited to notice that it contains a reference to the poet's death ('I have been stilled at last'), to other people ('they stand at the door'), to something which the people observe ('the full-starred heavens'), and to a remark which they make about it ('He was one who had an eye for such mysteries'). It can then be shown that similar references are contained in each of the other stanzas, and the children can be called upon to identify these. In this way it can be made clear that all the stanzas offer variants of Hardy's speculation upon the circumstances which will attend his death; and thus the pattern of the poem is established.

And is that all? Will the teacher now be able to rest assured that the poem is understood? I think not. No doubt some of the children will understand it; but there will be others for whom it is desirable to pick up a phrase here and there, examine a metaphor, explain a reference. There is the first line, for example:

When the Present has latched its postern behind my tremulous stay——

Some of the children will need to be shown that the Present, in shutting the gate of Death, will shut the poet out, so that he will become a part of the Past. And 'tremulous'—why 'tremulous stay'? What does the word suggest about the way in which Hardy regards our stay on earth? Does it not suggest that he regards our hold on life as uncertain? And then the next two lines:

> And the May month flaps its glad green leaves like wings,
> Delicate-filmed as new-spun silk . . .

Will all the children at once be able to see those leaves as we would wish them to? For what leaves, in fact, are they asked to see? Even country children may have to think twice. These are 'new' leaves, and leaves which are new in the 'May month'—therefore not the leaves of (say) elm, horse-chestnut, or sycamore. The most common of the new May leaves are those of the ash, beech, and oak. But the leaves in the poem 'flap' in the wind—that is to say, they are delicately-suspended on their stalks; moreover they are shaped like wings, and are filmed over with silk. In short, they are beech-leaves, and Hardy wishes us to see beech-leaves blowing in a strong wind. And is it not better to see them clearly than to be content with a picture of vaguely-flapping wings?

So with the rest of the poem: the 'dewfall hawk' deserves a little consideration. Is it a hawk which comes with the dewfall? Or a hawk which comes as gently as the dewfall? Or both? Or take the case of two later lines:

> If I pass in some nocturnal blackness, mothy and warm,
> When the hedgehog travels furtively over the lawn . . .

The 'feel' of the first of these lines surely deserves to be considered—the word 'mothy' suggests so much more than 'full of moths': its thick suffocating sound goes far towards evoking a sultry atmosphere. And the second line—the one about the hedgehog—is interesting for its rhythm, which so effectively mimics the movement of the creature it describes. All these matters need to be picked up and given a close look (the phenomenon of the bell, too); and when that has been done, the poem needs to be read uninterruptedly again, and appreciated as a whole. Subsequently the children can recite it, record it on tape, hear other people's recordings of it, and return to it as often as they want to, and always with greater liking and an increasing sense of familiarity.

Before going on to speak of longer (narrative) poems, I should like to examine one more short poem, a more difficult one: *The Song of the Mad Prince*, by Walter de la Mare. It is in several prescribed anthologies —in, for example, *Rhyme and Reason* (published by Chatto and Windus), which also contains the poem by James Shirley mentioned below. Here is *The Song of the Mad Prince*:

Who said, 'Peacock Pie'?
  The old King to the sparrow:
Who said, 'Crops are ripe'?
  Rust to the harrow:
Who said, 'Where sleeps she now?
  Where rests she now her head,
Bathed in eve's loveliness'?
  That's what I said.

Who said, 'Ay, mum's the word'?
  Sexton to willow:
Who said, 'Green dusk for dreams,
  Moss for a pillow'?
Who said, 'All Time's delight
  Hath she for narrow bed;
Life's troubled bubble broken'?—
  That's what I said.

                    WALTER DE LA MARE

Now this poem may be described as a 'poem of mortality' (though
it is in fact a poem which rejects the idea of mortality), and for that
reason we can usefully preface it by a reading of Shirley's *Death the
Leveller*, which treats the theme of mortality in a conventional way.
We can follow this by some preliminary readings of Walter de la
Mare's poem, and then begin our discussion of it by trying to form an
idea of what, as a whole, it is about. With the help of our pupils we
discover that there are various comments in the poem, made by various
speakers: by the old King to the sparrow; by Rust to the harrow; by
the Sexton to the willow; and by the Mad Prince to himself. Then
arises the question 'What are they commenting *on*?'—and an examination of lines 5, 13, and 14 show that it is 'her' death and burial. To
complete this general survey, we must note the difference between the
remarks made by the Mad Prince (a difference observable in both
stanzas) and those made by the other speakers: the other speakers accept
the full implications of 'her' death, taking the view of mortality
expressed in Shirley's poem; but the Mad Prince does not.

The rest of our study of the poem involves a closer examination of
this difference. By question and answer we establish the meaning of the
old King's comment (the two words 'Peacock Pie') on 'her' death and
burial. What ideas do we associate with peacocks? The pride of living
and the flaunting of colours. But this particular peacock has suffered
the fate of less exalted birds: she has been 'baked in a pie'. 'Peacock Pie'

is, in short, the old King's way of speaking of beauty-in-the-coffin, or beauty-in-the-grave. The remark of the Rust—the rust on a scythe, perhaps—is not so easy to interpret, but it is essentially of the same sort: 'Crops are ripe' (*i.e.* 'she', in all her beauty, is ready for harvest), but the scythe is rusted (*i.e.* no lover will ever gather her). Such are the views of the King and the Rust. By contrast the Mad Prince (because he is crazed by love and grief, and cannot visualize death as it really is) sees her as still above ground—somewhere resting her head, 'bathed in eve's loveliness'.

If the children can get thus far, the rest of the poem offers no difficulty, because the second stanza traces the same ground with more explicitness and feeling. The Sexton's grim comment, made to the willow, means in effect 'Silence is the right name for it'. Against this third declaration of the finality of death, the Prince once more sets his audacious assertion; he tells us that she dreams in the dusk of the trees; she pillows her head on the moss; she is dead, yes, but only in the sense that she is freed from mortal suffering ('life's troubled bubble broken'). She has known no loss of consciousness, she lies in no ordinary coffin, but survives lapped round with 'all Time's delight'. We should not make the mistake of thinking that the Mad Prince regards her as, in the conventional sense, 'immortal', far less as 'gone to heaven'; she survives on earth, and her life henceforward will be an unbroken ecstasy. A mad thought? Undoubtedly; but it is the sort of thought which grief and crazed love will set up as a barrier against an unendurable truth.

In my discussion of the poem I have used terms which may well make it seem difficult to understand; yet if the right simple questions are asked, the meaning, in large part, can be made clear to quite young children. I think it would be wrong to suppose that because it is a 'mad song' the poem is a mere collection of haphazard observations; the Prince may have been mad, but the poet assuredly was not. No doubt there are those who will say, 'This is a delicious fragile thing, made half of nonsense, half of evocative images; what a pity to ruin it by dissecting it!' But that has not been my experience. I liked this poem when I was a child; but I like it more now that I have, as I think, come to closer terms with it. And so it has been with every poem with which I have for long lived familiarly.

So much for *The Song of the Mad Prince*; and now a word about note-making. The question is sometimes asked, 'What sort of note ought children to write on these short poems if they are studying them for an examination?' The answer of course is 'Ideally none'—an answer which I am sure will recommend itself to those teachers who, when they themselves were school-children, were content to read and re-read their examination poems with pleasure, and to make no more use of pen and pencil than was necessary to underline in the poetry-book the lines they particularly liked. Unluckily, this will not do for all children; there are many who need the sense of support imparted by notes written neatly in a note-book—not to mention the fact that the actual writing of such notes is an aid to memory. If the children insist on writing notes, then, I recommend this: that they record the title and the author of each poem, a one-sentence statement of what the poem is 'about', and, unconnectedly, as many short quotations from it as appeal to them, and as they are likely to memorize. And I really do mean short: phrases, half-lines, single lines—lines in twos or threes at the most. When they come to do their revision, and insist, as so many children do, on revising from their note-books instead of from their poetry-books, they will at least have a great many of the actual words of the poems before their eyes.

With regard to longer narrative poems—I mean poems like *Morte d'Arthur*, *Sohrab and Rustum*, *The Ancient Mariner*, and *Michael*—the first task is of course to read them, to read them often and aloud, and to try to make something of them as wholes. There may be difficult words here and there, and these the teacher should explain; but difficult words deserve less attention than the difficulty which children may find in making sense of the narrative or the theme. For example, on reading *The Ancient Mariner* most children realize that Death and Life-in-Death play a game of dice for the soul of the Mariner, and that Life-in-Death is the winner; but not all children perceive that what follows—the Mariner's survival on board a ship filled with the bodies of his dead associates—is the direct result of her victory. To the adult reader this is obvious enough; but children are less inclined than adults to 'look before and after' and relate together the separate parts of a long poem. This is true also of a poem with a theme or central idea. Take Words-worth's *Michael*, for instance: at the heart of the poem lies Michael's ideal of service to the land which he has inherited and which he loves— an ideal which is in itself an inheritance from forefathers who cherished it, and one which Michael wishes his own son to cherish in his turn ('I wished that thou shouldst live the life they lived'). Every part of the poem relates in one way or another to this. So that our greatest need, as teachers, is to ensure that we ourselves understand what might be called the poem's inner logic, and then devote some of our discussion-time to seeing that our pupils 'make the necessary connections'.

After a longer poem has been read and studied as a connected thing, it is a good idea to analyse it into the parts of which it is built, and even to write down those parts as a list of headings. I am suggesting some-thing very simple. For example, Tennyson's *Morte d'Arthur* might be divided as follows: (*i*) A description of the chapel and its surroundings; (*ii*) Arthur's narrative about the sword, and his command to Bedivere; (*iii*) Bedivere's first descent to the lake, and its outcome; (*iv*) Bedivere's second descent; (*v*) Bedivere's third descent, and the throwing of the sword; (*vi*) The carrying of the king to the lake; (*vii*) Arthur's farewell to Bedivere and his departure. Headings of this sort are a sufficient note-book guide when one is revising a poem—(much better, I think, than a long summary of the story, the very writing of which seems to imply that the poem cannot be mastered as it stands, but must be rendered into prose before it is fully intelligible). Afterwards, if more notes are wanted, and if time allows, the best plan is to summarize each section as a series of *linked quotations*. The prose links should be as few as possible, and the verse quotations short and numerous.

There are two ways of making and setting out this sort of summary, and the choice of way depends on the poem itself. One way— a way which to many people may seem exceptionable, in that it turns the poem into prose, even though into a prose made largely out of the poet's own words—involves stitching together mere phrases in a close continuous narrative. Like this:

Bedivere's First Descent to the Lake. Stepping out from the 'ruined shrine' and crossing the 'place of tombs', over which 'the sea-wind sang Shrill, chill, with flakes of foam', Bedivere stepped down through 'zig-zag paths' and at last 'Came on the shining levels of the lake.' There he drew forth the brand Excalibur, and held it so that the moon 'sparkled keen with frost against the hilt', which 'twinkled with diamond sparks . . . Of subtlest jewellery.' He stood for a while undecided, 'This way and that dividing the swift mind In act to throw', but at last he concealed the sword in the flags 'That whistled stiff and dry about the marge.' 'So strode he back slow to the wounded King.'

It will be seen that I have summarized the passage in some detail— in more detail than one would summarize much of the poem; but that is because the passage is of unusual interest and special effectiveness. Here is an example of the other way of making this sort of summary.

The quotations are in the main longer, and they are set out in lines as originally printed.

Wordsworth's Description of Michael

Michael is introduced to us as—

> 'An old man, stout of heart, and strong of limb,'

and we are told that—

> His bodily frame had been from youth to age
> Of an unusual strength.'

He knew the meaning of all winds, and was accustomed to be out in all weathers. Indeed—

> 'he had been alone
> Amid the heart of many thousand mists
> That came to him, and left him, on the heights.'

Nor is it true that the valleys, the streams and the rocks—

> 'Were things indifferent to the Shepherd's thoughts.'

The fields where he 'had breathed The common air', the hills which 'with vigorous step He had so often climbed'—

> 'Those fields, those hills—what could they less? had laid
> Strong hold on his affections'

and were indeed—

> 'A pleasurable feeling of blind love,
> The pleasure which there is in life itself.'

Now the making of either kind of summary has its own value, even if the writer never reads it again after he has written it. First, it acts as a rapid and selective survey; secondly, it helps to impress some of the words on the writer's mind; and thirdly, it provides practice in the introduction of quotations and allusions. If it *is* used for revision purposes, it also provides the next best thing to the poem itself. As to who should do the actual work of preparing the summary, this should depend on the competence of the pupils. Good pupils will do it for themselves once they have been started off and shown how—(perhaps, in the early stages, shown *which* quotations can be most tellingly woven into the general fabric); less good pupils will do better to have it done for them, rather than be allowed to make mere prose summaries in their own words.

In choosing the quotations which we intend to incorporate into our summary (whichever of the two kinds of summary we attempt), we should be guided by a desire not only to illustrate the course of the story, but also to place on record passages which are memorable in themselves—memorable because they are happily expressed, and because incidentally they illustrate some noteworthy features of the poet's style. My quotations above, from Tennyson's *Morte d'Arthur*, in fact do that. So that when preparing our summary we are concerning ourselves with 'content' and 'style' simultaneously; and that is as it should be. All the same, we may be uncomfortably aware that examiners sometimes concentrate on 'style' alone—by (it may be) asking for examples of 'light effects' and 'sound effects' in *Morte d'Arthur*, of the 'language of ordinary men' in *Michael*, of 'strong appeal to the senses' in *The Ancient Mariner*, or of 'vivid pictorialism' in *The Eve of St Agnes*. I am not myself sure whether this is a good and justifiable practice (would it not be preferable to enquire after likings, preferences, enthusiasms—less what 'appeals to the senses' and more what appeals to the reader as an entire person?). But I suppose that the children should be prepared for this sort of demand, and that the poems should be examined with an eye to some of their more discussible stylistic features. If this can be done without reference to such things as 'alliteration', 'onomatopoeia', 'vowel music', and 'a judicious mixture of labials and dentals, with a few sibilants thrown in', it is an advantage, I think.

I would like to conclude this chapter by stating what I believe to be some of the characteristics of a good 'English literature answer'. I do this while realizing that it is easier to give good advice than to persuade one's pupils to follow it. A good literature answer should—

(*i*) avoid an obviously contrived introduction, and come straight to the point;

(*ii*) be based on the text studied, and as often as possible demonstrate the candidate's familiarity with the text;

(*iii*) contain only selected material, and not everything, relevant and irrelevant, which the candidate can call to mind;

(*iv*) take account of all parts of the question it purports to answer, and answer those parts separately and in order;

(*v*) if the answer is to a question requiring a judgement or a decision, give that judgement not at the beginning but at the end;

(*vi*) be cool in utterance, and contain no unsupported ecstasies;

(*vii*) prove a liking of the text, not by merely protesting the candidate's enjoyment, but by showing his acquaintance with details;

(*viii*) incorporate all quoted matter without interrupting continuity;

(*ix*) have all quotations enclosed within inverted commas;

(*x*) not have imperfectly-remembered passages enclosed within inverted commas, but contain them within its own prose fabric, where they are still acceptable as 'allusions';

(*xi*) be honest.

On the last point I have perhaps some reserves. A year or two ago I was shown the following 'literature answer', which raises in the mind some doubts as to the wisdom of complete honesty. The question asked by the examiner was 'Which of the four narrative poems—*Michael*, *Peter Grimes*, *Lepanto*, and *The Prisoner of Chillon*—do you consider the best, and why?'

To pick out the best of the poems is difficult, because you can pick out faults in nearly all of them. The one I like best is *Peter Grimes*.

Now I don't choose this one because it is something which appeals to me, but because it is the one with the least faults. To show that this is the best, I will go through the poems picking out the bad points from all of them, and then summarize my conclusions.

Let us first take *Michael*. Michael is for a start a rather far-fetched character. He is too good to be true. The idea of never being ill and still full of energy at eighty is absurd, and only adds to the doziness of the whole thing. Home-made cheese and fresh oaten cakes every day could only turn a man into a physical wreck and he would not be full of energy. Above all, the theme of persevering over tragedy is rather too much for the average boy, and could even be made into a Tiny Tots story. Michael, then, is over-accentuated.

The Prisoner of Chillon is an artificial poem. I say this because it is well known that Lord Byron used to visit Geneva and thus had first-hand knowledge of the place and didn't have to formulate the idea in his head. This immediately rules out *The Prisoner of Chillon* as a contender.

Finally, *Lepanto*. Here is a perfect example of a tangled-up fairy tale. It only takes a short time to read, but at the end of that time you can only gather one thing—*i.e.* 'Don John of Austria is going to the war'. After you have read it six times you begin to realize what it is all about. You realize that you are reading a sort of historical account—you might call it a hysterical account. By the time you have finished reading it for the tenth time you are a little bored. So you have to cross *Lepanto* off the list.

This leaves you with *Peter Grimes*. Peter Grimes is an easy-to-imagine character. Number one point in his favour. The whole thing is quite possible and there is no exaggeration. Thirdly, the whole poem, although it is long, grips your imagination the whole time and appeals to most boys. Thus we can, I hope, see that as far as boys are concerned, *Peter Grimes* is easily the best poem.

On further thought, I don't consider that it is the writer's honesty which is wrong. It is his being entered for the examination at all!

CHAPTER II

THE SHAKESPEARE PLAY

*Theatre visits—Disc recordings—The first rapid reading of
the play—The preliminary discussion—The contribution of
each scene—Closer examination of the play: discovery of 'implications'—The longer speeches—The problem of linguistic detail—
The functions of the characters—The whole play reconsidered*

'. . . . and as a reward, children, for a year's diligent study of your
Shakespeare play, you are to be allowed to attend a performance of it,
given by the Swan Players, at the Bard's Own Theatre early in June.
The price of the tickets will be . . .' And the children pay their money
happily enough, and they attend the performance in due course, and
sit attentively and laugh at all the jokes; and in the interval the vesti-
bules and refreshment-bars are filled with young voices, seriously discussing the cowardice of Falstaff, or the weakness of Claudio, or
whether the Drunken Porter's scene was really written by Shakespeare. A new interest in the play is stimulated; and afterwards, too,
in the classroom, further discussion of the performance makes it clear
that many small matters have at last 'clicked into place', their relevance
for the first time clearly perceived. A public performance of a Shakespeare play, seen at the end of a year's study, is obviously of tremendous
value to all who attend it. But is not such a performance more valuable
still if seen at the beginning? Can we not more usefully begin with the
whole play, and then work from the whole to the parts?

True, it is a common enough practice to attempt a sort of synthesis
—to work through the play scene by scene, and by meticulous attention to detail try to establish in the children's minds a 'clear picture' of
the complete thing. But is this in fact a good practice? Consider the
difficulty of it. The play is read at the rate of, to take an extreme case,
one scene per week. Each scene, studied separately, has an obvious
relationship to a whole—but to a whole which at first cannot be more
than faintly apprehended. And such is the rate at which the work proceeds, that by the time the end of the play is reached the middle is but

half-remembered, while the beginning is almost forgotten. By contrast, a performance of the play, attended even before the book is opened, and assimilated during a comparatively short space of time, provides a vivid experience to which each separate scene, read however slowly afterwards in the less exciting conditions of the classroom, can easily be referred. I do not speak now of something which seems to me theoretically right, but of something which I have found to work well whenever I have tried it. I need hardly add that the ideal state of affairs is achieved when performances of the play can be attended at both the beginning and the end of the course of study.

Now in all this there lies a difficulty: that we may not command public performances of Shakespeare's plays just when and where we like. Very often we must have recourse to the next best thing, which is a disc recording of the play. I am writing at a time when recordings of all Shakespeare's plays are easily to be had—some of the plays are available in several recordings—and wherever the money is available, buying copies of these will prove very much worth while. Unless the school is itself 'putting on' the play which is to be studied for the examination, a disc recording of it should be regarded as indispensable.

As a preliminary to the study of the play, then, the children are allowed to hear a recording of it, following the words in their books. The playing may take as many as four lessons, and it is an advantage if these lessons follow closely upon one another. For the teacher it is an 'easy lesson', coming, possibly, at a time when he is feeling particularly energetic; and he longs to interrupt, to explain, to interpolate comments. But he does better to let the playing take its uninterrupted course, with only the briefest of introductory or recapitulatory talks before each session. One thing he can usefully do is to write up on the board a list of the chief characters, and add a few explanatory words about each. The purpose of these explanations is to soften the shock caused by the rapid introduction of so many unfamiliar names in succession. These blackboard notes should be on show during each playing of an instalment of the play.

After the theatre visit—or it may be the playing of the disc recording—comes the first reading aloud by the children. How this is done (with what zest and degree of finish) and where it is done (in the classroom or on the stage) will partly depend on the attitude of the class to drama lessons. Children of fifteen vary so much in this matter: one class will become clamorously excited at the prospect of 'doing a play', while another class, composed of pupils no less intelligent and no less sensitive to literature, will hang back, mutter excuses, or even ask 'Can't we do it sitting in our places?' Yet, as I pointed out in Chapter 8, it is better that the actors should at least stand before an audience; and as an absolutely essential minimum they should read the words aloud. The worst conditions occur when the children are merely asked to read the play silently (for homework, it may be), and are afterwards tested on it in the classroom.

The matter which I raised in Chapter 8—the matter of a correct reading of the words—is so important that I hope I may be pardoned for returning to it. I can best illustrate what I mean by referring to passages which, simple though they appear to be, are rarely understood at a first reading; for example, this in *Julius Caesar*, where Pindarus observes Titinius riding on horseback towards a troop of distant horsemen:

> *Pindarus.*   Titinius is enclosed round about
> With horsemen, that make to him on the spur;
> Yet he spurs on. Now they are almost on him.
> Now, Titinius! Now some light. O, he lights too.

Here the words 'some light' are seldom at first seen to mean 'some of them alight from their horses;' they are treated rather as a request for additional illumination; and a similar failure frequently occurs later in the play, in the following exchange:

> *Octavius.*   All that served Brutus, I will entertain them.
> Fellow, wilt thou bestow thy time with me?
> *Strato.*   Ay, if Messala will prefer me to you.

Here, of course, 'prefer' means 'recommend', and ignorance of this fact will lead to a complete misreading of the line. One value of the preliminary reading aloud, is that it enables such gross misreadings to be corrected before any further study of the play is embarked upon.

Obviously there is more than one way of studying a Shakespeare play; the way I am now recommending involves an approach to the play by seven stages. These are (*i*) a preliminary discussion, chiefly of the story and the plot; (*ii*) a brief consideration of each scene in turn; (*iii*) a closer examination of the play, act by act; (*iv*) a special study of some of the long speeches; (*v*) some consideration of the linguistic detail; (*vi*) a discussion of the characters in relation to the play; and (*vii*) a reconsideration of the play as a whole. The remainder of this chapter is concerned with a fuller account of these stages.

(*i*) *The Preliminary Discussion.* This should be simple, and should attempt to encompass the whole play, or most of it. Suppose that the play is *Twelfth Night*. An obvious starting-point is to show that many of the incidents of the play spring from two circumstances—Viola's being disguised as a man, and the fact that she is easily mistaken for her brother, and he for her. It is worth while pointing out to the children that the audience has foreknowledge of both these circumstances— that from the beginning they are, so to speak, 'in the secret'—and that the spectator's enjoyment comes from observing the false assumptions and the mistakes of those who are not so well informed as he is. Some of the scenes in which these 'false assumptions and mistakes' occur can then be recalled and briefly commented on (Olivia's wooing of Cesario; Antonio's rejection by 'Sebastian'; Andrew's challenging of Viola, and his ultimate discomfiture at the hands of her brother); and the discussion can close with a glance at the climactic scene, in which a simultaneous appearance on the stage of Viola and Sebastian leads to a clearing up of all the mysteries. A talk along these lines does not in fact account for the whole play, but it does account for those parts which are most essential to story and plot, and it paves the way for the second stage, which is in effect a much closer look at the play, scene by scene.

However, before leaving the first stage, I should like to say a word or two about one more play, *Macbeth*. Here, obviously, the preliminary discussion should be less in terms of plot and more in terms of people. Two persons of normal humanity and sensibility bring themselves to commit an appalling crime, the murder of a divinely-appointed king; the play shows them planning it, committing it, and then having to live with the guilt of it. A quick survey of the early part of the play reveals Macbeth as lacking in the resolution and the sickness of mind which such crimes require, and his wife as forcing herself to assume a callousness which is not natural to her. (Here it is relevant to glance at Lady Macbeth's estimate of her husband's true nature (in Act I Scene v); at her request, in the same scene, to be 'unsexed' and 'filled with direst cruelty'; at the fact that she at first plans to commit the crime herself (cf. 'my keen knife' and 'my dispatch'); at Macbeth's doubts and hesitations (Scene vii); at the way in which his over-heated brain conjures up the vision of a dagger (Act II, Scene i); at Lady Macbeth's need (Scene ii) to fortify herself with wine before she enters Duncan's chamber, and her ultimate inability to murder a man who resembles her own father; and at Macbeth's utter loss of self-control after he has killed the king.) The middle part of the play shows the gradual hardening of Macbeth's nature, as he accustoms himself to a life of guilt and violence; and the end shows the different ways in which the partners succumb to the pressures within and around them: Lady Macbeth by taking refuge in madness, Macbeth by growing for himself a shell of insensibility. It is important to point out that even the violent death of his wife leaves Macbeth unmoved, and that his speech beginning 'Tomorrow, and tomorrow, and tomorrow' is not a judgement on life in any general sense, but the judgement on his own life of one who has inhibited all tender feeling, and all remorse, to the point where he has deprived his very existence of meaning:

> Life's but a walking shadow, a poor player
> That struts and frets his hour upon the stage
> And then is heard no more: it is a tale
> Told by an idiot, full of sound and fury,
> Signifying nothing.

(*ii*) *Discussion of Scenes*. After the play has been surveyed in something of this manner (but in simpler language, of course), and the pages flicked over in the process, it is no bad idea to have a discussion of each scene separately, in an attempt to see in what way it contributes to, and is necessary to, the whole. There is no objection to brief note-making here (a one-sentence or a two-sentence statement on each scene); though the kind of note I have in mind is one which touches more on the function of a scene than on its contribution to the story. So, in *Macbeth*, we are early brought up against the Witches' scenes: what are they there for, and in what way are they essential to the play? These questions are not difficult to answer if we have taken the full measure of the task which Shakespeare set himself—to involve a humane man and a loyal subject in a 'motiveless' murder, and to show us the effects of the involvement. Whatever else the Witches represent, they are primarily a device for making Macbeth's actions seem reasonable and credible. Or consider the Drunken Porter's interlude. Is it necessary? How necessary it is we can easily see if we try omitting it; we then perceive that it separates, and so provides a contrasting interlude to, two scenes which are in several respects very similar (that is to say, they employ some of the same characters, are both concerned with the murder of Duncan, and both move to a climax of horror and uncontrolled utterance). Or take one more example, the scene with Lady Macduff and her son. The function of the last part of the scene is obvious: the murder of Lady Macduff and her son provides evidence

of Macbeth's growing callousness and brutality, of his determination
to enter on a new life of spontaneous and ruthless action. But what is
the earlier part of the scene for? The earlier part is needed to impress on
us the magnitude of the crime which Macbeth is about to commit:
its three carefully-planned stages prepare us for the horrifying climax.
First comes the talk with Ross, establishing the fact of Macduff's
departure and his wife's resentment at it; then follows the conversation
between mother and son, which enlists the spectator's sympathy for
both of them; then comes the brief visit from the anonymous Messen-
ger, to heighten tension and expectancy; and finally there is the
arrival of the Murderers themselves, a moment made moving by Lady
Macduff's thoughts for her husband's safety and her son's defence of
his father's good name. It would be a mistake to regard the first seventy-
eight lines of this scene as 'just so much talk'; and here, as with any
other of Shakespeare's mature plays, if we find ourselves thinking of
any part of any scene in such terms, we need to come back to our
question, 'What is the function of the scene? What is its contribution
to the play as a whole?'

(iii) *Closer Examination of the Play.* An examination of the play scene
by scene usually takes a considerable time, especially if it involves, as it
often must, a partial or a complete re-reading; but to establish the
function of a scene, and its relation to the whole, is not the same thing
as understanding it in detail, and the time now comes for a new series
of questions—questions which attempt to penetrate beyond the words
and discover some of the cross-references, allusions, and implications.
When Lady Macbeth says 'That which hath made them drunk hath
made me bold', what does this indicate that she has been doing?
And with what purpose? When she says 'These things must not be
thought After these ways; so, it will make us mad', what thought
must occur to the spectator who knows the end of the play? And
when she asks 'Why did you bring these daggers from the place?',
what do we reflect as to Macbeth's state of mind? There is also scope
for questions which refer to the staging of the play or to the gestures
of the actors. For example, when, at the end of the sixth scene of Act I,
Duncan says to Lady Macbeth 'By your leave, hostess', what action
should accompany his words?

There are several ways in which this third stage of the work can be
tackled. One way is to let the children read the play by themselves,
act by act in five successive weeks, and to follow each reading by a
'teaching test' of the kind described in Chapter 7. The children write

their answers to perhaps twenty questions, using the text of the play
for reference. Some of the questions will be hard ones, some easy,
but their purpose will always be to turn the pupils' eyes back to the
text, and help them to discover the 'not-immediately-obvious'.

Let us suppose that the children have revised the first act of *Macbeth*.
Here are the first ten of twenty questions which I have found to be a
useful test on it. (The page references are to Dent's 'King's Treasuries'
edition. Brief answers are added in brackets.)

1. *Scene* i, *page* 21. Exactly what is referred to by the 'hurlyburly'
mentioned in line 3? (The battle in which Macbeth is engaged at the
time.)

2. 'Anon' in line 9 means 'Coming at once!' Whom are the Witches
addressing? (Their familiar spirits.)

3. *Scene* ii, *page* 22. Why does Shakespeare have the news of Macbeth's success brought by two messengers? Why not all the news by
one? (Gives more variety and action to an otherwise tedious scene.)

4. *Scene* iii, *page* 25. What has made the Witches plan to pursue and
torment the unlucky Sailor, and what does this tell us about their
natures? (His wife has refused them chestnuts; it shows them to be evil
and malicious.)

5. *Page* 26. At what point in his first speech does Banquo suddenly
change his tone of voice? (Before 'What are these . . .?')

6. *Page* 27. What does Banquo, in his second speech, refer to when
he speaks of 'present grace', 'prediction of noble having', 'prediction
of royal hope'? (Macbeth's present title; the prophecy that he shall be
thane of Cawdor; the prophecy that he shall be king.)

7. *Page* 28. Why does Shakespeare make Ross and Angus enter at
this point, bringing the gift of a new title from Duncan? Would not
Duncan have waited until he met Macbeth at Forres? (It is more
startling that the first prophecy should be fulfilled almost immediately
after it is uttered.)

8. *Page* 30. In the whole speech beginning 'Glamis, and thane of
Cawdor', which persons is Macbeth addressing? (First himself; then
Ross and Angus; then Banquo.)

9. *Scene* iv, *page* 32. When Duncan says of Cawdor 'He was a
gentleman on whom I built An absolute trust' and Macbeth at once
walks in, what does the thoughtful playgoer reflect? (That Duncan
trusts Macbeth in the same way.)

10. *Page* 34. When Duncan says 'True, worthy Banquo . . . peerless

kinsman', what has Banquo just been saying quietly to him? (He has been praising Macbeth for bravery in battle.)

My remaining questions upon Act I are of the same kinds as these. Some teachers will think them hard questions; others will think them easy (it depends on the ability of the classes they have to teach); but whether the children find them easy or not is really beside the point. The point of a 'teaching test' is not that the children should earn full marks, but that they should learn as they go. Of course, if it is considered that they have not yet reached the stage where they can tackle such tests with confidence, there is the simpler alternative of putting the questions orally and arriving at the answers through discussion.

(*iv*) *The Longer Speeches.* (*v*) *The Problem of Linguistic detail.* The next two stages involve attaining a greater familiarity with the words of the text and a more detailed understanding of their meaning; and here I must confess that I cannot be as helpful as I should like to be. No doubt I could recommend teachers to work through the Shakespeare play line by line, word by word, glossing and explaining as they go, and I have heard of teachers doing this, and doing it very thoroughly. Such teachers are sometimes said to 'prefer a plain text' (*i.e.* a text with no printed notes), and it is to be suspected that many of them do so because, lacking any other method of studying Shakespeare, they are glad enough to fill in their time by supplying detailed marginal notes and a commentary. But is not this a waste of time? Or at the very least, would not some of the time be better employed in the kinds of work I have described here? I myself am very far from preferring a 'plain text'; on the contrary I prefer fully (though unobtrusively) annotated texts, with notes which the children can ignore at first, but to which they can refer when the time is ripe. Examples of such texts are Heinemann's 'Players' Shakespeare' series: the words of the play are printed on the right-hand page—the page which most people's eyes prefer for comfortable reading—and the corresponding notes are on the left. There are probably other publishers' texts which are as suitable and convenient.

One of the difficulties which children often find with Shakespeare is in following the line of thought through the *long* speeches (as distinct from the short ones). The rapid exchanges between one speaker and another they can understand; it is the long soliloquies and other meditative and more or less reasoned speeches that they so easily lose themselves in. Because these speeches give so much trouble, it was formerly the practice to ask even quite young pupils to make detailed paraphrases of them. This practice has now been abandoned, I think, and a good thing too: only the brightest children have ever been capable of making good paraphrases, and there seems little purpose in giving valuable time to a kind of work in which few but the teacher can excel. It is much more reasonable to ask the class for 'paraphrase-gists' or 'paraphrase-summaries'—that is to say, paraphrases which do not attempt to account for every word, but which follow the course of a speech in rapid and simple outline. Even here, some care should be exercised in the choice of speeches—not necessarily the most difficult, but those which contain the most essential information as regards plot, character, or motive. So, with *Macbeth*, Act I, Scenes iv and vi, one would not bother oneself much about the complimentary speeches of Duncan and his hostess; their complication arises from the courtliness of the language, but their content does not demand close scrutiny. It is different with Macbeth's speech 'Two truths are told', or with his 'Is this a dagger . . .?', or with Lady Macbeth's 'Glamis thou art, and Cawdor'; these speeches throw light on the true natures of their speakers and help us to understand the dire ultimate effects of their delinquency. Such speeches deserve 'gist-summarizing' from end to end. Other speeches again—for example, such a speech as 'If it were done when 'tis done' (Act I, Scene vii)—require to be paraphrased in part: the earlier lines I would ignore entirely; the rest, from 'He's here in double trust' onwards, I would discuss with the class, until we had produced together some such version as this: 'There are two reasons why I should respect the confidence he places in me: first, because I am a relation and a subject of his; secondly, because I am his host and responsible for his safety. Besides, Duncan has been so good and virtuous a king that people will be appalled at his murder and feel compelled to pity him. Nothing justifies his murder; only my own ambition urges me on.' This, judged by the strictest standards, is an inaccurate and incomplete paraphrase; but it does follow the main line of thought; and that is as much as we should expect at this stage and with such young children.

So much for 'paraphrase-summaries'; and now some words about 'linguistic detail'. The whole question would probably not be such a vexed one were it not the practice of some public examiners to print passages from the plays and follow them by questions. When, as so often happens, these include questions on the meaning of difficult words and phrases, the candidate who has not slaved through his text

from cover to cover must take his chance—the chosen passage may
be one with which he has detailed acquaintance, or it may not. Much
depends here on the good sense and the fairness of the examiner. The
fairest questions are probably not those which are mere tests of 'vocabulary', but those which depend partly for their answers on a good knowledge of the play. The difference can be illustrated by words and
phrases in this extract from *Twelfth Night*, where Viola tells Orsino
how Antonio intervened in her 'duel' with Sir Andrew:

> *Viola.*   He did me kindness, sir, drew on my side;
> But in conclusion put strange speech upon me:
> I know not what 'twas but distraction.

Here it is entirely reasonable to ask candidates to interpret 'drew on my
side' and 'put strange speech upon me', but it is perhaps less reasonable
to ask for the meaning of such a hard word as 'distraction', even
though it occurs more than once in the play. In the case of the two
phrases, the language difficulty is lessened by the support received
from easily-recalled incidents; in the case of the single word, the
candidate is forced to rely on his recollection of a footnote or a marginal note.

What are we to do, then, about annotating our text in detail—in
those cases, that is to say, where the text is not, or is not sufficiently,
annotated already? The most rapid (but still very slow) way of doing
this is by using the method called 'Paraphrase Reversed' which I
described in Chapter 8. The teacher supplies the 'meanings' and the
page-numbers, and the pupil identifies the words and the phrases,
underlines them, and writes the 'meanings' against them. To 'do' a
whole Shakespeare play in this manner—even if one confines oneself
to the really obscure words and expressions—can take from six to
eight lessons; and it is very questionable whether the time would not
be more profitably spent upon a further two uninterrupted readings of
the complete play. After all, our chief desire at this stage is that the
children should enjoy the play, and want to return to it in later life;
and I should not be prepared to contradict those teachers who claimed,
of their less able pupils, that the sort of annotation I have described
would put them off Shakespeare for ever.

(*vi*) *The Functions of the Characters.* On an earlier page, speaking of
the characters of a novel, I suggested that we should beware lest we
carry our studies to the point where we treat the characters as 'real
live persons', capable of having an independent existence outside the

novel's pages; we ought rather to ask ourselves in what way each character 'serves' the novel's story, or plot, or theme, or in what way he provides variety or entertainment. If this should be our attitude towards the people in a novel, it ought even more, surely, to be our attitude towards the people in a Shakespeare play; for Shakespeare's plays are all more or less poems—dramatic poems, that is, (even where Shakespeare employs prose he employs it in the highly-selective manner of a poet); and we do not expect poems to attempt even as close a presentation of reality as novels do. Of the majority of Shakespeare's characters we cannot help admitting that they do not act and speak like ordinary people; they act and speak like 'people in a poem' and according as the conventions of poetry allow. So that while it is a fact that Shakespeare's characters often create an *illusion* of being 'extraordinarily true to life', when we look more closely at them, we discover that this 'truth to life' resides not so much in their words and deeds, as in the human feelings and situations which those words and deeds so powerfully re-create.

Let me try to show this by an example. In Act IV of *Julius Caesar*, Brutus remarks to Cassius—

> There is no terror, Cassius in your threats;
> For I am armed so strong in honesty,
> That they pass by me as an idle wind
> Which I respect not;

and in Act V, when Antony declares that he does not intend to 'die on Brutus's sword', Brutus replies—

> O, if thou wert the noblest of thy strain,
> Young man, thou couldst not die more honorable.

If the scenes in which these speeches occur were taken as a direct transcription of life, we would be forced to conclude, of Brutus, that Shakespeare wishes us to see him as priggish, vain, and much too conscious of his virtues. But the rest of the play does not bear out such an interpretation. Clearly, what Shakespeare wishes us to see is a Brutus high-minded, stoical, humane, and self-forgetful. Every character in the play is potentially an instrument of this purpose of Shakespeare's, and it is entirely within the conventions of poetry that Brutus himself should be one of the instruments. So that when Brutus utters those two speeches, he is not uttering unworthy boasts—he is merely directing the audience's attention to what, at that point, Shakespeare wants them to think and feel about Brutus himself.

Our pupils can be excused, then, from the task of writing the customary character-studies, the 'lists of good and bad qualities'. None the less, they ought to give some thought to at least the chief characters in their play, asking what their functions are; and as a preliminary to this they should make themselves acquainted with the principal appearances of those characters on the scene. This involves making reference-lists ('indexes') of the kind I described in Chapter 9; and very necessary the making and learning of such lists is, too, for how can our pupils even begin to discuss a play's characters intelligently unless they can recall the separate occasions on which the characters speak? I have known examination candidates be asked to choose the rôle they liked best in their play, and then say how they would perform it; and they have been balked at the outset because, while capable of discussing their chosen character in a general way, they have been quite unable to recall his separate appearances. So, a page-numbered 'index' for each character; and if the children can commit these to memory, they will have the preliminary equipment for answering any questions about the characters which the examiner may care to ask.

The 'functions of characters' is more a matter for classroom discussion than for note-making, I feel, and the kind of discussion we hold will depend a good deal on which play we are studying. Suppose that the play is *The Tempest*. It will not be difficult for our pupils to discover that each of several not very lively characters contributes some part to the small complexities of the story; but *The Tempest* cannot be said to yield much at 'story' level, and closer examination reveals that this is a play with its theme very much to the fore, and that Prospero, Caliban, Sebastian, Antonio, and Gonzalo (these in particular) exist primarily as contributors to Shakespeare's difficult and severe debate on the relative importances of 'nature' and 'nurture' in promoting the 'good life'. We pass rapidly on, glad that *The Tempest* is not usually set for study for first examinations. *Henry IV, Part I*, on the other hand, frequently is. In this play we have a much more interesting and dramatic plot, and we can profitably give time to discussing how the King, the Prince, Hotspur, and Falstaff are separately involved in it; yet even here we find a theme—not so obtrusive as that of *The Tempest*, yet surely deserving a glance; for it is through the medium of these four characters that Shakespeare conducts an enquiry into the nature and limitations of the nobleman's 'sense of honour'. The difficulty with this theme, for children, is that the play contains no nobleman of whom we can sufficiently approve to allow him to be the measure of the defects of the others. None the less, the theme should not be entirely neglected, and this involves giving (for example) Hotspur—'the king of honour'—a more critical look than he sometimes gets. Or take another play, *Julius Caesar* (I choose plays and characters almost at random): what are we to say about Portia, and Lucius, and Brutus's lesser followers? Clearly, these 'serve' neither the plot nor any theme; their function is different again. It is to 'serve' one of the characters—the main character in fact, the tragic Brutus; by showing him in his personal and domestic relations they reveal more of his inner worth and, by implication, the magnitude of his sacrifice in opposing Caesar. Or *Twelfth Night*. This is a 'play of several clowns'; and Feste, Toby, Malvolio, and Andrew—apart from the ways in which they contribute to the development of the plot—have to be taken account of as 'incidental entertainers'. I give these examples, not to make the study of characters seem more difficult than it is, but in order to show that each person must be judged as a separate case, and that to the question 'What is the function of this character?' there can be more than one sort of answer.

(*vii*) *The Play Reconsidered*. Interesting and absorbing as all these studies are, they should not be carried on to the point where there is no time left for a final re-examination of the whole play. Time should be reserved for another general discussion and a last reading. And this final discussion will of course be fuller and more informed than the preliminary one was. By the time this stage is reached, the brief account of *Twelfth Night* given on page 154 will be seen to be inadequate; closer study of the play will have revealed it as possessing an at first unsuspected dignity and stature—qualities which derive, not from the practical jokes and the mistaken identities, but from the serious treatment of loyalties and loves. And it is on these loyalties and loves that the last discussion will centre. Our pupils will look again at the loyalties—at Antonio's devotion to Sebastian, and at his grief on discovering that the 'goodly outside' of his idol has apparently no heart or soul within it; and at Viola's loyalties, too—her loyalty to Orsino, expressed in her sad silence and in her persistent wooing on his behalf; and her loyalty to Olivia, shown when she tells a lie rather than betray Olivia's secret to Malvolio. And the loves also: Orsino's, which is at first a 'love of being in love'; Olivia's, made candid by its suddenness and excess, and yet free from the taint of immodesty; and Viola's, passionately outspoken at the last, and looking her lover straight in the eyes. All these should be reconsidered, and the speeches in which they are asserted should be read again and savoured.

Both the loves and the loyalties gain in effect from their being placed side by side with the baser attitudes of some of the other characters— with Maria's mischievousness, Toby's malevolence, Andrew's cowardice, and Feste's spite. These are the 'comic' characters, certainly, and they provide a certain amount of amusement, but it will be noticed that the 'noble' characters do little more than tolerate them; at no point does their bad conduct receive endorsement or earn approval. Olivia in particular never utters a word which does not display a delicacy and correctness of feeling, and she is quick to condemn discourtesy to a guest and the abuse of a servant.

A last survey of *Macbeth* will perhaps not be so very different from the first, and will probably be little more than an amplification of the account given on page 154. Of *Macbeth*, obviously much more can be said than has been said here; but not to these children, nor at this early stage in the study of so complex a play.

CHAPTER 12

MISCELLANEOUS MATTERS

Talking—Handwriting—Spelling—Punctuation—Vocabu-
lary work—Précis Writing

IT IS a view commonly enough expressed nowadays, and one not
much disputed, that all good classroom practice in the teaching of
English rests on a triple basis of Writing, Reading, and Talking, and of
these three, TALKING is usually considered not less important than
the others. But when I add that this is a view which I myself share, my
reader may well feel that he has reason to raise his eyebrows, for a
glance at the pages before him will show that, as compared with
Writing and Reading, Talking is dismissed most summarily. It is with
this book as with Sir John Falstaff's tavern-bill: 'One half-pennyworth
of bread to this intolerable deal of sack!' A couple of pages of Talking
to this intolerable deal of Writing and Reading! For this lack of proportion in my treatment of the three topics I shall shortly offer what I
hope will seem an adequate excuse.

Of course there can be no questioning the value and importance of
Talking in a child's education, and yet to expatiate on that importance
is also to expound a difficult doctrine. It can be interesting to sit at a
Conference where a visiting lecturer takes up the matter, and with
more or less of gentleness and tact berates his teacher-audience for the
small part that Talking plays in their classroom procedures. 'Talking
should be at the root of all education, and especially of education in the
mother tongue. Whatever else it is or is not, the classroom should be a
Talking Place.' The reactions of the teachers to such remarks are
almost invariably hostile: some, it is true, merely look uncomfortable,
knowing that their own classrooms, for the most part, are not 'talking
places' but 'shutting-up' places; but others exchange angry murmurs
—'He ought to come along himself and try teaching *my* lot!'; while
others again are loudly resentful, and can barely wait for the end of the
lecture to bombard the lecturer with objections. I recall one such
Conference where lecturer and teachers were near coming to blows.

The trouble is that both sides stand on perfectly good ground. The lecturer knows, and perhaps better than his audience, that to encourage talking is to promote growth—growth not only of the child's capacity to use English but also of his mind and personality, and of himself as a social being. The teacher knows, and usually better than his lecturer, that to give free rein to talking is to turn to confusion that good order which he has worked so hard to achieve. And the conditions which will satisfy both sides are nothing less than those in which a self-disciplined class of children feel themselves free to speak at any time without fear of restraint, and yet voluntarily hold their tongues when appropriately they should. To establish such conditions is not easy—it is in fact the last and hardest task of the teacher of English. As with other such difficult matters, success in this is ultimately bound up with the relationship between the teacher and his children—with, on the one hand, the teacher's patience, his affection, and his readiness to listen and to defer, combined with a firm grasp of the immediate purpose and a consciousness that ultimately it is he, not the children, who is in command; and with, on the other hand, the children's liking, their respect for one another, and their acceptance of the teacher as a person from and with whom they want to learn. These are the ideal conditions; yet how often, after a teacher has striven for them, he is forced to say of one class 'They're too timid—I wish they'd relax and chat more freely!', and of another, 'The trouble is, as soon as you start a discussion you get a riot!' For the achievement of these ideal conditions is not something which depends on the efforts of one teacher alone: a multitude of influences in the shape of parents, other teachers, other associates, individual misfortunes and general upheavals may have gone to make a class what it is. We are perhaps too ready to blame ourselves when, in this matter of Talking, a class falls short of what we would have it be.

One thing is certain—that the teacher's problem is not to be solved by his dividing his lessons into two sorts, 'silent lessons' and 'oral lessons'. It is surely a perverse approach to the matter of Talking—though I think a not uncommon one—to say, 'Today for a change we'll have an Oral Lesson'. Even more perverse if that 'oral lesson' turns out to be, as so often it does, a mere debate—debating being an activity so formal and ordered as to be remote indeed from the spontaneous conversational exchanges which constitute true Talking! Let debates be banned from the classroom and sent along to the lecture-theatre, which is their proper place; for indeed, the solution to the problem of Talking does not lie in that direction. The solution lies in our trying to make conversation a part of as many kinds of work as we possibly can. And that, in fact, is my chief excuse for devoting so little space to Talking, as distinct from Writing and Reading. If we conduct our Writing and our Reading on sound lines, Talking will look after itself—for Talking will permeate everything we do.

To finish this note I should like to make mention (this is to a large extent a recapitulation) of some of the ways in which Talking can be made a part of our everyday classroom life. First, there is informal talking pure and simple—the kind we all take part in at the beginning of a term, say, as a preliminary to our settling down to work. It soon comes out that Jones's rabbits have had babies, and little by little the various other items of news and gossip follow. Similar informal exchanges—exchange of opinion or comment chiefly—are likely to occur when the class re-gathers after some school event or other (the taking of the school photograph, or the performance of the junior play). The odd spaces of time before, after, and between lessons should not be neglected: it is then that Smith shows you his jet aircraft, and James the mouse up his sleeve. And it is then that the shy child or the stuttering child comes up to talk to you.

Then there are the various kinds of talk associated with written work: the preparatory discussions which are often an essential part of the composition lesson; the discussions, conducted by the children themselves, of the compositions which are read out for criticism; and those other discussions which must precede the rewriting of badly-expressed work. These are described in Chapters 3 and 4. To them should be added the oral work associated with the administering of grammar and other exercises; it is a waste of time to have too much of such work done in writing, particularly when the 'answers' are nothing more than short sentences, phrases, or single words. Where the work is simple enough, it is a good idea to put the whole direction of it into the hands of one bright pupil, with the teacher merely in attendance to correct any mistakes on his deputy's part. The new 'teacher' begins by asking the pupils for a satisfactory interpretation of the instructions at the head of the exercise (such instructions are usually rather formally worded), and then chooses individuals to do parts of the exercise in turn. Children are often more at ease and more freely spoken when being 'taught' by one of their own number.

Finally there are the conversations and discussions which are associated with literature lessons. These include the incidental discussions which develop in the course of the reading of a short story, a novel, or a play, (and which are often only loosely connected with it), as well as the strictly relevant discussions (of story, plot, characters, theme, and larger issues) which are referred to in Chapters 7, 9, and 11. With these go the discussions of poetry. (The short questions devised by the teacher for the elucidation of a poem should seldom be answered in writing except in an examination, for discussing poetry should be above all a social affair.) And there is the whole business of play production, which, as I have already suggested, with plays of mere entertainment can safely be left to the children themselves. So can the improvised plays and the prepared duologues. These last are useful in cases where there is not much acting-space in the classroom. Seated in pairs, the children devise simple duologues (as it might be between a hairdresser and his customer), rehearse them, and subsequently speak and act them before the class.

These are only some of the kinds of talking which make up part of the day-to-day study of English language and literature. But the very making of a list of them seems clumsy: our aim should be to have 'oral work' become so much a part of our lessons that we cease to speak or think of oral work as such. I have already said that I think Talking should permeate all our classroom activities. Ideally, I suppose it should do more than permeate them: it should become integrated with them.

Does HANDWRITING really matter? Does it really matter whether children write badly or well? That is a question which I have often heard debated by teachers—by beginner-teachers, particularly, who frequently end by answering with an emphatic 'No'. And it is well that the question should be debated, for if we do not, at the outset of our teaching career, look past the surface to the 'soul of things', we are unlikely ever to do so at all. And yet it might be better to give a more guarded answer. Does handwriting really matter? Certainly hand-writing matters less than spelling and punctuation; and spelling and punctuation matter less than clear expression; while clear expression itself matters less than the ideas the child is trying to express. Yet all these things matter in their varying degrees; and perhaps we would do better to reshape our question: not 'Does it matter?' but 'How much does it matter?'

One reason why teachers should encourage their pupils to give attention to neatness is that children do not always regard as separate things the effort they put into their handwriting and the effort they put into the work of invention and expression. Often it is all a single effort; and when we allow their handwriting to deteriorate we sometimes find that the quality of their work also goes down; while conversely, when we insist that they improve their writing, we find them taking more pains with the ideas and their expression. Of course, there will always be the two extreme types of child—the child of brilliant ideas who just cannot be bothered to set them down neatly, and the child whose ideas are few and flat, and who attempts to compensate for his deficiencies by taking pains over the presentation of them. But between these extremes there are the many children who, as I have already said, regard the work in its various aspects as a single task, and do it well or ill according to their natures, abilities, and inclinations.

Most of the children who come up from primary schools bring with them a neat, round, and rather laborious hand. They have perhaps been accustomed to working at a slow pace and making a neat exercise-book their first object. In their new school they find that much more written work is required of them, and that they are required to work at a faster pace. This is as it should be. But one of the effects of this increase in the amount of their written work is that they need to develop a more rapid and more easily-flowing script; otherwise their handwriting goes to pieces altogether. The majority of children meet this challenge successfully, and the handwriting which in the course of six months they develop, though less neat than that which they brought with them, is quicker and more continuous, and, although smaller, is yet sufficiently legible. This is particularly the case with children who were already writing well in their junior school.

During the first three years of a child's life in a secondary school, he can be helped to take greater care with his handwriting if, from time to time, he is awarded separate marks for the neatness of his work. The giving of neatness marks involves very little trouble, and experience shows that such marks act as a real stimulus to effort—and not only effort with handwriting. The one difficulty for the teacher is to decide what to do with the marks after he has awarded them. Everybody knows that neatness marks, added to the marks already given for more solid achievements, can play havoc with a 'final order-of-merit', and may even have the effect of promoting some of the least able pupils to positions near the top of the class. In the circumstances, the best thing to do is keep a separate record of these marks, each class having a record book of its own. There is no need for the teacher himself to keep this book; a willing pupil can always be found to enter the marks as they are awarded. When at the end of the term the marks have been added up, the teacher can, if he wishes, award a Neatness Prize.

SPELLING. In Chapter 4, when speaking of the correction of other errors, and in particular of errors of expression, I postponed to a later page a discussion of the correction of misspelt words, and this is a matter to which I would now like to turn. The practice of indicating such errors by an 's' and requiring the children to write 'corrections'— which is the most usual way of dealing with the matter—has always struck me as unsatisfactory; the child can probably, and the teacher almost certainly, be more profitably employed, the first than in hunting up the misspelt words in his dictionary and transcribing them, the second than in making sure that the child has hunted up *every* misspelt word and has transcribed it correctly. However, although I think the usual practice an unsatisfactory one, I am not going to argue that 'spelling isn't really important'; only that it is more important with some children than with others, and that our approach to the question should vary with the children we have to teach.

We shall see the question more clearly if we concede the fact that— in spite of what we teachers would prefer to believe—the majority of the children who spell correctly do not acquire the skill from their teachers, but learn it of their own accord. Certainly it would be possible, with the help of daily drills of the most rigorous kinds, to turn even bad spellers into competent ones; but that would mean giving to the business of spelling a great deal of the time which ought to be spent on more worth-while occupations. And it really would involve a great deal of time, for it is observable that if a child reaches the age of eleven and is already a determinedly bad speller, nothing short of a labour of Hercules will turn him into a determinedly good one; whereas if, at the age of eleven, he already spells well, the likelihood is that, with only a little additional help from his teacher, he will retain that ability to the end of his life. Unlike his less gifted brother, the good speller is capable of self-improvement; he is constantly making new mistakes, it is true, but he is also constantly correcting them in the light of further experience; and since it is he, and only he, who is likely to have a 'useful writing life' ahead of him, it is for him, if for anyone, that a special effort should be made.

It comes to this, then, that if at eleven the children spell really badly—as slow-learning children frequently do—and show small likelihood of improvement, the teacher's most sensible course is to abandon spelling lessons altogether, and concentrate his attention on the task of securing written work of greater vitality and interest. In thus changing the direction of his efforts, he need not feel that he is failing in his duty to his pupils; teachers report that an increased liveliness in the children's written work almost always follows the change.

For children of average or more-than-average ability, the following way of treating misspelt words will be found effective and sufficient.

When the teacher is marking a child's composition, he of course observes that such-and-such words are misspelt, and any of these words which appear to him to be common words, such as a child of that age ought to be able to spell correctly, he himself writes out correctly in the exercise-book margin. Then, every so often, (every term, perhaps, or at the end of each half-term), he hands a piece of paper to each child in the class, and asks him to copy these words on to it. If the teacher has written carefully, and the children have copied correctly, the lists will provide the teacher with a record of all the common words misspelt by the members of that class during the past term (or half-term).

When the teacher comes to collate these lists—which he can do immediately after collecting them, merely by laying them out side by side on his desk and casting his eye over them—he will observe that there are a number of words which occur on several, perhaps on many, lists. These words will very likely include 'sincerely', 'fortunately', 'occasion', 'argument', 'occurred', 'travelling', 'address', 'surprise', 'interrupt', 'therefore', 'immediately', 'possess', 'privilege', 'safety', 'professor', and 'extremely', as well, perhaps, as some simpler words such as 'across', 'except', 'fifth', 'until', and 'truly'. Altogether he may find some thirty to sixty common words which have been misspelt by several of his pupils, and it is these words which he makes the subject of the tests or drills which he now administers.

When administering a spelling-test a teacher should remember that a difficult word means more to a child if he hears it used in a sufficiently broad context, and that the more the meaning of the word comes home to him the more easy it is for him to 'visualize' its spelling. With a class of the youngest children, I personally narrate a short story, introducing one of the difficult words into each sentence as I go, and pausing at the end of each sentence while the children write the word down. With older children it is sufficient to dictate a series of unconnected sentences, with one of the difficult words contained in each.

The children can check these tests themselves, referring to lists which the teacher writes on the blackboard, and themselves rewriting any words which they have spelt wrong. They can afterwards study the lists as a special task, and learn the correct spellings by heart.

PUNCTUATION is like spelling, in that it is a thing which calls for a certain amount of attention, but also one which should not be allowed to loom so large as to overshadow things of greater importance. We certainly should not ignore it altogether; for punctuation marks are a guide to a reader's eye and therefore to his understanding. Full stops, commas, semi-colons and speech marks, for example, are used to divide the printed words into groups and tell us to which group each word belongs. So that in this matter, as in other subsidiary matters, we ought occasionally to find time to give our pupils such help as they appear to require.

How much help they do in fact require will vary from pupil to pupil. Many children 'pick up their punctuation' just as they 'pick up their spelling'—though only in a rough-and-ready sort of way. No child punctuates really accurately without first making a closer study of the rules and customary practices than the words 'pick up' imply. Luckily there is a fair amount that can be taught by rule. The questions to ask before we start are 'Is it worth it?' and 'Can the pupils profit by it?' If we are sure that the right answers are 'Yes', we need feel no qualms about occasionally taking time off from more important matters, and making punctuation the subject of special study.

And how best can this be done? The ideal conditions undoubtedly exist where the teacher is able to work with his pupils individually. Each child can be shown his own mistakes, and can be made to see how his work is improved by the correct placing of stops, as by other alterations. But to give individual attention in this way is not usually practicable. Most teachers have no choice but to accept the alternative of punctuation exercises, and of these the most popular has always been the exercise which requires the insertion of punctuation into an unpunctuated passage. This particular kind of exercise has become so widely practised that it is interesting to find that modern enlightened opinion has thought fit to condemn it.

The challenge came a few years ago, when one of our large examining boards set itself to reform the syllabus of its G.C.E. examination in English at Ordinary Level. The syllabus then in existence required examinees to write an essay, to make a summary, to answer some 'comprehension' questions, and to do one of several sorts of language and grammar exercise. All those who had an interest in the examination, and especially teachers, were invited to send in criticisms of this syllabus and to suggest improvements. Criticisms were duly offered, and were collated, and a new syllabus was evolved. But when the new syllabus arrived, teachers were somewhat taken aback, for at first sight there did not appear to have been any change made. The examinees were still required to write an essay, to make a summary, to answer some 'comprehension' questions, and to do one of several sorts of language and grammar exercise. However, teachers were quickly cheered by discovering that there was an innovation. At the end of the amended syllabus there appeared this warning announcement: *No question on punctuation will take the form of an exercise in inserting punctuation into a continuous unpunctuated passage.* To this startling reform the united wisdoms of many teachers and the greybeard deliberations of the university authorities had ultimately conduced. In future no question on punctuation was to take the form of an exercise in inserting punctuation into a continuous unpunctuated passage!

Of course, the amended syllabus did not say on what grounds this kind of work, which for many years had been accepted as good practice, was now by implication condemned. The objection which can most reasonably be made to it is that people do not normally punctuate like that; they do not normally insert marks of punctuation into other people's writings; they insert them into their own, and not as an afterthought but as part of the actual process of composition. So that the best test of a person's ability to punctuate is one which requires him to punctuate his own work as he goes. But whatever the objection may have been, it is difficult to see why this particular kind of work should have been singled out in such a manner. One would have thought, to say the least, that there were other matters in the syllabus in more urgent need of reform; and speaking for myself, I was not much disposed, on the strength of this disrecommendation, to look upon the practice as an entirely worthless one.

However, while it is not an entirely worthless one, it is also not an absolutely necessary one. There are other ways of teaching and testing punctuation besides requiring the insertion of stops into an unpunctuated passage. Here is one of them.

Let us suppose that the class are reading, as a class reader, a reasonably modern book punctuated according to modern practice. Such a book, if it has dialogue as well as narrative, will provide numerous examples of the correct uses of speech marks, commas, full stops, semi-colons, and so on. The teacher decides that he wishes to teach, let us say, some of the uses of commas, and he may wish to concentrate attention upon one use in particular—perhaps the use of commas in separating the members of a series. He chooses a passage from the book with care, as it might be this one (from *Sea Hunters*, by Frank Robb, published as a class reader by Longmans):

> They regarded the little craft, Watts with interest, Cope with affection. She was beautiful, but only to a seaman who could see past the stubby deck-house, the dingy, scarred paint and the clutter of gear that littered her deck, to the clean, functional lines of the hull itself . . .
>
> All these and a hundred other skills had gone to her building. The far corners of the world had supplied the materials. Oregon from Canada, jarrah from Australia, oak from England, pine from Norway; iron, steel, copper and brass, manilla and hemp and canvas. All these had been grown and cut, mined and smelted, sawed, shaped, forged, wrought and sewn to make her. She had drawn on the industry and skill of all lands and peoples, her designers had planned well, and her builder had wrought honestly, so that Cope, her skipper, could say, as he did now, 'I'd take her through anything.'

Teacher and class examine the passage together, and decide for what purpose the writer has used each comma (or pair of commas as the case may be). In the first sentence, the two commas are seen to separate off two adverbial phrases. In the second sentence, the series of three items is conventionally punctuated ('see past the . . . deck-house, the . . . paint and the . . . gear . . . ,') but is complicated by the commas separating pairs of adjectives '(dingy, scarred' and 'clean, functional'). In the following paragraph there is, first, a series of phrases doing the work of nouns, followed by a series made up of single nouns, a noun-pair, and a noun-trio. Verbs are treated similarly in the fourth sentence of the same paragraph: the series involves single verbs, pairs, and trios. Finally comes a sentence containing, in its first part, a series of three short statements; and, in its second part, a phrase in apposition and a parenthesis. So that several different uses of commas can be studied here, but with the use of commas in series predominating.

When each case has been discussed and explained, the children are asked to close their readers, and the passage is read aloud by the teacher, a sentence at a time. The children take it down from dictation. In reading, the teacher makes no unnatural pauses at the commas, which the children insert as judgement and memory direct. The dictation over, they check their work by reference to the printed book. Then, as a 'follow-up' exercise, they take down from dictation another and similar passage, but this one they have not studied before, or even seen.

The uses of other marks of punctuation can be treated in the same way.

It may appear that the exercise I have described here is not much different from the one which has been condemned; but there is this difference—that the children do not all the while have the whole passage under their eyes. They are thus forced to consider the words of the passage *as they come*, and to punctuate accordingly. The conditions under which the marks of punctuation are inserted by the pupil are, in fact, not unlike those under which the author inserted them in the first place. And in that lies the special character of the exercise.

It should not be necessary for me to write much about exercises designed to enlarge VOCABULARY, beyond suggesting that it would be a mistake to spend more than a little of our valuable time on this sort of work. True, on the surface of it, nothing would appear to be more laudable than a desire to enrich a child's vocabulary and so, as one feels, extend his means of expression; yet in fact, when one looks at the nature and scope of the exercises and tests which purport to do so, one is forced to conclude that few kinds of school work are ever embarked upon with less real deliberation, less intelligent consideration of the principles involved, and less ultimate effectiveness.

Of course, there is general agreement among educationists as to what should be the basic vocabulary of all persons, children and adults alike—the words of Basic English; but I have not heard tell of any research which establishes the order in which the *less* 'basic' words ought to be introduced, nor the stages at which it is appropriate that they should be added to a child's word-stock; nor can I think that the conclusions of any such research would have universal validity; for who, after all, is to determine the vocabulary needs of any particular child, or the stages of his growth at which particular words should be introduced? But one thing I am sure of—that if any such research has been done, its conclusions have been generally ignored by the devisers of the vocabulary tests to be found in most text-books and set in most public examinations. There the devisers have always been allowed free rein, sometimes indeed testing for words which, in their own uninformed judgement, the pupils 'really ought to know', but most often contenting themselves with certain small-value tests of long-established kinds.

What these kinds are I need hardly explain to anyone who is at all familiar with the ordinary run of text-books and examination papers. There is the test which requires a word in place of a phrase (a word for 'able to use both hands equally well'); the test which requires the provision of a related word (an adjective related to the verb 'adhere'); the test which requires a word of opposite meaning to the one supplied (the opposite of 'bankrupt' or of 'urban' or of 'fragile'); the test which requires a word of similar meaning to that supplied (a word similar to 'arrogant' or to 'concise' or to 'prohibit'); and there are all those tests which, starting from single words or pairs of words, require the pupil to supply definitions of them or illustrations of their use. And as a special case—but so well entrenched in our practice that I must not omit it—there is the test which requires the pupil to supply the 'appropriate collective noun'. No test so well-established as that which asks for the 'appropriate collective noun'! As I write I have before me one of the proposed syllabuses for the new C.S.E. examinations, and here, sure enough, it turns up, as impudent as ever—the suggestion that the candidates should be tested on their 'knowledge of collective nouns—e.g. "covey".' Those coveys of partridges! Those braces of pheasants and gaggles of geese! Within the next fifty years the wild life of Britain may dwindle to the point of extinction, as with the encroachment of industry our partridges and pheasants and wild geese depart to find breeding space on kindlier shores; yet still these creatures will live on, collectively as well as individually, in our English text-books, and still the nouns which identify them will be deemed an essential part of the vocabulary of every well-instructed British child!

What an absurdity it all is! And in any case, how hopeless to attempt the systematic introduction of a 'useful vocabulary'! For (to put it simply, and to carry simplicity to the point of silliness) 'useful vocabulary' cannot really be useful unless we happen to have a use for it. In Chapter 3 I spoke of the natural and proper way in which a new word should be added to our vocabulary—not 'first hunted up in the dictionary and then employed in a specially-written sentence', but 'discovered in one meaningful context and used purposefully in another'. In such a way, I suggested, nearly all the useful and permanent additions to our vocabulary are made. And I would hold to that. There is abundant evidence to show that, whether as listeners or

as readers, when we learn a new word we do so because we are impelled by a need to understand something; and that, whether as speakers
or as writers, when we use a new word we do so because we are
impelled by a need to communicate something. It is a truism that
all our language practices are closely bound up with our needs and
interests, and once we have accepted this truth we shall not feel it
necessary to bother our pupils with vocabulary exercises of any kind
whatever.

I confess to having myself devised such exercises, attempting in
particular to introduce a range of general vocabulary of a kind which
one would expect educated people to need. I doubt whether many of
the words thus arbitrarily introduced ever manage to 'stick'. For the
child, as for the adult, the chief source of new words must always be
the books he reads and the people who talk to him, and the chances of
his retaining them in his vocabulary must depend upon his need to use
them in speech and writing. This, of course, gives a tremendous advantage to children who are well read and who frequent the society of
educated people. But for the child not so advantageously placed, the
alternative does *not* lie in vocabulary exercises. Almost invariably he
would be better employed in silent reading.

For the sake of completeness I conclude this chapter by making
a mere mention of PRÉCIS WRITING. I am offering no advice regarding it because no single topic has been so exhaustively treated
elsewhere, particularly in School Certificate text-books, where the
instructions on 'how to make a précis' are usually intended for teacher
and pupil equally. There is, for example, full treatment of the subject
in *Comprehension and Précis* by Frank Whitehead (University Tutorial
Press), and rather less full treatment in *English Four* and in *Précis and
Comprehension*, both by Raymond O'Malley and Denys Thompson
(Heinemann Educational Books).

CHAPTER 13

GRAMMAR

An ancient controversy—Children learning to write—A child's stock of sentence-patterns—Analysis essentially investigatory—Analysis will not help children to write better—Useful grammar—The uses to which it can be put—A grammar lesson—A 'follow-up' lesson—Further examples and exercises

'MUCH OF the ancient and wearisome controversy about grammar is no more than shadow-boxing. It is only reasonable to suppose that a knowledge of the structure of sentences is useful at a certain stage in learning to write. To this knowledge most experienced teachers of English would add an acquaintance with the parts of speech and their functions.' This extract from Ministry of Education Pamphlet No. 26, (*Language: Some Suggestions for Teachers of English and Others*), expresses a traditional conception of the value of grammar teaching, and also, by implication, a desire to maintain the *status quo* as it is in many schools. Common enough as this conception is, the source of the extract is surprising, for the Ministry of Education do not usually lag behind the times; they have always been able to draw upon the services of excellent advisers; and it would be churlish not to admit that their recommendations are often enlightened and eminently practicable. Yet here, surely, the Ministry falls short; the very tell-tale expressions 'It is only reasonable to suppose' and 'at a certain stage' give the game away. For do we not usually say 'It is only reasonable' when we have not sufficiently thought out our reasons? And do we not say 'at a certain stage' when we are not prepared to say at *which* stage?

'It is only reasonable to suppose that a knowledge of the structure of sentences is useful at a certain stage in learning to write.' And for a great many teachers, who interpret 'a knowledge of the structure of sentences' as 'an ability to analyse in an accepted way sentences of lesser or of greater complexity' this appears an eminently reasonable statement. What, indeed, could at first sight seem more reasonable? The children take the sentences to pieces, find out how they are made, and thenceforward construct their own sentences according to the patterns they have investigated. It is on an assumption that this is what actually goes on that much of the grammar teaching of today is based. Yet the statement quoted, and the assumptions associated with it, do in fact suggest a general ignorance of the real processes by which children, from the first tentative 'utterances' onward, develop their mastery of the written language.

Underlying many people's conception of these processes is the quite unwarranted belief that children, when engaged in the writing of sentences, are performing acts of deliberate *synthesis*. People observe a child, in his beginnings, to set down childish sentences of a few words each; and they also observe that as the same child grows older he becomes capable of 'utterances' which are more and more complex in structure. This leads them to speak of his 'gradually building up longer sentences', or of his 'joining his ideas together more skilfully', or even of his 'learning to put Subject to verb and add an Object'. In taking this view of the child's increased writing skill they entirely overlook the fact that the pattern made by the words of a sentence—be it a short sentence or a long one—is a single and complete thing, which the writer either has or has not grasped *as a whole*, and which he either has got or has not got under his control. The growing and intelligent mind, all eyes and ears, is for ever busy acquiring and mastering such patterns, unconsciously classifying each sentence heard or read with others of similar structure, until a whole group of similar sentences becomes generalized into one non-verbal or only partly-verbal pattern—a pattern which is retained in the mind as an item of more or less accessible stock, capable of taking on a fully verbal form at the call of a need for utterance. These processes of assimilation, classification and digestion are, of course, involuntary; their rapidity and effectiveness depend partly upon the child's verbal intelligence and partly upon the nature of his 'speaking' environment. From the talk that he hears and the stories that he reads he assimilates his sentence-patterns as wholes; if his grasp of those patterns, as shown by his compositions, is faulty, it can be strengthened only by greater familiarity with those patterns as wholes—that is to say, by his continuing to be alive in a world in which people and books 'speak' to him things he wants to hear.

By what means, then, can we, as teachers, increase a child's grasp of the numerous sentences-patterns? The answer is that we can do very little *directly*—i.e. by enforcing his attention to the various parts of which, we allege, the sentences are composed; but that we can do much *indirectly*—by talking to him, by letting him talk to ourselves and to others, by encouraging him to read well-expressed and memorable matter, and then by allowing him to write upon such subjects as have engaged his interest and attention. Small faults in his writing we can correct with some hope that they will be avoided in future—and in the correcting of them, as I shall indicate, some 'grammar' may be useful—but the 'grasp' and the fluency of the competent writer can be born only out of the activities of listening, speaking, reading, and writing, and then only to the extent that the child's innate aptitudes allow. What help, indeed, could ever be expected to come from the mere splitting up of a sentence and the naming of its parts? The chief need of the mind is to hold those parts not as separated but as joined and related. The act of composition itself is much less an act of synthesis than one of recall.

Before leaving the subject I am ready, however, for the sake of argument, to allow that an enlightened study of the structure of sentences can be useful at a certain stage in learning how to write; the question then arises whether our traditional methods of 'study' are sufficiently enlightened to be successful. Consider this typical 'examination sentence'—'On the last occasion when he was in Oxford he saw in a shop a book containing what he wanted but costing, alas, more than he could afford.' The accepted procedure compels us to distinguish three subordinate clauses ('when he was in Oxford', 'what he wanted', 'than he could afford'), and one main clause ('On the last occasion he saw in a shop a book containing but costing, alas, more'). No one who reads that last clause can maintain, unless he has a perverse sense of humour, that these four clauses are the 'parts' out of which the sentence is 'constructed'. Further, when we come to examine the sentence with an eye to discovering what really are its 'parts'—*i.e.* the word-groups into which it falls when spoken—we find that some of the groups ('On the last occasion when he was in Oxford', 'more than he could afford') are not classifiable by the traditionally-accepted method of clause-analysis.

At this point, a well-informed reader may comment, 'All very true—but have we not now the New Grammar?' For of course, the fact that the traditional method does not always separate a sentence into 'natural groups' is no new discovery; linguists have been at work on the matter for some years, and by the close study of English as it is spoken by ordinary people have evolved a grammar with new groups and categories. Would not a study of this new, more intelligent grammar—which does treat English as if it were English, and not as if it were

Latin—be useful in our schools? But to ask such a question is to mis-understand the case against classroom grammar generally, whether it be new or old. The study of English grammar remains an essentially *investigatory* activity; it is the proper province of linguists; and it is *not* the province of school-children, for the reason that they have on hand a task in which it can give them almost no assistance—the task of learning to write. It is an odd fact—but not so very odd, when you come to think of it—that even the exponents of the New Grammar do not always express themselves in clear and competent English!

The foregoing notes are but a small part of the case against analysis as we still practise it in our schools. The observant teacher, however, has no need to read these notes. He has already found out that, while there are some of his pupils who can analyse correctly and also write well, there are also those who are expert 'analysers' but find difficulty in writing any but the most halting English; while there are others again who cannot distinguish between a phrase and a clause and yet can write correctly and fluently. Having made these discoveries he has long since abandoned hope that 'a knowledge of the structure of sentences', as it is generally understood, can ever be 'useful at a certain stage in learning to write', and has set his hopes elsewhere.

When it comes to 'an acquaintance with the parts of speech and their functions', the Ministry pamphlet is on more solid ground. Indeed, many teachers today regard 'grammar' as essentially a number of terms which can be used, for convenience, in the discussion of the faults or the virtues of a piece of writing, or in the elucidation of it. They do not believe that a knowledge of the meaning of these terms has any value in itself; they regard the teaching of them as preliminary work—as the provision of a technical vocabulary which will facilitate discussion of language questions and problems.

Therefore, before introducing a grammatical term to a class, the teacher asks himself, 'Is this going to be a useful term for a child to handle? Do I myself make use of this term when discussing children's work with them, or when sorting out the difficulties which arise from the reading of prose or poetry?' If the answer is 'No', he may very reasonably wonder whether he is not about to waste valuable time. And even if the answer is 'Yes'—even, that is to say, if the grammatical term is obviously a useful one—there still arises another question, 'Is it worth while? Are the children bright enough to grasp the meaning of this term and to appreciate it when the word is used rapidly in a casual context? Or would it not be better, on occasions when I might use it,

N

to have recourse instead to a paraphrase?' Undoubtedly in some cases it would indeed be better. Some children spend the whole of their school career in attempting merely to master the grammatical terms, and there is no time left—nor has the teacher the inclination, nor, alas, does he always see the need—to put the grammatical terminology to use in a discussion of a child's or of an adult's writing. A grammatical terminology is of little value unless it can be learned rapidly and confidently; that is why (except indeed when University examination regulations compel it to be otherwise), we direct our grammar teaching to only the brightest of the children.

I have spoken of the 'convenience' of grammatical terms, and there is no doubt that, in the conversation of educated people, their use often *is* convenient. We may be discussing the use of commas in, say, a sentence of this kind—'Towser, come here, sir!'; and very convenient it is to be able to point out that a comma can be used 'in order to isolate a noun in the vocative case'. The penalty for this ease of reference—a prepaid penalty in this case—is the having learnt the meanings of 'noun', 'vocative', and 'case' (with 'isolate' thrown in for good measure). Or to take another example: imagine that we are discussing the unsatisfactoriness of this sentence—'The brown and white Siamese cat which lives in the house next door but one spits'; the lack of balance of the sentence can more easily be shown if we are able to say that, beginning with a very long Subject, it ends in a predicate of a single word. Again, so easy an explanation is dependent upon the children's having previously mastered some difficult terms—Subject and predicate. In the minds of those teachers who have discovered, through hard experience, the difficulty of establishing such terms in the *unhesitating* vocabulary of many children, there arises the question which is the most recurrent of all those associated with grammar teaching—'Is the game worth the candle?' Often the answer is simply 'No'.

In my own practice as a teacher, I find that—apart from their limited use in the correction of faulty sentences—I make the most frequent use of grammatical terms when teaching punctuation and when teaching poetry! This may seem odd; but it must be remembered, first of punctuation, that to discuss the correct placing of punctuation marks is much easier if we understand such terms as Subject, predicate, vocative, apposition, sentence adverb, and parenthesis; and secondly of poetry, that to be able to separate Subject from predicate, or merely to determine to what part of speech a word belongs, is essential if we are to unravel the orthodox complexities of Wordsworth's *Prelude* or the less orthodox complexities of Hopkins's sonnets. However, these facts can hardly be cited as evidence of the need to teach grammatical terminology to all and sundry. As I have already indicated, bright children will always find more use for grammar than dull ones; and I should add that advanced students will always find more use for it than children who are still mastering the rudiments of English.

To the children who can make good use of them, what terms should we teach? I tentatively suggest these: noun, verb, adjective, adverb, preposition, pronoun, personal pronoun, relative pronoun, case, singular, plural, Subject, predicate, Object, imperative, active, passive, phrase, clause, transitive, intransitive, and the names of some tenses. Several of these terms I myself do not use very often in class. An ability to distinguish Subject from predicate is useful when one is discussing the sense of a complicated sentence. There are a good many other terms (such as vowel, consonant, symbol, accent, phonetic) which are to be found in the preliminary pages of any good dictionary, and which claim equal rights with grammatical terms to be part of a school-child's vocabulary. But of all these terms, let this be noted—that the work which a knowledge of their meanings facilitates is essentially critical, essentially investigatory, and in no sense inventive. Such terms can have little to do, unluckily, with the early stages of 'learning to write'.

I would now like to describe some of the work we can do in grammar lessons. Let us suppose that we wish to introduce to the class the use of one or another of the terms given above. The lesson falls into four parts, which we can entitle as follows: (*i*) illustration, (*ii*) discussion, (*iii*) deduction, (*iv*) writing. The first part of the lesson involves the examination of a passage which contains several examples of whatever it is we intend to talk about—nouns, or pronouns, or adverbs, or some of the various tense-forms—and which is also of sufficient general interest to focus the class's attention. After reading and examining the illustration we proceed to the second part of the lesson, a discussion of some aspect of the passage which leads us, by stages, to the third part, in which we are able to deduce principles and even sometimes formulate a definition. The lesson concludes with the fourth part, a written exercise, preferably involving original composition, in which the knowledge gained is put to use.

It will be seen that the procedure here described reverses that which is normally adopted when one is speaking to or writing for adults, in that here the illustration is given first and the statement of principles follows it. The object of this reversal, as will probably be clear, is to secure the children's attention before any abstract discussion is embarked upon. I now give an account of an actual lesson in which this procedure is adopted.

The lesson is a first lesson on Pronouns. The teacher begins by writing up, and then asking the children to read, some nonsense verses from *Alice in Wonderland*—verses which are not without interest in themselves and which contain several examples of pronouns of the various kinds:

> They told me you had been to her
> And mentioned me to him:
> She gave me a good character
> But said I could not swim.
>
> He sent them word I had not gone,
> (We know it to be true);
> If she should push the matter on,
> What would become of you?
>
> I gave her one, they gave him two,
> You gave us three or more;
> They all returned from him to you,
> Though they were mine before.

When the verses have been read once or twice, the teacher begins the discussion by enquiring if anyone can say what they are about. To this enquiry he probably receives some confused answers, well-meant attempts to supply a 'story' which isn't there; but the class is bound to be led, finally, to the conclusion that the verses as they stand have not very much meaning. Yet there is sequence in the words, and it is certain that the poem is about 'persons and things'. But what persons, what things? There are three things actually mentioned—'character', 'word', and 'matter'—and the words which name them are of course nouns. But there are other persons and things clearly referred to, and the class's next task is to pick out the words which refer to those other persons and things—'they', 'me', 'you', 'her', and so on. The class is told that these words are pronouns.

Having carried the discussion thus far, the teacher is in a position to help the class draw some conclusions regarding pronouns. In this poem there are many words which *refer* to persons or to things, but only three ('character', 'word', and 'matter') which *name* them. The other words

—the pronouns—refer to persons or to things in a vague way, but do not actually name them.

That is enough in the way of a definition, and the class proceed to the 'writing' part of the lesson, in which they can confirm their newly-acquired knowledge. The teacher sets before the class a conundrum:

> *They* say *I* am cracked, and my eyes won't close;
> But I haven't got beads for eyes, like *those*.

Which are the pronouns, he asks, and what persons or things do they refer to? There is general agreement that 'I' refers to a doll and 'those' to a soft toy such as a bear. There is some disagreement about 'they': does it mean 'children' or 'people in general'? After the difficulty has been fully aired, the children are asked to write (in prose or verse) similar conundrums, bringing in any pronouns they care to. When this writing has been done, each child reads his conundrum to the other children, who are expected to identify the pronouns and to guess to whom or to what each one is intended to refer. The whole exercise involves not only the identification of pronouns, but also the employment of them and the driving home of their essential character and limitations.

This matter of the 'limitations' of pronouns can be taken up in a subsequent lesson, where it can be shown what sorts of confusion arise from their indiscriminate use. Children enjoy reading a passage such as the following:

The Visit

'Come along in, my dear!' called out Uncle, as soon as I opened the door. 'Come along in, and give me those 'eavy bags!' I noticed that Uncle dropped his aitches. He picked them up at once, and I followed him into a dining-room filled with the smell of a real old-fashioned Irish stew. It had all sorts of things in it: a cat, a couple of puppies, a stuffed squirrel, and a horsehair sofa.

Auntie came forward to greet me. I handed her my hat and gave her a kiss; she flung it on the sofa, and invited me to sit down at the table.

Auntie then put some victuals before her husband, pointing out to him that his hands were dirty. But he began to eat them at once, saying that good food couldn't wait. I, too, began to eat.

Suddenly the cat sprang on to the table, and looked expectantly at Auntie. She purred loudly and scratched herself, so that Uncle said, 'Give 'er some of the fish-bones brought in by Mrs Noakes. Good old Mrs Noakes! She practically lives on fish-bones,' he added, turning to me. 'No wonder 'er whiskers are so long!'

When the children have read the passage through, they can go on to identify the pronouns, and then to discuss some of the personal pronouns in the third person ('them' and 'it' and 'she'). What is the first 'it' intended to stand for—the dining-room or the Irish stew? And what is the second 'them' intended to stand for—the victuals or the hands? It is possible to ask similar questions about the other pronouns, and the discussion easily brings out the fact that, if we are careless in our use of pronouns, we may write nonsense unintentionally. The next thing to do is to demonstrate the two alternative ways in which this 'pronoun nonsense' can be avoided—either by substituting a noun for a pronoun, or, where this involves a clumsy repetition, by changing the words or inverting the word-order. Finally, the children can be set to work on passages which have been rendered nonsensical or ambiguous by the misuse of pronouns, and can write improved versions of them. Extract (a) below is the beginning of a passage which can be improved by the replacement of pronouns by nouns.

(a)

I pushed my way on to the bus. I had just seen a suitable seat out of the corner of my eye—but too late! Someone had sat on it! Then I let fall my gloves. I searched amongst the passengers' feet, but could only find the one with a finger missing. Where was the other? The conductor rang the bell, but it could not be seen . . .

Extract (b) can be improved by an inversion or a re-wording of sentences 2, 3, 5, and 8.

(b)

I swerved past the astonished girl, and my cycle made straight for the pond. Just as she opened her mouth to scream, I rushed straight into it. Both wheels became embedded in the mud, much to the astonishment of two farmyard ducks. 'They will need oiling now,' I thought, as I scrambled off, entirely unhurt. Carrying the hen which had been the cause of the accident, the girl now approached. She was cackling loudly, and her feathers were dropping out. The girl said she was very sorry, but explained that a stray dog had chased the hen. The dog had given a great deal of trouble to her father, the farmer. He was a vicious beast, and deserved to be chained up.

The lessons on pronouns which I have just outlined will serve, I hope, as models for all lessons where the object is to introduce a grammatical term or establish a grammatical category. The two chief difficulties lie, of course, in finding suitable passages which can act as illustrations, and suitable exercises which can be used as 'follow-up' work; but several modern text-books contain useful material, and the teacher will derive pleasure from inventing material of his own.

Here is a connected passage—admittedly absurd but not, I hope, too absurd to be useful—which can be used as a means of introducing the principal tenses of verbs:

The Sailor's Rejoinder

'Mr Sparks,' snapped the captain at last, 'there's work for you to do. Will you help, and not hinder?'

'You ask me to help?' roared the old sailor, almost beside himself with fury. 'I am helping, sir. I was helping when you spoke. I have helped for this last hour. I reckon I help as much as anyone, sir. I helped all day yesterday. I shall help here all night. I shall be helping when the other fellows are asleep. What's more, sir, a fortnight come Thursday I shall have helped on this ship for fifteen years. Think o' that, sir. If others had helped, sir, same as me, we would have been away to sea by now.'

The sailor gulped and was suddenly silent, scared by his own bold speech. But the captain merely gazed at him for a moment—then muttered 'A helpful sort of man!' and turned away.

The passage is intended to provide a context for nine tenses of the verb 'to help'. Discussion centres upon the difference between the simple, the continuous, and the perfect tenses, and the concepts 'past', 'present', and 'future'. When these have been mastered, the children should be able to find the nine tense-forms (past simple, past continuous, past perfect, and so on) and enter them in a table. The composition work which concludes this lesson should involve the writing of a connected passage similar to (but shorter than) the one given above, with the object of introducing, in as natural a manner as possible, some four or five specified tenses of a given verb.

If the provision of suitable illustrative material is important in the early stages of these lessons, the provision of 'follow-up' work is hardly less so, for it is through such work that the pupil is enabled to strengthen his hold on his new knowledge, and also to perceive its language applications. I would like to devote the remainder of this chapter to the description of one or two 'follow-up' exercises associated with the learning of the parts of speech.

For young beginners who are trying to establish the concept of a noun, there is the simple exercise of writing a series of nouns which outline a well-known story or nursery-rhyme—like this:

> Boy—errand—market—sale—cow. Encounter—butcher. Exchange—cow—beans. Boy—home. Mother—anger. Beans—window. Boy—bed.

Or this:

> Father—mother—discussion—lack—money. Decision—expedition—forest —abandonment—children. Children—eavesdroppers. Decision—collection —pebbles. Morning—family—departure—forest. Boy—trail—pebbles.

Or this:

> Youth—cat—bundle—journey—road—London. Milestone—rest—despair. Youth—attention—sound—bells. Bells—encouragement. Youth—continuation—journey.

Some children will include in their series words which are not nouns, but that does not much matter; their 'stories' can still form a basis for discussion. First, the writer's class-mates can guess *which* well-known story is intended, and secondly they can criticize it, trying to find in it words which, in such a context, cannot possibly be nouns. All the while they are taking a firmer hold of the concept of a noun, and they are also putting nouns into use.

A similar exercise can be used to establish the concept of a verb. It involves the thinking-up of suitable one-word verbs and their insertion as stage-directions in playlets either provided by the teacher or invented by the children themselves. Plays are the only literary form in which verbs occur in isolation (and in italics, and between brackets); such directions as (*Laughs*), (*Pauses*), and (*Sits*) are self-sufficient in a play, and the act of supplying them forces the child to concentrate his thoughts on the 'true nature' of a verb. But once the child is sure of his verbs, he should pass on to the more ambitious exercises, one of the most useful of which is that which requires the improvement of a 'flabby' piece of writing by the strengthening of its 'flabby' verbs. The ideal source of such writing is a child's essay, but if a suitable piece is not forthcoming, a specially-written piece can be made to serve. Here is an example of the sort of writing I mean:

> Rex came downstairs in the dark, trying not to awaken the rest of the family, and went into the kitchen. Unluckily he fell over a chair which was in the doorway, and the noise attracted the parrot where she half slept in her cage. She at once said 'Hallo, Polly!' so loudly that her cry promised to have a bad

effect upon all his plans. Luckily she soon went again into a stupor, and the shriek of a passing train, just outside, came in time to cover Rex's further noises as, with caution, he moved back the bolt of the house door.

With the help of the children, and as a piece of oral work, the teacher first picks out and underlines those verbs or verb-equivalents which lack the force or the precision required by their context. Afterwards the class can rewrite the passage and improve it. An improved version might read as follows:

Rex crept downstairs in the dark, trying not to awaken the rest of the family, and tiptoed into the kitchen. Unluckily he stumbled over a chair which stood in the doorway, and the noise aroused the parrot where she dozed in her cage. She at once screamed 'Hallo, Polly!' so loudly that her cry threatened to ruin all his plans. Luckily she soon sank again into a stupor, and the shriek of a passing train, just outside, came in time to drown Rex's further noises as, with caution, he slid back the bolt of the house door.

Exercises which test both the recognition and the use of adverbs are not difficult to devise, and the following three exercises, though they involve nothing more than a rearrangement of words, are a little more exacting than they might at first appear. The children are required to find in passage (*a*) six adverbs of Manner, in passage (*b*) seven adverbs of Time, and in passage (*c*) seven adverbs of Place, and then to rearrange the adverbs in each passage so that each adverb is in its proper position. The mere discovery of the adverbs is not difficult, but the task of rearranging them—especially in passages (*b*) and (*c*)—sets twelve-year-olds thinking very hard about the meaning of the passage and the meaning of the adverbs they have to insert. And that hard thinking is something which they can usefully do.

(*a*)

The car swerved aimlessly so as to avoid three people who were walking briskly across the road. In doing so it roughly missed a lamp-post and came to rest sharply. The driver got out and stepped narrowly towards the offending persons, ordering them rather abruptly to stop.

(*b*)

Yesterday we have been to the cinema. We intended to go often, but it was such a bright day that we played tennis instead. Tennis is a game which we usually play because there is so great a demand for the tennis-courts; today there are as many as a dozen people waiting their turn. We seldom avoid the cinema except on rainy days, and repeatedly we only see films which have been then recommended by our friends.

(c)

I have been looking back for Jim but I cannot find him. He was inside a minute ago, but I think that he may have gone everywhere for a walk. If you see him in the town, please ask him to hurry about. A letter has arrived for him, and I think it has important news somewhere. I am sure you will find him out here.

I will conclude by describing one or two of the exercises which can be used as an aid to the study of adjectives. And at this point I ought perhaps to forestall criticism by admitting that some of these exercises (those I have just described, and those I am about to describe) are of a kind which are often frowned upon, a kind involving the supplying of single words—mere word-puzzles—a filling-in of gaps. I am aware that these are regarded as limitations; but there are times, so it seems to me, when even exercises of this sort can be both exacting and intelligent, and if we do not expect them to do the things they cannot—above all, if we do not look upon them as substitutes for original composition— we shall not go far astray. The following three exercises, each involving the insertion in a short passage of the five adjectives supplied, set out to differentiate the three kinds of work which adjectives can do. In (a) the adjectives indicate number or quantity; in (b) they select particular persons or objects from others of the same kind; and in (c) they tell us about the natures or the qualities of things.

(a)

After hard thinking and hours of toil we still had hope that we would ever escape from the prison-camp. Previous prisoners had tried, but only Australian private had been successful.

   (*Insert* little, one, several, many, much)

(b)

The man to make the ascent of the peak chose the time of the year when avalanches were not to be feared. The attempt, a year later, was made by a party of five, but of these five the man to reach the top was General Fenning.

   (*Insert* next, only, principal, first, coldest)

(c)

It is useless to hunt the rhinoceros with a spear, especially one made in England. This creature has a hide through which it is very difficult to pierce. In spite of its movements it is capable of extremely onslaughts on its enemies.

(*Insert* unwieldy, African, resolute, plated, tough)

A different sort of exercise, and one testing not only an understanding of the work of adjectives but also a feeling for their descriptive power, is that which requires the children to insert ten adjectives of their own choosing into a given passage, and in that way to make it a fuller picture of what is described. Either passage (*a*) or passage (*b*) below can be used for this purpose.

(a)

Simon found his brother and sister with their noses glued to the window of a baker's shop. Within there was a display of cakes such as would be bound to appeal to children: fruit tarts with pastry and cherries; meringues with cream; raisin cake cut so as to show the fruit inside, and, less luxurious but hardly less appetizing, some currant buns. Over these hovered wasps, evidently undecided whether they should settle in jam or in cream.

(b)

The people who travelled with him in the railway compartment were certainly rather unusual. There was a fellow with a nose and a hat; a woman with spectacles and an ear-trumpet, through which she sometimes blew as if it were an instrument; a woman, probably her daughter or her sister, who ate peanuts with speed from a bag; and a boy who ran about the compartment, making remarks about the passengers and throwing his cakes out of the window.

It might seem a simple enough task to supply ten adjectives to either passage, and indeed, most twelve-year-olds have little difficulty in finding adjectives as such; but they vary considerably in their ability to supply adjectives which are genuinely contributory: one child will write 'thick cream', 'dark raisin cake', and 'shiny currant buns', and thus show that he has appreciated the needs of the context; while another will write 'sickly cream', 'stale raisin cake', and 'small currant buns', and thus show that he has not. The exercise, if done well, will reveal not only a knowledge of grammar but also intelligence and imagination.

Now a last exercise—one which involves deleting from the given passage ten adjectives which do very little useful work. Again, not so simple an exercise as it seems; it compels a close reading and a careful consideration of all the words.

Paying a quick annual visit to the Cornish town, as I do every April, I was surprised to find the steep, almost perpendicular banks of the river already covered in green verdure. The early spring had come even sooner than usual, and in sheltered places the bluebells, protected from wild gales, had opened right out into full flower. The tree-trunks on those slopes are always covered with a mossy growth of grey lichen, which I suppose is encouraged by the favourable salt winds of the region. It has been shown to be a proved fact that certain mosses thrive in a salty air.

This, then, is what I would call 'useful grammar'—useful, that is, to those children who can profit by it. How much time ought one to devote to such work? I would suggest an occasional lesson—one lesson a fortnight, perhaps—for the first three years of the course. That ought to be quite enough time for building up a small vocabulary of grammatical terms, of a kind that will be useful to children when discussing the nature and qualities of any sort of writing, whether their own or someone else's, whether prose or poetry.

CHAPTER 14

GATHERING UP THE LOOSE ENDS

Supplementary reading—Class and school libraries—Testing knowledge of a supplementary reader—What other class-books?—Internal examinations—The need for a separate Composition paper—Its constitution—The Literature paper—The school magazine—Who should write it?—What should it contain?—Its contents discussed in detail—The use of symposia. The teacher of English—This book

IN THIS chapter I should like to pick up the ends of some matters embarked upon in earlier pages, and to extend their threads a little further; and in doing so I am reverting to the two broad topics which occupy the major part of this book—reading and writing. First I shall say something about supplementary and private reading; then I shall speak about the school's internal examinations, in which both reading and writing are tested; and finally I shall come back to the question of the *use* of writing, and resume the discussion, began in Chapter 2, of the contents of the school magazine.

To publishers engaged in general publishing who have also educational departments, it must be a great comfort, faced with the increasing disinclination of adults to read books of any kind, to know that in the schools at least there continues to be a steady market for their wares. In the schools at least, if not elsewhere, there is a reliable buying public, and every extension of state education opens up fresh prospects. But 'buying public' is not necessarily 'reading public'; children who are the sons and daughters of non-reading parents will hardly be expected to be the keener readers for that; and resistance to reading can be as widespread in school as it is in the world outside. The teacher can indeed stand over his pupils while they read aloud to him; but beyond that he can do little to promote reading without their full-hearted co-operation—without, above all, their taking pleasure in literature and recognizing it as supplying a deep-felt need.

And that is what, often enough nowadays, they do not do. The need is not there, or in any case it is not felt to be there. How should it be? In recent years the primitive excitements which children formerly derived from popular reading and from the cinema have become available, and in increasing quantities, from a much more powerful source, television, and the quantity of ready-to-hand vicarious experience which television now supplies makes it seem absurd to children that they should give up potential viewing-time to tedious and effort-demanding works of literature. The children's fantasy-life is already satisfied, without the need for 'good books'; and in terms of real experience, too, as opposed to vicarious, their lives seem to them already full and complete. What young adolescent is prepared to drool and dream over the vaporous love-affairs of nineteenth-century lovers when *real* love affairs—and love, as it seems, much more to the purpose —are to be had with the boy or the girl round the corner? The pity of all this is that these crude and premature satisfactions, whether we think of the children's fantasy-life or of their real life, are in a way stultifying: they actually stand in the way of children developing the desire to share the experience which imaginative literature sets out to convey. It is not just that these children needs must love the lowest when they see it (that is a common enough plight); it is that, in loving the lowest, they soon lose the capacity for loving anything else, or in any other way.

In face of these difficulties, what else can we do after ensuring that our pupils have read their class reader? Beyond the class reader there is the supplementary reader; beyond the supplementary reader the class library; beyond the class library the school library; and beyond the school library the public library. And the farther we go from the class reader, the less power we have, not merely to choose their reading-matter, but to ensure that they read anything at all. So our first care should be to see that there is a good supply of supplementary books to back up those which are to be studied in detail. This is easier to achieve if we do not spend too much of our book allowance on Courses, books of tests and exercises, and comprehension-books; ideally each class of children should have, in addition to the novel or story chosen for special study, at least two other prose readers for spare-time reading, and there should be a new issue of books at the beginning of each term; so that in one year each child has a chance to read at least nine novels and stories from the school's general stock. I have never quite managed to bring about this state of things in my own school, although some years ago, before the price of books rose so disproportionately, I came very near to doing so; but I still look forward to the day when I shall see all my classes thus equipped.

And what of libraries? Most schools have central libraries of their own, and the enlightened policy which many local authorities nowadays pursue in the matter of financing school libraries means that librarians are able to stock them as never before. Yet—I hesitate to make a general statement about this, for the shape of things inevitably varies from school to school—has not enlightenment come too late? Are these larger and better-equipped libraries being more extensively used than were the small libraries of ten years ago? Certainly some of the teachers who have spoken to me on this matter agree that they are not. 'Our store of books increases every year,' said one teacher; 'but the supply of enthusiastic readers gets smaller and smaller.'

It was to forestall the coming-about of this state of things that we in my school (I hand on our experience for what it is worth) some while ago instituted class libraries as a supplement to the central library. These libraries are not the usual collections of Biggles books and children's annuals brought along by the children themselves; they are small libraries bought with library money and consisting of about thirty-five books each—that is to say, enough to supply all the children of a class with one each. The books are selected with care. Thirty-five books will easily go into a small cardboard packing-case, and they can be carried by the teacher into the classroom. If you are not sure that the horse will go willingly to the water, you must bring the water to the horse.

Even then you will not always make him drink.

The kind of 'travelling' library I have described is not suitable for Sixth forms; yet even Sixth-formers do not always go willingly to the school library, and for them a Paperback Library, housed not too far from their classroom, is a good alternative. None of these small libraries need interfere with the work of the school's central library; what a school's chief librarian sometimes laments is that there are classes in his school which appear to have no library users at all, and the institution of form libraries is intended to remedy that.

Before I leave the subject of supplementary reading I should like to mention a simple test that can be used in connection with it. It is not a test that can probe very deep; in fact, it does little more than find out whether or not the book has been read through. What is more, it is applicable only to novels and tales of a certain sort—those which have a fair number of characters who reside in or visit a fair number of places. But it is an amusing test which it is easy to set and mark, and it makes a rapid and light survey of a novel as a whole. I give it for what it is worth. It is called 'Establishing Relationships'.

Let it be supposed that a middle-school class has been given *Pride and Prejudice* as a supplementary reader. When the time for the test comes, the teacher draws on the blackboard as large a circle as he can manage, and marks the circumference with points or small crosses. Against each point he writes the name of a person or a place mentioned in the novel. These names are written horizontally, and just outside the circle. Then, for his first question, he joins two of the points by a line—say, 'Lydia' and 'Mr Bennet'. The line need not be a straight one; indeed, as more and more lines appear, it is convenient to give the children the pleasure of finding their way through a tangle. After the teacher has drawn each line he rubs a little of it out, and inserts in the gap the number of the question—in this case, 1. The children's task is to write down the relationship between Lydia and Mr Bennet—*i.e.* daughter and father. If there is a family relationship between the persons whose names are joined, the children must give it. If there is no family relationship, they must tell of any significant incident which connects the two persons. If the line joins the name of a person to the name of a place, the children must say when or in what circumstances that person came to be in that place. If there is no known connection between the two items, the children must write 'No connection'.

The test can in fact find out a little more than might at first appear. 'Lydia'–'Mr Bennet' would present no difficulty; nor would 'Lydia'–'Brighton'. But 'Lady Catherine'–'Longbourn' might be a different matter, for it would demand a recall of the one occasion when Lady Catherine visited Longbourn (in order to forbid Elizabeth to marry Darcy). And if one felt the need of a few teasers, there would always be relationships like 'Kitty'–'Eastbourne' (Mr Bennet declared that he would not let his daughter Kitty go nearer to Brighton than Eastbourne!). Nor is there any harm in introducing a few 'duds'—*i.e.* in enquiry after relationships which do not exist. But I have never had difficulty in finding enough matter for fifteen questions (usually the maximum number which I can manage in the space available); and the marking of the test is straightforward if one insists, first, that a family relationship must always take priority, and secondly, that any other relationship mentioned must be a significant one from the point of view of the novel as a whole.

In cases where the children read supplementary readers at their own pace, the tests may be written down on sheets of cardboard, and handed out as they are needed.

When we are buying books for a new school, or for a new class in an old school, the prose readers—stories, novels, and the like—should be our first concern, for these are the books which the majority of the children will take to most readily. After them will come the poetry-books; it is a matter of prestige to have a good poetry anthology on our store-room shelves, or in our pupils' desks; and if, as occasionally happens, the poetry-books get less use than the other books, there is at least this advantage, that they do not need frequent replacement. In addition to these, we should try to get some suitable plays. I have already dwelt on the difficulty of finding, for children of eleven to fourteen, plays which are really worth the trouble of reading and acting, but in view of the popularity of the drama lesson with the majority of children, it is probably better to have bad plays than to have none at all. Perhaps the day will come when our dramatists will turn themselves to the task of writing good plays specially for children —though the prospect of this seems remote in times when to the writing of plays we devote some of our lowest intelligences.

After we have provided prose readers, poetry, and plays, the time has come to pause, and ponder very hard. What are we to do about the Courses, the books of exercises, the grammars, and the comprehension tests? Have not educationists laboured to show that many such books give little help to the young reader, and almost none to the young writer? And if proper time is given to the kinds of work described in this book—kinds which do not demand the use of any school-books except stories, plays and poems—will there be any time left for ordinary text-books? Is it not a fact that even many of the people in text-book business (you can be 'in show-business' so I don't see why not 'in text-book business') are not convinced that their products are of value in helping children to read and write? To sum up, is there any place whatever for text-books in our classrooms?

Before we answer the last question with an emphatic No, we must be sure that we have the right to do so. This right, in my view, is the prerogative of those who have known the conditions of many years' continuous class-teaching. In common humanity, we ought not to speak slightingly about the small value of text-books unless we ourselves have for many years taught without them. To carry on, day after day, the kinds of work which I have described in the first eleven chapters of this book—constantly helping the children to write

o

better, to read more intelligently—requires a drive and an initiative not paralleled by the teaching requirements of any other subject. It exhausts the energy of the strongest souls; the strongest cannot help turning an occasional wistful eye on teachers of other subjects, who, more fortunate, are *not* denied occasional recourse to books in which their work is done for them. Strong-minded indeed is the teacher of English who pushes all text-books away from him, crying 'I will *not* —they are evil—a wicked waste of time! For the fifth time this week I will get down to it, and once more stir up my rebellious children to yet another fit of creative writing!'

Of course there is much in most text-books which is of small practical value—much that is mere 'busy work', as I think the Americans call it. But while admitting that many of the people in text-book business are not convinced of the value of their products, I feel bound to add that many of those who are not so convinced nevertheless continue to write text-books; and in doing so they are not, I think, entirely inconsistent or hypocritical. They work on in the hope of devising better kinds of book—kinds more genuinely related to the business of reading and writing. If text-books are not absolutely necessary, they are not all absolutely bad; the teacher has to learn discrimination—between books, and between the various contents of one book. The kinds of text-book work most worth considering are those which, as it were, 'look towards' better writing, or which, by whatever means, conduce to better reading; the kinds least worth considering are the merely analytical or investigatory, those which point nowhere, the kinds with no intelligent applications. In the best text-books of today we see the germs of the good text-books of the future—books which will act as companions to, and in some cases contain long extracts from, worth-while reading matter, and will use that matter as a guide to further reading, and as a starting-point for discussion and for various kinds of continuous writing.

If there is one kind of text-book we shall decide to dispense with before all the others, it will be the comprehension-book—the books of very short prose passages, each of them followed by up to fifty questions. I once asked a publisher what these books were for. 'The theory of it is,' he replied with a smile, 'that these books force the children to consider the chosen passages slowly and carefully, and that having acquired, by the prolonged use of such exercises, the care and patience which the work demands, they will afterwards bring the same qualities of mind to bear on any other reading they do.' These words, or words like them, were the substance of his reply; but I did not fail to notice his smile. And indeed, it doesn't work. Try it for yourself. Choose a pupil who you know reads rapidly and carelessly; take him away from his Biggles book, or his Saint book, or his James Bond, or whatever else commands his attention, and set him down to a prolonged course of comprehension-exercises; and after that, let him return to his Biggles books, his Saints, and his James Bonds. Will he at once bring to bear on his favourite reading all his newly-acquired disciplines? Quite the contrary. He will apply himself to his old books with, if anything, even greater rapidity and carelessness, as if resolved to make up for so many weeks wasted on unpalatable 'comprehension'!

It does not need much experience to teach us that comprehension-books can do little to transform a careless reader into a careful one, and that their value as teaching aids is small. The proper use of comprehension-exercises is not as teaching aids but as tests; and as tests they have their proper time and place. Their time is the end of the school year, and their place is the examination room. In the annual examination in English literature they are at home.

When we come to the task of planning our internal examinations we shall probably decide to set separate papers in English composition and English literature. True, some people declare separate papers to be unnecessary: all writing, they say, proceeds from reading, and a completely satisfactory course (and therefore examination) in reading and writing can be built around the study of works of literature. But this is a point of view which ignores both the peculiar limitations of a great many children and also a particular trend of our times. Perhaps not a very large proportion of the country's school-children can be said to make a real success of writing, but that proportion is much greater than the proportion which makes a success of literature (in the sense of responding to it, valuing it, and being as it were transformed by it). And this is not necessarily the fault of the teachers. Indifference to literature may indeed be fostered by bad teaching, as it may by an unfavourable environment; but indifference to literature may also spring from causes more inherent—from a lack of interest in the 'things of literature' (the things human and humane which are the pre-occupations of the novelist, the playwright, and the poet), from an irremediable deficiency of the imagination (which means that the child is unable to propose clearly to himself the experiences of which the artist treats), and from an inability to respond to words in any but their primary senses. The notion that there are numerous children (rich and poor, clever and not-clever, over-privileged and under-privileged) who are beyond the reach of great imaginative literature is not a popular one with us teachers because, as lovers of literature, we would prefer to believe that it is a heritage which all can share. But observation does not support this belief. And the abolition of English composition examinations and the putting of all children through the English literature mill—a course of action which some people advocate—would be a cruelty and an injustice to many of the children, and would prevent them from showing their special aptitude in those sorts of writing which do not demand a 'literary' mind.

We say that reading precedes writing. But does it? If we think in terms of our primitive ancestors, we have to admit that writing must have preceded reading; and of the children of today—here I touch upon what I have already referred to as a particular trend of our times —it must be observed that, while they certainly learn to read before they learn to write, many of them go on writing, and writing with ever increasing fluency, long after they have ceased to read. It is perhaps not sufficiently realized that great numbers of today's children early abandon literature, and indeed almost all kinds of reading except text-books and instruction-manuals, and yet retain and further develop remarkable facility in writing about matters within their observation and experience. I do not pretend to be able to explain why; it may simply be that there is more well-expressed English 'in the air' than ever before. But I am certain it is a mistake to suppose they cannot write well except under the influence of books. Much of their writing, and some of the best of it, is written 'out of life'; and is that not perhaps as we should prefer it to be? In this book I have not hesitated to put Writing before Reading.

When the time comes for our end-of-the-year examinations then, we can properly set two examination papers, one in English language and one in English literature. In the first of these two, there is no reason why we should not ask for two or even three pieces of original writing, deliberately contrasted with one another as to type and subject-matter. Many teachers hesitate to make free composition the chief or only kind of task prescribed in a composition paper, arguing that the marking of compositions is a subjective matter, and that it would be unfair to make our whole judgement of a child's ability depend upon it; but the difficulty of establishing standards of good writing is often much exaggerated, and it is one of the purposes of this book, and of others like it, to help people to establish such standards. Two experienced teachers who have discussed the matter beforehand seldom have difficulty in agreeing how to 'place' any one composition in a batch. In addition to these 'free' compositions we may, if we desire it, include a question of a more controlled type; any type will be suitable so long as it is genuinely 'compositional'. Summary-writing and sentence-making are both of them suitable tests for this purpose, and of the latter I will write a few words more.

The test in question will easily be recognized as of an established kind. The children are given a series of groups of short sentences. Each group has to be studied, and then the information contained in it has to be incorporated into a single long (sometimes complex) sentence. Here, as an example, are six groups of short sentences arranged so as to make a 'story':

(The children were old enough. They could make a journey alone. Their father judged so. They could go to the seaside.) (They set out. They went gaily. They made their way to the station. They bought tickets.) (The train came in. The children had waited for only a few minutes. They had stood on the platform.) (They were lucky. Tom said so. They had a compartment to themselves.) (The journey was a slow one. The train stopped at many stations. The children reached their destination at midday. They did not reach it earlier.) (They left the station. Then they made their way down a long road. This road was lined with shops selling seaside novelties. They came at last to the beach.)

And here are six sentences which might be made out of six groups:

The children's father judged that they were old enough to travel alone to the seaside. So they set out gaily to the station, where they bought their tickets. After they had waited for only a few minutes on the platform, the train came in. Tom said they were lucky to have a compartment to themselves. The journey was a slow one, for the train stopped at many stations, and the children did not reach their destination until midday. On leaving the station, they made their way down a long road lined with shops selling seaside novelties, and came at last to the beach.

This kind of sentence-making used to be called synthesis—it was supposed that the children joined the ideas together, and in this way made longer sentences from the short ones. And were this indeed the case— were it actually a fact that the process of composition involved a linking of one idea to another—then sentence-making could truthfully be called, what I said in Chapter 13 it was not, an act of deliberate synthesis. But what goes on in the child's mind can certainly not be called synthesis, and hardly even sentence-making; what happens is that the child surveys the information before him, and then summons from his accumulated stock of sentence-patterns a pattern which will accommodate that information. The test, when properly done, is therefore hardly even a test of manipulative skill—rather a test of the ability to retain and reproduce at will patterns of greater or less complexity. But it *is* a test of ability in English composition—and a good one, I think.

And now, what of the English literature examination? What sorts of question are appropriate here? At first thought, this might seem not difficult to determine: the questions we should set ought surely to be questions on the books studied during the year, whether prose, verse, or drama; they should be imitations of the questions ordinarily set in public examinations. But before proceeding along these lines, we should perhaps ask ourselves what, precisely, we are seeking to test. Is it a knowledge of books which may already have been adequately tested during the school year? Or is it the children's reading ability, as it may have developed as the result of a year's maturation and further practice? If it is the latter, we would do better to forget the books which the children have already studied, and turn our attention to reading-matter which has not yet come under their eyes. And surely that will be the wiser course; for what we want to test is not their memories of books now behind them, but the qualities of mind which they will bring to books of the future.

This is where comprehension-exercises come into their own; for these exercises, as I have already said, are our best means of measuring progress in reading. An English literature examination paper, I suggest, should include at least one 'unseen' passage of prose and one of verse; and if questions on previous reading are included, they should be questions on supplementary reading—private or 'home' reading—and should be of a sufficiently general nature to apply to books of many kinds. It is one effect of regularly including a private-reading question in the end-of-year examinations that such reading becomes established as part of the course in English, and the reluctant but examination-fearing pupil is compelled to read at least one book on his own!

In earlier chapters I have tried to explain what sorts of question seem to be suitable for asking on passages of prose or verse, and I need say little more about them here. The passages themselves should not be too simple, I think—they should present some degree of challenge to the children—and their subject-matter should be within the range of the children's interests. Passages of mere description, as of a landscape, an empty street at noonday, or an old house, tempting as they are to the teacher because of the ease with which they can be questioned on, are unsuitable for comprehension-tests: such passages do not lie at the heart of a child's reading nor at the centre of a novelist's achievement. Passages which give the teacher a chance to ask 'logical' or deductive questions should also be avoided; an English literature examination is not just an intelligence test. The most suitable passages are those which concern themselves with some definite human situation—which have strong so-called human interest. There should be action and feeling, and the writing should be of the kind which says some things by implication. This gives the pupil a chance to feel his way into a situation and display some measure of sensitivity.

Turning now to the school magazine—obviously it would not be proper in me to say 'The magazine ought to be this' or 'It ought to be that'; for the shape of each school's magazine is something that decides itself, or is moulded by the wishes of the head teacher, the judgement of the editor, or the abilities and tastes of the contributors. What I want to describe here is a particular sort of school magazine—one which sets out to absorb a good deal of the children's writing, and one which the children will eagerly read. Its chief characteristics, to be very brief, are these: that it is edited by the teachers and written by the children (not, as some are, edited by the children and written largely by the teachers); that it really is a *school* magazine—in that it devotes itself to the life of the school and the life of the pupils; that it addresses itself to the children primarily; and that it speaks with the voices of a large number of them. Such a magazine is achievable even in a school where the pupils are of only moderate ability.

In order to represent a large number of contributors, the magazine must, of course, eschew the 'single' contribution, and make as much use as possible of the symposium—the group of contributions, in number anything from three to fifty, all upon the one topic. Such a symposium can consist, at the one extreme, of three or four full-length essays, or, at the other extreme, of fifty snippets. And there are intermediate possibilities—a dozen items of paragraph length, for example. As a general rule, the longer the contribution, the smaller the number that one gathers into a single symposium.

Let me now mention some of the subjects which I think will be found suitable for symposia of the various kinds; and I will start with subjects which lend themselves to essay treatment. There is of course the performance of the school play, an account of which is a feature of most school magazines. The writing of it is often entrusted to a member of the teaching-staff, or to a responsible senior pupil, or even, when the editor wishes to be on the safe side, to the producer himself; but interesting as such an account often is, it cannot usually compete for interest with a group of three or four shorter essays—one from the producer, perhaps, one from an actor, one from a stage-helper, and one from a member of the audience. Then there are the reminiscences of school life written by children about to leave school—an excellent symposium can often be made out of some three or four of these. Again there is the school journey, the week spent in Paris or in Switzerland; a selection of the best accounts (or of long extracts from them) is likely to be more interesting, and, because of the different ages and interests of the contributors, more varied, than an account from a single hand. Another subject for essay-length treatment—suitable for use in schools which have Sixth forms—is the visit to a University for the purposes of examination or interview. I need hardly add any more to this list of subjects, because it will soon be seen that several of those mentioned below as suitable for briefer treatment can also be included here.

So we come to the symposium of shorter contributions—contributions of two-paragraph or one-paragraph length. I have already described two of these symposia in Chapter 4: 'Schoolboys' Diary' (or 'Schoolgirls' Diary') and 'In and Around the School'. There need never be any shortage of contributions to these two features; if the matter is organized beforehand and a wide enough net is thrown out, there will be plenty of matter to choose from. Other such features are 'Reports from Participants' (a variant of the 'Diary', the contributors being pupils who have taken an actual part in school functions or informal activities); 'What Are the Societies Doing?' (a collection of reports written by magazine 'reporters' who have been allowed to drop in at meetings of the school societies); 'School Occasions' (another but more formal variant of the 'Diary'); 'Letters to the Editor'; 'Short Talks with the Editor' (paragraph-length letters on school topics with paragraph-length replies); 'Reporters Out in the Lunch Hour' (a gathering of short reports, suitable for a day-school magazine, which tell how various groups of pupils pass the lunch-hour); 'The Right Reading for a Boy (Girl) Like Me' (paragraphs on the pupils' reading-preferences); and 'Advice to Our Successors' (short accounts of the special problems associated with being in such-and-such a class, addressed by members of that class to those who will succeed them). Some of the topics proposed earlier for essay-length treatment can be used here as well, as can also some of those proposed below for even briefer treatment.

It is the symposium made up of snippets, or of a mixture of paragraphs and snippets, which is capable of comprehending a really large number of contributions; for here one can bring together under one title the tiny contributions of as many as fifty children. Moreover, here is a good way of representing some of the youngest pupils, whose essays may not always be good enough to be printed in their entirety. Because of the ease with which contributions are obtained, it is often necessary to limit the request for contributions to a few classes—the first-year children, perhaps, or the fourth forms. The contributions come in as essays or as paragraphs, of course—it is the editor who does the snippeting. Topics which are suitable for this short treatment include these: 'New Pupils' Accounts of their First Day at the School'; 'The Ideal Prefect and the Ideal Schoolboy (Schoolgirl)'; 'What We Thought of the School Play'; 'The Ministry Inspection'; 'Improvements in Me After a Year' (by children who have reached the end of their first year in the school); 'What We Hope to Get out of Our Education'; 'Parents' Evening'; 'Open Day'; 'Thoughts in the Examination Room'; and 'On Taking Home My End-of-Term Report'. Where the symposium consists of numerous snippets, it is better to classify them under several headings. So, the children's comments on the school inspection might be classified under such headings as 'The Inspectors Expected', 'The Inspectors Inspected', 'The Inspectors in Retrospect', and 'Miscellaneous Comments'.

Up to now, in suggesting topics suitable for symposia, I have concentrated on school matters as such; but I think that the range may legitimately be widened to include topics relating to the children's world and daily doings. And if this extension is accepted, a whole new series of topics comes within scope—topics to do with home life, leisure-hours, and friendships. Here, without further comment, are some more topics suitable for essay, paragraph, or 'snippet' treatment: 'I Read Last Week'; 'The Schoolboy's (Schoolgirl's) Meals'; 'How I Spend my Spare Time'; 'Last Saturday'; 'Entertaining a Foreign Boy or Girl'; 'Friends Out of School'; 'The Girls (Boys) of Today and What I Think of Them'; 'My Family Watching Television'; 'What My Family Read'; 'Schoolboy (Schoolgirl) Chores'; 'Our Heroes in

Fiction and on Television'; and 'Family Arguments'. I have seen lively and absorbing writing on all these topics—indeed, on all the topics mentioned in this chapter. If an editor plans in advance, and is prepared to read a great deal of manuscript, he cannot fail to have enough material; on a topic involving much interest and feeling, such as an inspection, he can usually be assured of getting enough suitable material from a single class, and the problem confronting the maker of symposia is often not so much what to include as what to leave out. One last remark—an editor should be careful not to include in his magazine too many symposia of the snippety kind. No doubt, many a child is pleased to be represented in his magazine by even a single sentence; but whenever the quality of their writing warrants it, some of the children should be represented at much greater length. A well-balanced issue of the magazine might include two symposia of essays, two or even three of long paragraphs, and one of snippets.

There remains the question of 'original contributions'. Since the proposed magazine is to be devoted solely to the in-school and out-of-school doings of the pupils, there should obviously be no place in it for the miscellaneous essays, the facetious articles, the crossword puzzles and the jokes which are so often a blemish on a magazine's contents. But I think an exception should be made of any writing which is perceived to have genuine merit *as* writing—literary merit, as they say; for such writing is, after all, representative of one aspect of the children's life. Only it is best printed under a separate heading, a little apart from the 'school' and the 'home' contributions; some such title as 'Recent Writing' or 'Junior Writing' or 'Samples of Work' is usually suitable. And even here the symposium is not out of place. Under such a title as 'Junior Writing' it is possible to assemble three or four meritorious pieces on a common topic—'Cousins', or 'The Child Next Door', or 'Conversation in the Kitchen', or 'The Youngest and the Oldest Members of My Family'.

Poems, of course, claim a place in most school magazines in a section of their own. They rank as literary contributions, and so are one of my exceptions; certainly no magazine editor, so far as I know, has ever tried to insist that even the poetry should all be about the school life or the out-of-school life of the pupils!

In bringing this book to a close, I had thought to write some words about the teacher of English, trying to describe the ideal teacher whom I hold in my mind—one who is essentially an abstract of colleagues past and present, of other teachers whom I have known and admired, and of the best of those who taught me when I was young. But now I come to attempt this task, I find myself pondering on qualities which are those not so much of the good teacher of English as of the good teacher of any subject whatsoever. Perhaps I can clarify my thoughts by saying that those qualities which in the good teacher of any other subject seem desirable, in the good teacher of English seem essential. And the first of these essentials is affection for the children he teaches. Very little can be accomplished without this. The teacher of English should be fond of all children—not, like Lewis Carroll, liking 'all children except boys', nor, of course, liking all children except girls; and his affection should not be the morbid concentration which exudes from a lonely and thwarted nature, but rather the overplus of a heart already fulfilled by ordinary satisfactions. If it is not that, it may bring a curse and not a blessing; for the burden of one teacher's undivided affection is something no single child should be expected to bear; in the long run it makes him bewildered and uncertain, it makes him conceited and difficult for others to manage, and it blinds him to his own limitations. And because of the personal nature of English as a subject—because it deals in things of the mind and the spirit—it behoves the teacher of English more than of any other subject to shield the individual pupil from the full force of his own liking. At a time when the child is struggling to come to terms with so many of life's complexities, he should be ready to accept the influence of as many teachers as possible, and not reject all save the influence of one.

I have said that a teacher should be affectionate; when I add that he should be wise I have obviously said all that there is to say. But wise with what sorts of wisdom? The wisdom of 'knowing his subject', certainly; but also—I say this almost apologetically—the special wisdoms which come of spending a year or more at a good training college or Institute of Education. Apologetically; first because I number among my friends several fine teachers of English who never underwent training; secondly because (this must be something peculiarly British) in this country the question 'How much training should I have?' is often answered not just by the simple 'None' but by the scornful 'As little as possible'—as though being trained were the surest way of *unfitting* oneself to be a teacher! That is not my own belief, and has not been my experience; if there is any teacher who is the worse for professional training it is certainly not the teacher of English.

What are they, then, these wisdoms which my ideal teacher learns rapidly in a good training college—but only with difficulty or not at all if he goes untrained into teaching? First, he learns to ask, and to tentatively answer, such fundamental questions as 'Exactly what ought I to be teaching?' and 'What is the true nature of good English?' and 'Why does literature matter?'; and from time to time throughout his teaching career he asks those questions again and confirms the answers. Secondly, he familiarizes himself with the teaching methods of his own day, and in doing so avoids the pitfall which awaits the untrained teacher—that of, for want of better guidance, adopting the methods of those people who taught him when he was a boy. Thirdly, he discovers that each year of a child's life should be regarded as life in its own right, and not just part of a 'state of becoming'—not just part of a troublesome immaturity which must be hustled away with all speed, in order that the true life of the adult may come on; and this discovery teaches him tolerance and forbearance. Lastly, he learns not to press on his pupils his own high standards, whether in language or in literature, or to scorn the children's more uncertain ones; for a censorious habit of mind is something from which every child winces. The resolute purveyor of 'good English' may purvey it to such effect that he dries up his pupils altogether; the resolute purveyor of 'good-literature-and-nothing-but-the-best' may breed in his pupils a distaste for all literature, or may turn them into prigs.

And in the midst of these general preoccupations, the ideal teacher does not disdain the bread-and-butter aspects of his craft, the aspects with which this book chiefly deals. Humdrum as they are, they should never be neglected. When I was a boy at school, in the Sixth form, it was one of our innocent aspirations (an aspiration peculiar to those innocent times, the days of *Tarzan* and *The Blue Lagoon*) to be cast ashore with a beautiful girl on a desert island. One day, when we were discussing this matter amongst ourselves in the classroom, a master who overheard us mildly remarked, 'But after a while you would be looking for other things to do.' It is in the spirit of this remark that I have written this book. I do not belittle the special excitements which the teaching of English provides, the types of work loosely called active and creative. Only they are not the whole of English. It is for the teacher who will sometimes be 'looking for other things to do' that I have written these sober pages.

INDEX